The Problem of Pornography

The Problem of Pornography

Susan Dwyer

McGill University

Wadsworth Publishing Company

I(T)P™ An International Thomson Publishing Company

Belmont • Albany • Bonn • Boston • Cincinnati • Detroit • London • Madrid • Melbourne
Mexico City • New York • Paris • San Francisco • Singapore • Tokyo • Toronto • Washington

Philosophy Editor: *Tammy Goldfeld*
Editorial Assistant: *Kelly Zavislak*
Production Services Coordinator: *Debby Kramer*
Production: *Scratchgravel Publishing Services*
Designer: *Cloyce Wall*
Print Buyer: *Karen Hunt*
Permissions Editor: *Bob Kauser*
Copy Editor: *Robin Whitaker*
Cover: *Harry Voigt*
Compositor: *Scratchgravel Publishing Services*
Printer: *Maple-Vail Book Manufacturing Group*

Printed in the United States of America.

For more information, contact:

Wadsworth Publishing Company
10 Davis Drive
Belmont, California 94002, USA

International Thomson Publishing
Berkshire House 168-173
High Holborn
London, WC1V 7AA, England

Thomas Nelson Australia
102 Dodds Street
South Melbourne 3205
Victoria, Australia

Nelson Canada
1120 Birchmount Road
Scarborough, Ontario
Canada M1K 5G4

International Thomson Publishing GmbH
Königswinterer Strasse 418
53227 Bonn, Germany

International Thomson Publishing Asia
221 Henderson Road #05-10
Singapore 0315

International Thomson Publishing Japan
Hirakawacho Kyowa Building, 3F
2-2-1 Hirakawacho
Chiyoda-ku, Tokyo 102
Japan

1 2 3 4 5 6 7 8 9 10—01 00 99 98 97 96 95

Library of Congress Cataloging-in-Publication Data

The Problem of pornography / [edited by] Susan Dwyer.
    p. cm.
    Includes bibliographical references.
    ISBN 0-534-22044-4
    1. Pornography—Social aspects.   I. Dwyer, Susan.
HQ471.P76   1994
363.4'7—dc20   94-18082

Contents

v

PART FOUR

Pornography and Speech Acts

Preface

There is no getting around it: pornography is something about which reasonable people disagree. It is, therefore, a topic rich in pedagogical potential. The difficulty is not just that people cannot come to a consensus about what pornography is—although that is certainly a factor. On closer inspection, disputes about pornography usually reveal much deeper disagreements about the proper relation between morality and law, about sex and sexuality, about feminism, about constitutional interpretation, about the validity of certain kinds of empirical research, and so on. Thus, the topic of pornography raises important questions that cut across a number of disciplines, including at least: philosophy, law, women's studies, psychology, criminology, and sociology. *The Problem of Pornography* is designed with such questions and disciplines in mind.

As I discuss in the Introduction, thinking about pornography has changed dramatically in recent years. Just over twenty years ago, feminists' contributions to the debate about pornography served to shift attention from "old-fashioned" arguments about sexual morality to matters of more substantive political import. Increasingly in the last decade, traditional liberal approaches to the topic have been shown to be limited. Pornography is no longer just about the morality of nonprocreative sex or masturbation. It is no longer just a feminist issue. Nor is it just about free speech. In my view, the change in thinking and writing about pornography is the result of sustained theoretical reflection on the compatibility of complex equality and liberty and on the limits of the law in a pluralistic society. The papers for this anthology were chosen to represent the contours of this new debate. New debates give rise to new questions, and the essays in Part Three (Pornography, Sexuality, and Politics) and Part Four (Pornography and Speech Acts) represent attempts to answer these questions. For example, do feminist arguments against heterosexual pornography count against gay male pornography as well? Do these same arguments cast women as victims or as sufferers of false consciousness forever alienated from their sexuality and in need of special state protection? Finally, what philosophical sense can be made of the claims that pornography *is* the subordination of women or that pornography *silences* women?

The anthology is deliberately theoretical and is intended to provoke critical reflection and thoughtful responses rather than rhetoric. Discussions of pornography are often fraught with emotion. But it is important that as teachers and students we do the best we can to organize both our thoughts and our feelings. Theory helps in this endeavor. I have found that students readily see the complexity involved in thinking about pornography and quickly come to appreciate the value of articulating arguments for one position or another. Among other things, theory allows them to grasp a point of view they do not share and thus provides a framework within which they can begin to make sense of their own beliefs. Perhaps more important, by adopting a theoretical perspective, we can all come to recognize what it is to have reasoned and substantive disagreements with one another.

No one will agree with *all* the views expressed in this collection. But that, too, is one of my objectives. I am acutely aware that ideological bias can affect the selection of material for such an anthology, and, of course, my own thinking has influenced what I have included. Insofar as is possible, then, the essays have been chosen so that no one view emerges as dominant. In the end, it is really my experience in the classroom that influenced my decision to include these papers rather than others.

The juxtaposition of some pairs of papers is intended to encourage comparison. For example, in Part Two, Rae Langton's paper is critical of Ronald Dworkin's conclusions concerning the regulation of pornography, and in Part Three, John Stoltenberg and Thomas Waugh clearly disagree about the status of gay male pornography. Ellen Willis and Mariana Valverde address and sometimes take issue with Catharine MacKinnon's work. However, the order in which papers of such pairs appear, or indeed the order of all the papers, should not be taken as evidence of my endorsement of a particular piece or approach.

The Problem of Pornography contains two features that will make this anthology useful in a wide range of classes, both in Canada and in the United States. First, there is a comprehensive bibliography, organized by theme to encourage student research and to facilitate teaching. For example, the major topic heading "I: Pornography and the State" is further subdivided into "A. Law—United States," "B. Law—Canada," "C. Freedom of Expression," and so on. In addition, a wide selection of material concerning feminist critiques of pornography and feminist and nonfeminist responses to them is included along with citations for work on child pornography and violence against women. The second feature of note is the Legal Appendix. It is intended as a simple reference guide to the treatment of pornography in a legal context. It provides an annotated comparative chronology of relevant Canadian and U.S. Supreme Court decisions interspersed with a number of salient legal "milestones"—for example, the definition of pornography employed in the anti-pornography civil rights ordinance drafted by Catharine MacKinnon and Andrea Dworkin.

Acknowledgments

My students in Contemporary Moral Issues at McGill University provided the inspiration to put this book together. Their interest in hard questions and their willingness to consider seriously a variety of arguments have confirmed my view that philosophers can and ought to make a contribution to discussions of public policy. For help with the bibliography I thank Leslie MacAvoy and especially Patrick Miller, who was an invaluable research assistant. Jeff Lord provided a mine of information on gay pornography. I should also like to acknowledge the helpful suggestions made by several reviewers: Robin S. Dillon, Lehigh University; Lynn Pasquerella, University of Rhode Island; Lani Roberts, Oregon State University; Steve Smith, Claremont McKenna College; Roye Templeton, University of Maryland, Baltimore County; and Barbara Wall, Villanova University. Finally, thank you to my life's companion, Paul Pietroski, for helping to make that life such an emotionally and intellectually rich one.

Susan Dwyer

Constructing the "Problem" of Pornography

1. Introduction

Any serious discussion of pornography quickly leads to two queries: Is pornography somehow problematic (for example, morally, socially, or politically)? If so, precisely what sort of problems does pornography present? Such questions have elicited a variety of responses, and in this book you will find some of the most recent answers to them. But thinking about pornography has changed significantly over the last thirty years. I believe we better appreciate the current debate about pornography when we understand the substance and motivation for previous approaches to the topic as well as the reasons those approaches have been rejected and/or replaced. Hence, the aim of this introduction is to outline and explain some of the several ways in which the problem of pornography has been constructed or formulated.

2. Pornography as a Business

One cause of the rapidly changing nature of the debate about pornography is the rapidly changing nature of pornography itself. The history of pornography goes hand in hand with the history of media technology. For example, it was the advent of the printing press in the sixteenth century that first made possible the publication and mass circulation of sexually explicit prints and books,[1] and the first pornographic films emerged along with advances in photographic reproduction in the late nineteenth century. In the earliest days of home video technology, pornography accounted for approximately 75 percent of sales,[2] and today guests in many hotels can readily access a variety of pornographic films. Cable television and interactive computer software have also been utilized by producers of pornography. Sex is now to be had even over the telephone. The availability of sophisticated technology has certainly been a major factor in the massive growth of the pornography business. Annual turnover is now estimated to be approximately $10 billion internationally. Furthermore, many film and photographic equipment companies advertise in pornographic magazines, and although much of the production and dissemination of pornography is still limited to certain "red light" districts or the back of video stores, it would be a mistake to think that pornography is in any way a "fringe" enterprise.

Like many businesses, the pornography industry has diversified as it has grown—arguably, in response to consumer demand. The range and content of pornography have changed dramatically. Today, pornography extends from "soft core" magazines like *Playboy*, to "hard core" films depicting explicit sexual acts—including vaginal and anal intercourse, fellatio, and cunnilingus—between persons of opposite genders as well as persons of the same gender. Most pornography currently available is heterosexual, but there is a substantial market in gay male material, and a growing one in lesbian pornography. In addition, there is a considerable amount of pornography specifically tailored to particular audiences—for example, fetishists of various sorts, sadomasochists, pedophiles, and so on. A point of some controversy concerns just what percentage of all this material contains violence. At least this much can be said: pornography that combines explicit sex and violence is readily available, and much of this type has entered the market since the late 1970s.

---

[1]For detailed historical accounts of the emergence of pornography see Lynn Hunt, ed., *The Invention of Pornography: Obscenity and the Origins of Modernity, 1500–1800* (New York: Zone Books, 1993); and Walter M. Kendrick, *The Secret Museum: Pornography in Modern Culture* (New York: Viking, 1987).

[2]John Tierney, "Porn, the Low-Slung Engine of Progress," in *New York Times*, Sunday, 9 January 1994, sec. 2. For more details on the dimensions of the pornography industry, see Gordon G. Hawkins and Franklin E. Zimring, *Pornography in a Free Society* (Cambridge: Cambridge University Press, 1991); and David Hebditch and Nick Anning, *Porn Gold: Inside the Pornography Business* (London: Faber and Faber, 1988).

3. Pornography's Effects

Pornography's intended and most direct effect is to produce sexual arousal. But participants in the pornography debate have been more concerned with a range of other effects that pornography is alleged to have—for example: that it causes men to rape and sexually harass women and (sometimes) children; that it contributes to an environment in which its consumers are indifferent to the real needs of women or fail to take women seriously. A different claim is that pornography facilitates the harmless satisfaction of otherwise dangerous sexual desires.[3] This suggestion that pornography has a "cathartic" effect on its consumers often figures in arguments against the restriction or prohibition of pornography, whereas anti-pornography theorists tend to focus on the claim that pornography has significant negative effects. In other words, empirical considerations play a role in arguments both for and against pornography. So the success of these arguments partly depends on what can be established about the connection between pornography and various types of behavior and attitudes.

That there is some connection between rape, say, and pornography is undeniable. It is well-documented that some sex offenders admit to being incited by pornography; some even use it during the commission of their assaults.[4] However, it is unclear what generalizations can be made about the connection between the consumption of pornography and sexual violence against women. Does all pornography *cause* men to torture and rape women? Does the use of pornography make men more callous towards women? Is pornography uniquely responsible for the attitude that women are either sexually insatiable or timid virgins awaiting sexual initiation? Researchers have provided conflicting answers.

In 1970, the U.S. Commission on Obscenity and Pornography reported that empirical studies on the effects of pornography were insufficient to establish that pornography is a central causal factor in sexual violence. But in 1986, the Meese Commission concluded that "the available evidence strongly supports the hypothesis that substantial exposure to sexually violent materials . . .

---

[3]See, for example, G. L. Simons, "Is Pornography Beneficial?" in *Pornography without Prejudice* (London: Abelard-Schuman, 1973), 85–103.

[4]See, for example, Catharine A. MacKinnon, "Francis Biddle's Sister: Pornography, Civil Rights, and Speech," *Feminism Unmodified: Discourses on Life and Law* (Cambridge, Mass.: Harvard University Press, 1987), 185–186, 291 n. 107; and *Pornography and Sexual Violence: Evidence of the Links* (London: Everywoman, 1988).

bears a causal relationship to antisocial acts of violence and, for some sub-groups, possibly to unlawful acts of sexual violence."[5] In Canada, the "official" view about pornography's effects has been somewhat more consistent: In 1978, the Standing Committee on Justice and Legal Affairs declared, "The clear and unquestionable danger of this type of material is that it reinforces some unhealthy tendencies in Canadian society. The effect of this type of material is to reinforce male-female stereotypes to the detriment of both sexes."[6] In 1985, the Special Committee on Pornography and Prostitution, despite accepting that a causal connection between pornography and sexual violence had not been established, recommended the criminalization of violent pornography "because of the seriousness of the impact of this sort of pornography on the fundamental values of Canadians."[7]

Investigation into the effects of pornography is subject to a number of difficulties not unlike those which beset other social scientific research. Various biases operate in the design of experiments and questionnaires and in the interpretation of their results;[8] the same "expert testimony" is employed in very different, often opposing, political and pragmatic arguments.[9] Such uncertainty renders problematic the appeal to such research in arguments for either restrictive or permissive policies on pornography. And, theorists on all sides of the debate are now far less inclined to rest their cases on empirical claims alone. This is not to imply that current thought about pornography takes empirical matters to be irrelevant to philosophical or legal arguments. Indeed, several contemporary theorists urge us to take a *broader* view of empirical data. For example, Catharine MacKinnon argues that the empirical impact of

---

[5]Attorney General's Commission on Pornography, *Final Report*, 2 vols. (Washington, D.C.: U.S. Government Printing Office, 1986), vol.1, 326.

[6]House of Commons, Standing Committee on Justice and Legal Affairs, *Report on Pornography*, no. 18, 22 March 1978, 4.

[7]Special Committee on Pornography and Prostitution in Canada, *Pornography and Prostitution in Canada*, vol. 1 (Ottawa: Supply and Services, 1985), 103. More recently, the Supreme Court of Canada argued that, although the evidence of a causal connection between pornography and violence against women is inconclusive, Parliament has a "reasonable basis" for restrictive legislation. See *R. v. Butler* [1992] 1 S.C.R. 452, 613; and the Legal Appendix.

[8]See, for example, Ferrell M. Christensen, "Cultural and Ideological Bias in Pornography Research," *Philosophy of the Social Sciences* 20 (1990): 351–375; and, Alison King, "Mystery and Imagination: The Case of Pornography Effects Studies," in *Bad Girls and Dirty Pictures*, ed. Alison Assister and Avedon Carol (London: Pluto Press, 1993), 57–87.

[9]For discussion on the use of experimental studies by the Meese Commission see Daniel G. Linz, Edward Donnerstein, and Steven Penrod, "The Findings and Recommendations of the Attorney General's Commission on Pornography: Do the Psychological 'Facts' Fit the Political Fury?" *American Psychologist* 42 (1987): 946–953.

pornography extends far beyond its direct and indirect effects on consumers: it also encompasses what has to happen to real people in order to make pornography and the social and economic facts of women's inequality.[10]

4. The Traditional Approach: Pornography as a Moral Issue

Pornography used to be a sort of litmus test for where one stood on the political spectrum. Conservatives claimed, sometimes on the basis of religious considerations (for example, the alleged sinfulness of masturbation or non-procreative sex), that pornography is something disgusting and immoral. Liberals, with varying degrees of enthusiasm, declared pornography something to be tolerated; and a few self-proclaimed sexual radicals argued for less state control over sexually explicit material. In any case, disagreements about pornography used to be fairly straightforward because, by and large, people focused on a single feature of pornography—namely, its sexual content. Arguments for both restrictive and permissive social policies hinged on moralistic claims about the public dissemination of graphic depictions of sexual activity.[11] To the extent that pornography was thought to be a problem at all, then, it was thought to be a problem about the proper boundaries of sexual morality.

Arguably, for the first half of the twentieth century, philosophical and legal opinion about pornography mirrored the simplicity of this commonsense disagreement. In law, sexually explicit representations were (and continue to be) dealt with under the rubric of obscenity. For a long time, obscenity statutes were justified on the grounds that they were necessary to protect the moral fabric of society. For example, Patrick Devlin is well known for arguing that one legitimate purpose of the criminal law is to preserve the moral code of the society whose code it is.[12]

---

[10]See Catharine A. MacKinnon, *Only Words* (Cambridge, Mass.: Harvard University Press, 1993), 3–41.

[11]A representative selection of liberal and conservative arguments about pornography appears in Douglas A. Hughes, ed., *Perspectives on Pornography* (New York: St. Martin's Press, 1970). See also Fred R. Berger, "Pornography, Sex, and Censorship," *Social Theory and Practice* 4 (1977): 183–209.

[12]Patrick Devlin, "Morals and the Criminal Law," in *The Enforcement of Morals* (Oxford: Oxford University Press, 1965), 1–25. And see the Legal Appendix for early definitions of obscenity.

When the problem of pornography is constructed in these terms, the following sort of argument is likely to be advanced by anti-pornography campaigners: Because (i) pornography is immoral, and (ii) the purpose of the law (including the criminal law) is to protect the moral well-being of society, then (iii) the state should prohibit the production, display, and sale of pornography. On the other side, a variety of strategies are available to the advocate of less-restrictive policies. Such a person could take issue with (i) and claim that pornography is morally innocuous. Alternatively, she could concede that pornography is immoral but argue directly against (ii) on the grounds that the enforcement of morality is none of the state's business. Finally, it is open to anyone to reject the very way in which this argument is framed. That is, someone might object to formulating the problem of pornography in this manner; and this is precisely what has happened.

Popular opinion about the immorality of nonprocreative sex and masturbation was transformed during the "sexual revolution" of the 1960s, and many people claimed that pornography is a valid form of expression, not simply "smut." In addition, the view that the legislation of morality—especially *sexual* morality—is a legitimate objective of the state was subject to intense criticism.[13] Accordingly, the problem of pornography was recast as a battle between an "authoritarian" state, on the one hand, and beleaguered sexual radicals, on the other. As a radical form of expression, pornography was defended against governmental interference for the same reasons that the expression of political dissidents was defended. As Catharine MacKinnon has recently put it, the pornography debate was "one of governmental authority threatening to suppress genius and dissent."[14]

Two elements are notably absent from these traditional ways of thinking about the problem of pornography. First, very little detailed attention is paid to the *context* in which pornography is produced, sold, and consumed. Second, no specific mention is made about the particular impact that pornography might have on *women*. A significant change in the construction of the problem of pornography was brought about when these elements—context and gender—were emphasized.

---

[13]See, for example, H. L. A. Hart, *Law, Liberty, and Morality* (London: Oxford University Press, 1963).

[14]MacKinnon, *Only Words*, 8.

5. Pornography as Harmful to Women

As Laura Lederer reports,[15] two factors were instrumental in women's initial organization against pornography: an increase in the combination of sex and violence in pornography (and other media) and the explicit recognition of widespread violence against women. In the 1970s, feminists began to document the *systematic* nature of this violence, and many were tempted to infer that there is a direct connection between representations of violence against women and actual violence against women.[16] Indeed, some feminists agreed with Robin Morgan, who went so far as to say, "Pornography is the theory, rape is the practice." Now, this way of looking at pornography has implications for the sort of argument that can be made against pornography. In order to make these implications clear, we need to turn more directly to matters of free speech.

A right to free speech is enshrined in both the U.S. Bill of Rights and the Canadian Charter of Rights and Freedoms,[17] and rightly or wrongly, pornography is widely considered to be a form of speech or expression. Hence, any argument for the restriction or prohibition of pornography must make clear why this particular type of expression is deserving of less protection than others. Such an argument may be made in slightly different ways, but each is likely to depend on (i) a view about why freedom of expression is valuable at all, and (ii) a view about the way(s) in which pornography differs from other forms of expression. So, why is freedom of expression important, or put another way, how is its protection to be justified?

There appears to be no single answer to this question. A right to freedom of expression has been variously defended: in terms of the necessity of a "marketplace of ideas" for the discovery and/or test of truth;[18] on the

---

[15]Laura Lederer, "Introduction," in *Take Back the Night: Women on Pornography,* ed. Laura Lederer (New York: William Morrow & Co., 1980).

[16]See, for example, groups like Women against Violence against Women (Toronto, 1977), Women against Violence in Pornography (San Francisco, 1978), and Women against Pornography (New York City, 1979).

[17]The relevant guarantees are the First Amendment to the United States Constitution, and section 2(b) of the Canadian Charter of Rights and Freedoms. See the Legal Appendix for a statement of these provisions.

[18]Classic sources here are John Locke, *A Letter Concerning Toleration* (1689) and John Stuart Mill, *On Liberty* (1859). See also Justice Wendell Holmes in *Abrams v. United States,* 250 U.S. (1919) 616, 630.

grounds that bad consequences are likely to ensue upon the suppression of speech; in terms of the role of free speech in democratic self-governance;[19] and finally, in terms of the connection thought to exist between an individual's ability to express herself freely (and hear others do so also) and her dignity and moral autonomy.[20] It is not obvious that these justifications are or need be mutually exclusive. But one point of difference among them deserves mention. The last idea—namely, that freedom of expression is connected to human dignity—has it that freedom of expression is good in and of itself. However, all the other justifications just mentioned are *consequentialist* justifications; that is, they appeal to the likely outcomes of allowing or not allowing free speech. According to these views, then, the value of free speech is a function of the value of the end to which it is thought to be a (necessary) means—for example, the discovery of truth, the avoidance of tyranny, or the possibility of democracy.

No matter how the right to free speech is defended, it is rarely defended as an absolute right—that is, as one that may *never* be infringed or overridden.[21] But, of course, what counts as a sufficient reason to limit the right to free speech in any particular instance will vary according to how that right is justified in the first place. Suppose, for example, that we defend the right to free speech on the grounds that it is essential to the pursuit of truth; then we might be able to argue for the restriction of some form of expression by showing that it plays no role in furthering that goal. In any case, the right to free speech is justified on quite substantial grounds, and anyone who wishes to argue that pornography ought to be restricted has to show that there are very good reasons to do so. (These matters are discussed in more detail in the introduction to and the essays in Part Two, "Rights, Equality, and Free Speech.")

Now that we understand something of the commitment to free speech that lies in the background of discussion about pornography, we are in a bet-

---

[19]See, for example, Alexander Meiklejohn, *Free Speech and Its Relation to Self-Government* (New York: Harper, 1948); and Martin H. Redish, "The Value of Free Speech," *University of Pennsylvania Law Review* 130 (1982): 591–645.

[20]For this "constitutive" justification of free speech see Ronald Dworkin, "The Coming Battles over Free Speech," *The New York Review of Books*, 11 June 1992, 55–58, 61–64.

[21]Notable exceptions here are Justices Hugo Black and William O. Douglas. See, for example, Black's dissent in *Beauharnais v. Illinois*, 343 U.S. 250 (1952); E. Cahn, "Justice Black and First Amendment 'Absolutes': A Public Interview," *New York University Law Review* 37 (1962): 549–563.

ter position to grasp the way in which early feminists constructed the problem of pornography. They argued that pornography is harmful to women. Surely, if it could be established that pornography is causally responsible for violence against women, this would constitute a good enough reason for pornography's restriction or prohibition. There is indeed philosophical precedent for just this sort of argument.

In *On Liberty*, John Stuart Mill defended freedom of expression on the grounds that an unfettered exchange of ideas is essential to the attainment of truth. He argued that the restriction of speech and expression would likely have nothing but bad consequences: it would permit the rise of authoritarian government; it would hinder the critical examination of moral and political ideas; and so on.[22] But Mill was aware of the dangers of completely unconstrained liberty, and in *On Liberty* he also articulated what has come to be known as the harm principle. Very roughly, the idea is that the state is not justified in prohibiting actions (that is, limiting its citizens' liberty) unless it can be proven that those actions are harmful *and* that the benefits of prohibiting such actions outweigh the costs of allowing them. In these terms, someone who would argue *for* the prohibition of pornography would bear the burden of showing (i) that pornography has demonstrably harmful effects and (ii) that the benefits of prohibiting pornography are greater than the costs of permitting a free market in pornography. Within this framework, someone who would argue *against* the prohibition or restriction of pornography could adopt any of the following three strategies. First, she could point to evidence that pornography is not harmful, or not *as* harmful as its opponents would make out, and so deny that the costs of a permissive policy on pornography warrant the restriction of free speech. Second, she might agree there is reason to believe that *some* pornography is harmful but argue that this is not sufficient to warrant the censorship of *all* pornography. Or, third, she might invoke what philosophers call a slippery-slope argument: If pornography is prohibited on the grounds that some of it might be harmful, do we not then set a dangerous precedent for the restriction of other forms of expression about which we might be suspicious?

---

[22]Mill thus appears to advance what I earlier called a consequentialist justification of free speech. As a utilitarian, Mill was certainly apt to rely on consequentialist arguments. However, I believe there is sufficient evidence in *On Liberty* and in his *Utilitarianism* to attribute to Mill a *constitutive* justification of free speech—that is, one that emphasizes the role of freedom of expression in the realization and maintenance of an individual's self-respect and dignity.

As we saw above, the empirical evidence does not univocally support the claim that pornography is causally responsible for violence against women. Although there is a large amount of anecdotal evidence implicating the consumption of pornography in sexual violence against women, taken together it is still not considered sufficient to justify state intervention. An anti-pornography advocate might try to respond that, of all forms of expression, the restriction of pornography represents an exception to the general requirement of establishing demonstrably harmful effects. In order to do this, she or he would have to show how pornography differs in *principled* ways from other types of expression. Otherwise the singling out of pornography as a legitimate target of state control appears to be entirely arbitrary; and it is the threat of arbitrariness that underlies slippery-slope objections to state interference with free speech.

In short, given our current knowledge of pornography's effect, when the problem of pornography is constructed as representing a conflict between freedom of expression and probable harm to women, no argument for its restriction is likely to prove successful. This result has led many people, especially feminists, to question the adequacy of a "liberal" approach to the problem of pornography. The liberal approach focuses on abstract rights and liberties, often to the exclusion of the substantive realities of women's lives. Moreover, it is precisely this way of thinking about the problem of pornography that compels the sort of cost-benefit analysis I outlined above, and it therefore places a very heavy (perhaps unattainable) burden of proof on those who would argue for pornography's restriction or prohibition. Thus, a new type of argument against pornography has emerged. Like the harm approach, this new and highly influential way of constructing the problem of pornography—the sex discrimination model—is inspired by feminist thought. However, it is important to note that it does not represent *the* feminist position on pornography; nor need it be the *only* adequate way of conceiving of the issue.[23]

---

[23]See, for example, the essays in *Pleasure and Danger: Exploring Female Sexuality*, ed. Carol Vance (London: Pandora Press, 1992), and in *Bad Girls and Naughty Pictures*, ed. Alison Assister and Avedon Carol (London: Pluto Press, 1993); and Elizabeth Fox-Genovese, "Pornography and Individual Rights," in *Feminism without Illusions* (Chapel Hill: University of North Carolina Press, 1991), 87–112.

6. *Pornography as a Form of Sex Discrimination*

Although it has proved very difficult to establish a definitive causal connection between violent pornography and the incidence of rape and other sexual assault, feminists (and others) have continued to insist that the widespread display and consumption of pornography contribute to a cultural and social environment that is damaging to women. Pornography conveys certain messages about what women are like and about what they want from sex. In particular, much of what is currently available suggests that women are primarily sexual creatures, that they are essentially submissive, that they want to be humiliated and hurt, and that they derive sexual pleasure from being treated in these ways. As Helen Longino puts it in "Pornography, Oppression, and Freedom: A Closer Look" (Part One), pornography lies about women's sexuality. It presents a distorted view of women, which, if accepted as the truth by men who consume it, is likely to affect the ways in which those men respond to and behave towards women in general. Some may choose to rape women; others may adopt the attitude that women are just sex toys and are thus not to be taken seriously. These general attitudinal effects of pornography, it is argued, have far-reaching implications for women's ability to participate fully and equally in the political process. For if women are perceived to be nothing but sexual creatures, it is unlikely that their fellow citizens will be inclined to give them power (for example, elect them to high governmental office).

Now, it might be argued that pornography is not unique in having these effects. As Ronald Dworkin suggests in "Liberty and Pornography" (Part Two), much of mainstream advertising also presents a distorted and potentially damaging view of women. Indeed, Dworkin believes that the negative effects of advertising and soap operas are likely to be greater than the negative effects of violent pornography. He writes:

> Television and other parts of popular culture use sexual display and sexual innuendo to sell virtually everything, and they often show women as experts in domestic detail and unreasoned intuition and nothing else. The images they create are subtle and ubiquitous, and it would not be surprising to learn, through whatever research might establish this, that they do indeed do great damage to the way women are understood and allowed to be influential in politics. Sadistic pornography, though much more offensive and disturbing, is greatly overshadowed by these dismal cultural influences as a causal force.

Suppose Dworkin is right about the effects of television and advertising—namely, that they are more potent than violent pornography in molding attitudes about women. Consistency would then demand of someone who argues for the restriction or prohibition of pornography solely on the basis of its attitudinal effects that she also be committed to the legitimacy of substantial state interference with advertising and television. Now, the state certainly does exercise some control over both of these media, but few people who value free speech would be happy to see the state's power extended in this way.

At the end of the last section, I suggested that a proponent of a restrictive policy on pornography could concede that pornography is a form of expression and that freedom of expression ought generally to be protected, but could nonetheless try to argue that pornography is a special form of expression. I said that such a person would have to persuade us that pornography has some distinctive feature(s) that sets it apart from expression of other sorts. Given the background commitment to free speech in both the United States and Canada, it is only in this way that a person proposing the restriction or prohibition of pornography could avoid the force of slippery-slope objections like Dworkin's above. The hypothesis that pornography causes sexual violence against women has not been definitively established. We have just seen that a weaker claim—namely, that pornography uniquely contributes to a hostile environment for women—also cannot be sustained. What, then, might be suggested as a way of singling out pornography from other forms of expression in such a way as to make an argument for its restriction or prohibition more plausible?

The newest turn in the pornography debate is to argue that pornography is not merely a form of expression with potentially bad effects. Some theorists encourage us to think of pornography also as a *practice*, specifically as a practice of sex discrimination. Catharine MacKinnon, Andrea Dworkin, and Susan Cole[24] argue that pornography is more than just a form of expression, and they insist upon a broader understanding of pornography's empirical dimensions. Pornography *is* a form of expression: it has, in legal terms, expressive content or a message. But pornography has the content it

---

[24]MacKinnon, "Francis Biddle's Sister: Pornography, Civil Rights, and Speech," 163–197; Andrea Dworkin, *Pornography: Men Possessing Women* (New York: Plume, 1989); Susan G. Cole, *Pornography and the Sex Crisis* (Toronto: Amanita, 1989).

has only because certain things happen to particular people. As MacKinnon says, "Suppose that the sexually explicit has a content element: it contains a penis ramming into a vagina. Does that mean that the picture of this conveys the idea of a penis ramming into a vagina, or does the viewer see and experience a penis ramming into a vagina?"[25] Her point is that the production of pornography, especially photographic magazines and films, requires that real things, some of which are dangerous or abusive, happen to real women and men. Furthermore, MacKinnon argues, pornography *delivers* its message in a unique way. Because pornography is primarily a tool for masturbation, when men become aroused and orgasmic using pornography, they are performing a sex act. In other words, to the extent that pornography's message is grasped by its consumers, it is grasped through sex. On these grounds, we are encouraged to construe pornography in very inclusive terms: *pornography* does not refer just to a collection of magazines, films, and books; the term also encompasses the conditions required for its production, its use, and its ultimate effects. It is this broader focus that underlies the view, espoused by MacKinnon and others, that pornography not only says certain things, it also does certain things. It is a form of expression that is also a particular activity.

This understanding makes possible a different sort of argument for the restriction or prohibition of pornography. In particular, it permits an argument that does not rely on (i) denying that pornography is a form of expression, or (ii) rejecting the importance of protecting free speech, or (iii) indeterminate empirical studies about the negative effects of pornography. It so happens that in the United States there is considerable jurisprudential precedent to the effect that some forms of expression or speech do not fall under First Amendment protection *because* these forms of speech are also forms of discriminatory conduct: "social life is full of words that are legally treated as the acts they constitute without so much as a whimper from the First Amendment."[26] Among these "exceptions" to the First Amendment are: "fighting words," or words "which by their very utterance inflict injury or tend to incite an immediate breach of the peace,"[27] and various utterances that, produced in a certain context, in fact constitute discriminatory

---

[25]MacKinnon, *Only Words*, 24.
[26]MacKinnon, *Only Words*, 12.
[27]*Chaplinsky v. New Hampshire*, 315 U.S. 568, 572 (1942).

behavior—for example, "'help wanted—male,' 'sleep with me and I'll give you an A,' 'fuck me or you're fired.'"[28]

In Canada, the situation is slightly different. Hate propaganda—that is, speech which willfully promotes hatred against any identifiable group on the basis of color, race, religion, or ethnic origin—is illegal.[29] However, in *R. v. Keegstra*,[30] the Canadian Supreme Court ruled that hate propaganda *does* fall under the protection of section 2(b) of the Charter. Nonetheless, it argued, this expression can be legitimately restricted under section 1, which states the following perfectly general constraint on all the rights and liberties in the Charter: "The Canadian Charter of Rights and Freedoms guarantees the rights and freedoms set out in it subject to reasonable limits prescribed by law as can be demonstrably justified in a free and democratic society." Hence, three ways of making the desired argument about pornography would be: in the United States, (i) to show that pornography is relevantly similar to other forms of unprotected expression; and in Canada, (iia) to show either that pornography is hate propaganda or (iib) that its restriction is legitimate in a free and democratic society. Let us look briefly at (iia) and (iib) first.

Several feminists have suggested that we ought to construe pornography as a form of hate propaganda;[31] and in 1978, the Fraser Committee in Canada wrote, "If one accepts the argument that pornography is an expression of misogyny, then use of the hate propaganda section of the *Code* in this connection is particularly attractive."[32] But it is not obvious that pornography satisfies the legal definition of hate propaganda, as it appears in the Canadian Criminal Code. Section 319(2) makes the *willful* promotion of hatred against an identifiable group a crime. Thus, in order for pornography to be actionable under the rubric of hate propaganda, it must be established

---

[28]Catharine A. MacKinnon, *Only Words,* 13–14. MacKinnon cites, in order, the following case law for these utterances: *Pittsburgh Press Co. v. Pittsburgh Commission on Human Relations,* 413 U.S. 376, 379 (1973); *Alexander v. Yale University,* 459 F. Supp. 1, 3–4 (D. Conn. 1977), aff'd. 631 F.2d 178 (2d Cir. 1984); *Stockett v. Tolin,* 791 F. Supp. 1536, 1543 (S.D. Fla. 1992).

[29]See section 319(2) of the Canadian Criminal Code.

[30]*R. v. Keegstra* [1990] 3 S.C.R. 697.

[31]See, for example, Margaret Atwood, "Pornography," in *Contemporary Moral Issues,* 2nd ed., ed. Wesley Cragg (Toronto: McGraw-Hill Ryerson, Ltd., 1987); Susan Brownmiller, *Against Our Will: Men, Women and Rape* (New York: Simon & Schuster, 1975); and Susan Griffin, *Pornography and Silence: Culture's Revenge against Nature* (New York: Harper & Row, 1981).

[32]Special Committee on Pornography and Prostitution in Canada, *Pornography and Prostitution in Canada,* vol. 1 (Ottawa: Supply and Services, 1985), 319.

that it is the conscious intention of those who produce pornography to promote hatred against women. Not only would this be very hard to do; it is also probably untrue that the deliberate intention of pornographers is to promote misogyny. (Their intention to make a profit from the sale of this material is undeniable.) Pornography has thus not been addressed legally in Canada as a form of hate propaganda.[33] However, the second argument available in a Canadian context—namely, that pornography is a form of "protected" speech that nonetheless may be legitimately restricted in a free and democratic society—has been made.

In 1992, the Canadian Supreme Court unanimously ruled[34] that, although the obscenity provision of the Criminal Code (section 163) constitutes an infringement of the right to free speech guaranteed under section 2(b) of the Charter, the prohibition of certain types of pornography is warranted in light of the threat they are presumed to pose to other Charter values—especially to equality and dignity. The Court conceded the indeterminacy of the empirical evidence linking pornography with violence against women but argued that it is reasonable to hold that the dissemination of certain forms of pornography is both directly and indirectly harmful to women. Thus, the current situation in Canada is that material which depicts "explicit sex with violence" or "explicit sex without violence but which subjects people to treatment that is degrading or dehumanizing" is legally obscene and is thus prohibited. Sexually explicit representations that do not depict violence, degradation, or dehumanization are not illegal.

Let us now turn to the U.S. context. I suggested above that a potentially successful strategy for the anti-pornography advocate would be to show that pornography resembles, in the relevant respects, other forms of speech or expression that the Supreme Court has deemed unprotected. Some forms of speech do not fall under the protection of the First Amendment by virtue of the sort of conduct they constitute—for example, the verbal incitement to violence and various forms of discrimination that are realized by words. This strategy is adopted by Catharine MacKinnon in her essay "Francis Biddle's Sister: Pornography, Civil Rights, and Speech" (in Part One), in which she argues that pornography, understood broadly as a practice that traffics in women's bodies, is a form of sex discrimination. (Because MacKinnon draws

---

[33]On the desirability of treating pornography as a form of hate propaganda, see Law Reform Commission of Canada, Working Paper 50, *Hate Propaganda*, 1986.
[34]*R. v. Butler* [1992] 1 S.C.R. 452.

on the work of Andrea Dworkin, let us call this the MacKinnon-Dworkin approach.) This argument embodies two further claims. First, requiring, as it sometimes does, the coercion and abuse of women for its manufacture, and leading, as it sometimes does, to the rape and assault of women, pornography is said to subordinate women. Second, it is claimed that pornography silences women: by creating and maintaining a social hierarchy in which women are believed to be inferior and essentially sexual, it prevents women from being heard authentically—that is, it robs their speech of power. Arguably, too, pornography is used against women to prevent them from speaking.[35]

The MacKinnon-Dworkin approach to constructing the problem of pornography differs from earlier feminist anti-pornography arguments in at least the following respects. First, it is underpinned by a far more complex and sophisticated theory of gender and of the social construction of sexuality (see Andrea Dworkin's and MacKinnon's essays in Part One). Second, although it, too, is motivated by the alleged negative effects of the end-products of pornography (for example, magazines and films), the MacKinnon-Dworkin approach emphasizes an inclusive understanding of pornography's empirical dimensions. MacKinnon and Dworkin urge that we pay as much attention to the production of pornography as to its consumption and the effects of that consumption. Third, and most important, MacKinnon and Dworkin suggest that pornography does more than simply give men bad ideas about women or cause men to harm women; they claim that pornography itself *subordinates* and *silences* women. Thus, MacKinnon and Dworkin do not construct the problem of pornography as a conflict about sexual morality and the state's role in enforcing it. Nor do they see it as a conflict between the good and bad consequences of free speech. By attributing to pornography itself the power to subordinate and silence women, MacKinnon and Dworkin argue that pornography poses a substantial threat to women's equality—so much of a threat, in fact, that women's equality is unimaginable while pornography continues to exist.

If the MacKinnon-Dworkin analysis is plausible, an argument for a prohibitive policy on pornography based upon it would not be immediately vulnerable to the objections raised against the earlier feminist analysis (discussed in the previous section). Furthermore, if the claim that pornography silences

---

[35]See the testimony presented at the Public Hearings in Minneapolis in *Pornography and Sexual Violence: Evidence of the Links* (London: Everywoman, 1988); and Linda Lovelace, *Ordeal* (Secaucus, N.J.: Citadel Press, 1980).

women can be established, then even the most ardent defenders of free speech will have to take note. This, at any rate, is the hope. However, Dworkin's and MacKinnon's arguments have been subject to considerable criticism.

From within feminist theory, the account of gender and its role in the social construction of sexuality, which underpins MacKinnon's approach in particular, has met with objections.[36] As the essays by Ellen Willis and Mariana Valverde in Part Three show, there is plenty of debate among feminists concerning the proper way to formulate the problem of pornography and about what theoretical and strategic position that problem ought to occupy on various feminist agendas. Not all contemporary feminists share MacKinnon's view about what pornography is; far less do they agree on what ought to be done about it.

Neither has MacKinnon's account met with legal success. In 1983, Catharine MacKinnon and Andrea Dworkin drafted a model anti-pornography ordinance for the city of Minneapolis. The ordinance was premised on a detailed definition of pornography (which appears in the Legal Appendix) and was devised to allow individual women (and others who could show they had been treated *as women*) to seek damages from the consumers, producers, and distributors of pornography, which they could demonstrate had been harmful to them. This ordinance was passed by the City Council but vetoed by the mayor. A somewhat modified version of it was proposed in Indianapolis in 1984 with more success, but it was immediately challenged as unconstitutional. Two lower courts determined that the ordinance was indeed unconstitutional, and the Supreme Court summarily dismissed the appeal to this ruling. (See the Legal Appendix for details.)

Finally, a cluster of philosophical problems also arise. Not long after the MacKinnon-Dworkin ordinance appeared, philosophers began to raise questions concerning the coherence of the claims that pornography *is* the subordination of women and that it *silences* women.[37] How is it possible, they asked, that *pornography* as such could do such things? Isn't subordination something that only *people* can do to other people? How could mere

---

[36]See, for example, Drucilla Cornell, *Beyond Accommodation* (New York: Routledge, 1991), chap. 3.

[37]See Melinda Vadas, "A First Look at the Pornography/Civil Rights Ordinance: Could Pornography Be the Subordination of Women?" *Journal of Philosophy* 84 (1987): 487–511; and W. A. Parent, "A Second Look at Pornography and the Subordination of Women," *Journal of Philosophy* 87 (1990): 205–211.

representations rob women of the power of effective speech? These objections—along with responses to them by Rae Langton and Jennifer Hornsby—are discussed in detail in Part Four. Langton and Hornsby attempt to show how speech act theory—a philosophical account of the workings of language that emphasizes the things we can *do* with words—can be used to good effect in defending the twin claims that pornography subordinates and that it silences.

This recent work on speech act theory and pornography certainly makes more plausible the claims that pornography subordinates and silences women. But nothing obvious about what can legitimately be done about pornography follows from the coherence of those claims. Even if it is intelligible to say that pornography is *capable* of doing these things, it does not follow automatically that pornography *does* do them. In his essay "Liberty and Pornography" (Part Two) and elsewhere,[38] Ronald Dworkin argues against the idea that the problem of pornography should be constructed as (i) a conflict between women's liberty to participate in the political process and pornographers' liberty of expression or (ii) a conflict between women's and pornographers' rights to free speech. As we have already seen, Dworkin is skeptical of the power of pornography—exclusively or overwhelmingly—to limit women's ability to participate in political decision making and action. Even if this were true, Dworkin argues, "the right to free speech [that] includes a right to circumstances that encourage one to speak, and a right that others grasp and respect what one means to say" is not a right (or rights) "that any society can recognize or enforce." In other words, a constitutional or Charter guarantee of free speech does not (and cannot) carry with it a guarantee of "a sympathetic or even competent understanding of what one says."

This new construction of the problem of pornography has certainly deepened our understanding of what sort of problem pornography presents, and it raises many new and interesting questions of its own. In particular, as the papers in this volume make clear, we need to think carefully about the language and concepts we employ in our discussions about pornography. Could it be, as Elizabeth Fox-Genovese has suggested, that any construction of the problem of pornography that focuses on *individual* rights and liberties will be insufficiently sensitive to considerations of community and to what we might call public morality? That is, might we not reach a better understand-

---

[38]Ronald Dworkin, "Women and Pornography," *New York Review of Books*, 21 October 1993.

ing of pornography, its effects, and what we ought to do about it if we were to focus even more fully on contextual matters?[39]

An insistence that we pay attention to the context in which pornography is produced and consumed is a central theme in the work of several feminist writers represented here. It is important to note that this context is the same context in which we must think about our rights and liberties. This idea is evident in Stanley Fish's essay, "There's No Such Thing as Free Speech and It's a Good Thing, Too" (Part Two). Speaking about free speech generally, Fish does not reject the importance of individual rights and liberties, but, he says, we must think about liberty and equality in concrete, not purely abstract, terms. Human beings, their freedoms, and their status relative to one another are matters of substance. People and their lives are shaped by the access they have or do not have to certain political goods, and effective argument on public policy (for example, what to do about pornography) must take these facts into account. North Americans *do* live in a world of inequality, and it is arguable that the abstraction and the (alleged) neutrality in existing laws make for bad application in actual cases. In the context of inequality, the deployment of neutral principles runs the risk of perpetuating that inequality. The ideal of neutrality—of treating like cases alike—naturally goes along with the ideal of justice as fairness. If we can assume, for the purposes of public policy, that all citizens are the same with respect to their access to basic civic goods such as free speech, then the neutral application of neutral principles is well-motivated. But it is precisely this assumption that is presently under attack and from a variety of quarters. Thus, it might be suggested that the problem of pornography is a special case of what may be the greatest challenge currently facing Western democracies.

7. Conclusion

We have considered three ways in which the problem of pornography has been constructed. The first saw the problem of pornography as a conflict between liberals and conservatives over the moral status of nonprocreative sex,

---

[39]See, for example, Michael Sandel, "Morality and the Liberal Ideal," *New Republic,* 7 May 1984, 15–17. Such skepticism regarding the efficacy of individualistic approaches to social policy is now widespread in contemporary thought and arises for issues other than pornography; for example, see Kathryn Pyne Addelson, "Knower/Doers and Their Moral Problems," in *Feminist Epistemologies,* ed. Linda Alcoff and Elizabeth Potter (New York: Routledge, 1993), 265–294.

masturbation, and sexually explicit representation; the second as a conflict between the value of free speech and the disvalue of probable harm to women. The third takes pornography to be a form of sex discrimination. I have outlined some of the arguments that go along with each of these ways of formulating the problem of pornography as well as some of the difficulties that beset them. In North America, our sexual morality has changed dramatically during this century, and given the reluctance of the courts to engage in legislating morality, perhaps it is better to recognize, as Catharine MacKinnon suggests, that pornography is "not [only] a moral issue."[40] However, the difficulty in establishing the causal connection between pornography and violence against women renders the simple harm-based approach inadequate. Finally, the sex discrimination construction of the problem of pornography opens up a host of new and nasty political and philosophical queries.

As the essays in this collection make vivid, thinking seriously about pornography is a complicated matter. Not only is it the case that pornography raises extraordinarily complex philosophical and legal questions; it has also been one of the most politically charged topics of our time. Perhaps where one stands on the problem of pornography, indeed, what one takes the *problem* of pornography to be, is still a litmus test—only now for very different things.

---

[40]Catharine A. MacKinnon, "Not a Moral Issue," *Feminism Unmodified* (Cambridge, Mass.: Harvard University Press, 1987), 146–162.

Characterizing Pornography

The four papers in Part One attempt to offer a clear characterization of pornography. Much of the debate about pornography has been a debate at cross-purposes, because people often mean very different things when they use the word *pornography*. So, for example, suppose you think "pornography" refers to pictures of naked people having sexual intercourse. And suppose your friend thinks "pornography" refers to depictions of sexual activity that are degrading and dehumanizing to women. It is likely that the two of you will give very different answers to the question, What, if anything, ought to be done about pornography? And your answers would differ yet again from those of a third person who thinks pornography is a certain kind of powerful and subversive political speech.

Pornography is not synonymous with *obscenity*. The latter term dates back to the late sixteenth century and refers to things that are highly offensive or morally repugnant. *Pornography*, on the other hand, entered the language only in the nineteenth century and is strictly defined as "the explicit description or exhibition of sexual subjects or activity in literature, painting, films, etc., in a manner intended to stimulate erotic rather than aesthetic feelings. . . ."[1] In ordinary usage, however, both terms are vague. And while

---

[1] *The New Shorter Oxford English Dictionary*, ed. Lesley Brown (Oxford: Clarendon Press, 1993).

obscenity has a statutory definition in both U.S. and Canadian law, little consensus exists about the exact meaning of *pornography*.[2] This does not imply that it is impossible to formulate a sufficiently clear and plausible definition to get a discussion going. But it does suggest that, if we are to have any serious debate about pornography, we must be explicit about what we have in mind when we use that term. In particular, we must be aware of the moral and legal implications of defining pornography one way rather than another. On the one hand, if someone defines pornography as a form of political speech,[3] then they could argue that, as speech, pornography is *prima facie* protected under the First Amendment of the United States Constitution, and under section 2(b) of the Canadian Charter of Rights and Freedoms. On the other hand, someone who thinks that pornography is the "undiluted essence of anti-female propaganda"[4] will have a very different view about what protection pornography ought to enjoy and about what ought to be done about pornography.

Since a main concern is the moral assessment of pornography, it is crucial that we distinguish between *descriptive* and *normative* characterizations of it. Descriptive and normative characterizations of things, persons, or events are best thought of as ways of talking about those things, persons, or events. Roughly, a descriptive characterization of an event, say, is one that does not use any evaluative terms. For example, "Jim sang an aria" neutrally describes the event of Jim performing a song. The same event can be normatively characterized in the following way: "Jim screeched and howled his way through thirty bars of Mozart." Now, with respect to pornography, to say that pornography is the explicit depiction or representation of human beings engaged in sexual activity is to offer a descriptive characterization. To say, as Catharine MacKinnon and Andrea Dworkin do, that "pornography is the graphic sexu-

---

[2]That obscenity is defined in law does not mean that the courts have always been sure about what actually constitutes obscenity. For example, in the Canadian Criminal Code, section 163(8), obscenity is defined as "any publication a dominant characteristic of which is the undue exploitation of sex, or of sex with any one or more of the following subjects, namely crime, horror, cruelty and violence." But what constitutes the undue exploitation of sex? A similar difficulty attends the U.S. test of obscenity, which appeals to the notions of community standards and prurient interest. See the Legal Appendix for the evolution of the various tests of obscenity.

[3]See, for example, William E. Brigman, "Pornography as Political Expression," *Journal of Popular Culture* 17 (1983): 129–134; and the opinion of Judge Frank Easterbrook in *American Booksellers Association, Inc. v. Hudnut*, 598 F. Supp 1316 (SD Ind 1984).

[4]Susan Brownmiller, *Against Our Will: Men, Women and Rape* (New York: Simon & Schuster, 1975), 394.

ally explicit subordination of women . . ."[5] is to offer a normative characterization. The latter definition, notice, already settles part of the question about
the moral status of pornography. It says that pornography *is* the subordination
of women, and, arguably, the subordination of any group of persons is morally suspect. The former definition, on the other hand, does not so clearly
have moral force. For it is not obvious that there is something particularly
morally troubling about the representation of human sexual activity.

The point here is simply that descriptive characterizations allow the claim
that *some, but perhaps not all,* pornography is morally problematic. Moreover,
they make it relatively easy to tell whether some piece of material—a photograph or film—is pornographic. Normative characterizations, in contrast, do
not permit the easy identification of pornography as such, since, for example,
people disagree about what constitutes subordination. Normative characterizations such as the one above also have the effect of rendering all pornography morally problematic by definition.

A natural way to try to characterize pornography is to contrast it with
erotica. This is Gloria Steinem's approach in her paper, "Pornography and
Erotica: A Clear and Present Difference." Steinem emphasizes that human
beings engage in sexual activity for reasons other than procreation. We sometimes have sex with each other in order to bond deeply with another person
or simply to experience pleasure. But because erotica and pornography are
both about sex without procreation, they are easily confused. Steinem draws
our attention to the etymology of the words *erotica* and *pornography*, reminding us that, although *erotica* has its roots in *eros* (passionate love), *pornography* originally referred to writing about prostitutes. Both pornography
and erotica involve representations of sexual activity, but, Steinem claims,
erotica can be distinguished from pornography by the presence of mutuality,
choice, and shared pleasure. The mark of the pornographic, on the other
hand, is the absence of choice and the presence of violence, dominance, and
conquest.

Steinem's suggestion is somewhat helpful, but reasonable people also disagree on what is erotic. So if pornography is to be defined in contrast with
erotica, we will need to reach consensus on the erotic before we can say what

---

[5]This is the beginning of the definition of pornography that MacKinnon and Dworkin
offer in their model anti-pornography ordinance. For the complete definition, see Catharine A.
MacKinnon, *Feminism Unmodified: Discourses on Life and Law* (Cambridge, Mass.: Harvard
University Press, 1987), 262 n. 1 and/or the Legal Appendix.

we mean by "pornography." More important, people disagree when a representation is one that depicts an asymmetry in power or an absence of choice. For example, can we conclude from a picture of a clothed man and a naked woman that the woman is not there by choice? Would a photograph of a woman masturbating alone be erotic or pornographic according to Steinem's characterizations?

You might think that the answer to these questions is "It depends." Photographs of the types described may be either erotic or pornographic, depending on who took them, where they are displayed, how the people came to be participating in them, and so on. In other words, we need to pay attention to the *context* in which such representations are made and consumed. This dimension of the task of characterizing pornography is taken up explicitly by philosopher Helen E. Longino. In her paper in Part One, Longino offers the following definition of pornography: "Pornography . . . is verbal or pictorial material which represents or describes sexual behavior that is degrading or abusive to one or more of the participants *in such a way as to endorse the degradation.*" This notion of endorsement is crucial to Longino's characterization. She argues that degrading sexual activity—for example, rape or sexual torture—can be depicted in ways that either implicitly or explicitly approve or recommend that behavior. One way in which such behavior is endorsed is presentation of it in a glossy magazine with the intention of providing sexual pleasure for the readers. Most people think that sexual pleasure is a good thing; and it is a fact in contemporary North American culture that a sure way to recommend anything—be it a car, a pair of jeans, or toothpaste—is to connect that thing with sex and sexual pleasure. Hence, when women are depicted as deriving sexual pleasure from humiliation, and when such depictions are marketed with the explicit aim of sexually arousing others, then that humiliation is endorsed. Longino does not claim that sex or sexual pleasure is morally problematic, but she does think that degradation and abuse are. Hence, any material that depicts such activities in an approving way (say, by sexualizing them) is problematic also.

An important aspect of Longino's paper is her argument that pornography lies about women's sexuality in general. Pornography, as she defines it, recommends the mistreatment of women and suggests that women themselves derive sexual pleasure from such abuse. Furthermore, in most contemporary manifestations of violent or degrading pornography, the fact that a woman is a woman appears to be sufficient to justify treating her in an abusive manner. In this way, Longino argues that pornography recommends the mistreatment of *all* women and that pornography is therefore immoral.

One thing we want a definition of pornography to do is allow us to determine, for any verbal or pictorial representation of sexual activity, whether it is pornographic. Longino's definition is helpful in that respect. It does allow us to distinguish between pornography and other sexual representations, and between pornography and what Longino calls "realism" (for example, a documentary film about rape). But it might be thought that Longino's definition does not go far enough. Although it would pick out depictions of sexual torture that are designed to arouse as pornography, it is not clear whether publications such as *Playboy* and *Penthouse* would be considered pornography. This indeterminacy is not a fault of Longino's definition, but rather is indicative of our uncertainty about what is degrading and abusive. There are clear cases, to be sure, but there are also many unclear cases. Are all nonviolent depictions of women in sexual poses degrading? An affirmative answer would require arguing either that all depictions of sex are degrading to any person involved in them, or that all depictions of women in sexual contexts are necessarily degrading to women.

Both Steinem and Longino emphasize that it is not simply the *sexual* content of certain representations that make them pornographic. They both focus on the *combination* of sex and violence or degradation. But perhaps we also need to think more deeply about the nature of sexuality itself. Andrea Dworkin and Catharine MacKinnon encourage us to do so.

Andrea Dworkin's piece is taken from the opening chapter of her book *Pornography: Men Possessing Women.* She writes, "The major theme of pornography as a genre is male power, its nature, its magnitude, its use, its meaning." According to Dworkin, male power is a complex system of interacting attributes, attitudes, and practices, comprising such things as men's superior physical strength, men's power to validate aspects of human experience selectively, and men's historical control of property and money. Most important, men and male interests define what is sex and sexuality for *both* sexes. This is what Dworkin means when she claims that men have the power of sex.

To make these abstract ideas more concrete, Dworkin describes in detail a photograph that appeared in *Hustler* magazine. She points out, one by the one, the aspects of the photograph that manifest the components of male power. The example is graphic and disturbing, but not obviously violent.

The magazine in which it appeared has a large circulation. Thus Dworkin's strategy is to show us how a "mainstream" representation of a woman in a sexual context can be problematic. Dworkin's main point is that "male power is the raison d'être of pornography; the degradation of the female is the means of achieving this power." Hence, like Longino, Dworkin sees the degradation of women as an essential component of pornography. But she goes further than Longino in construing this degradation as intrinsic to the very meaning of sexuality and sexual practices in a male-dominated culture.

At the heart of Catharine MacKinnon's work is the idea that, in male-dominated society, sex and sexuality are constructed in a way that is particularly damaging to women. In this excerpt from her speech entitled "Francis Biddle's Sister: Pornography, Civil Rights, and Speech," MacKinnon explains how she thinks pornography sexualizes violence against women. A central and organizing theme of pornography, according to MacKinnon, is gender inequality: women are depicted as being always sexually available and accessible to men, always eager to do whatever men want. Focusing mainly on violent pornography, MacKinnon argues that such material not only conveys a false message about what women want from sex (namely, cruelty and humiliation), but crucially is sex itself. Thus, pornography is more than just expression (or speech); it is also a practice (or activity). Perhaps the easiest way to understand this point is to think of the act of viewing pornography and being aroused by it as a sex act. Whenever a person watches a film of a woman being raped or tortured and is sexually aroused by that film, he or she is having sex. As MacKinnon writes, "Pornography is not imagery in some relation to a reality elsewhere constructed. It is not a distortion, reflection, projection, expression, fantasy, representation, or symbol either. It is a sexual reality." On the suppositions (1) that all pornography essentially embodies a power asymmetry between men and women, and (2) that pornography *is* sex in our society, then sex itself is problematic for women in our society. Here, as elsewhere, MacKinnon argues that pornography is best thought of as a form of sex discrimination. It is not only words and pictures but also uniquely capable of doing certain things. Pornography, by its very nature, subordinates women.[6] MacKinnon believes that the sexual subordination of

---

[6]MacKinnon's idea that pornography subordinates women has been criticized. See, for example, Ronald Dworkin, "Liberty and Pornography," *New York Review of Books*, 15 August 1991, 12–15 (reprinted in Part Two of this book); and W. A. Parent, "A Second Look at Pornography and the Subordination of Women," *Journal of Philosophy* 87 (1990): 202–211. Both the idea and the criticisms are addressed more fully in Part Four.

women through pornography is at the base of women's social and political oppression. So for her, the elimination of pornography is a necessary condition for achieving gender equality.

MacKinnon's paper is also important for her arguments about the ways in which women and their lives can be "invisible" from the perspective of the law. Since the law must be widely applicable, it is framed in terms of rather abstract notions and principles—for example, equality, liberty, and neutrality. However, MacKinnon argues that given the substantive inequalities that exist in our sexist and racist society, the law is often unable to be effective in righting injustices. Its commitment to neutrality prevents it from giving extra weight to the interests of some groups at the expense of others. MacKinnon argues that a commitment to neutrality assumes that all groups are equal to begin with, and she claims that once one recognizes that this is not so, the law in its current form seems rather inadequate.[7]

As we noted above, the way in which pornography is defined will determine to a great extent both what can and what ought to be done about it. If pornography is defined as a form of expression, albeit containing a fallacious and potentially dangerous message about the nature of women's sexuality, then a particular sort of argument will be required to support its restriction or censorship. In both the United States and Canada, there is enshrined in the law and in the popular imagination a solid commitment to free speech. Any suggestion that a particular piece of material ought to be censored or restricted is met with suspicion. Part Two deals with the topic of free speech in more detail, but the point to note here is that if pornography *is* taken to be a form of speech, then its constitutionally legitimate restriction will depend on showing that it is manifestly harmful. Given the explicit guarantees to free speech in both the U.S. Bill of Rights and in the Canadian Charter, those who would ban or restrict pornography bear the burden of proof. They must demonstrate that pornography is so immediately harmful to people that the state has a compelling interest in protecting its citizens from it. This has, as a matter of fact, been rather difficult to do. Empirical evidence concerning the effects of pornography is not definitive. Construing pornography as a form of sex discrimination, as MacKinnon recommends, allows the critic of pornography to claim that free speech arguments are beside the point. If such a definition of pornography is adopted, then the "problem" of pornography can be

---

[7]The notion of neutrality plays a central role in arguments concerning free speech, and it is addressed in Part Two.

separated from the criminal law, which deals with obscenity, and moved into the arena of civil rights. Indeed, MacKinnon and Andrea Dworkin have twice almost succeeded in getting civil anti-pornography legislation passed.[8]

The arguments presented in the following selections have been very influential. Thinking about pornography from a feminist perspective has changed the way in which arguments about pornography proceed (see the Introduction). But it would be a mistake to think that the views of Steinem, Longino, Dworkin, and MacKinnon constitute *the* feminist position on pornography. Many feminists have been highly critical of MacKinnon's and Dworkin's work in particular. Some of their objections are discussed in Part Three.

---

[8]The MacKinnon–Dworkin anti-pornography civil rights ordinance is discussed in more detail in the introduction to Part Four. See also the Bibliography, I: Pornography and the State, F. The Minneapolis Ordinance, for further reading.

GLORIA STEINEM

Erotica and Pornography: A Clear and Present Difference

Gloria Steinem is a writer, feminist activist, and journalist. She was the editor of Ms. *magazine from 1971 to 1987 and is the author of* Outrageous Acts and Everyday Rebellions *(1983) and* The Revolution from Within: A Book of Self-Esteem *(1992).*

Human beings are the only animals that experience the same sex drive at times when we can and cannot conceive.

Just as we developed uniquely human capacities for language, planning, memory, and invention along our evolutionary path, we also developed sexuality as a form of expression; a way of communicating that is separable from our need for sex as a way of perpetuating ourselves. For humans alone, sexuality can be and often is primarily a way of bonding, of giving and receiving pleasure, bridging differentness, discovering sameness, and communicating emotion.

We developed this and other human gifts through our ability to change our environment, adapt physically, and, in the long run, affect our own evolution. But as an emotional result of this spiraling path away from other animals, we seem to alternate between periods of exploring our unique abilities to forge new boundaries, and feelings of loneliness in the unknown that we ourselves have created; a fear that sometimes sends us back to the comfort of the animal world by encouraging us to exaggerate our sameness with it.

The separation of "play" from "work," for instance, is a problem only in the human world. So is the difference between art and nature, or an intellectual accomplishment and a physical one. As a result, we celebrate play, art, and invention as leaps into the unknown; but any imbalance can send us back to nostalgia for our primate past and the conviction that the basics of work, nature, and physical labor are somehow more worthwhile or even more moral.

In the same way, we have explored our sexuality as separable from conception: a pleasurable, empathetic bridge to strangers of the same species. We have even invented contraception—a skill that has probably existed in some form since our ancestors figured out the process of birth—in order to extend this uniquely human difference. Yet we also have times of atavistic suspicion that sex is not complete—or even legal or intended-by-god—if it cannot end in conception.

No wonder the concepts of "erotica" and "pornography" can be so crucially different, and yet so confused. Both assume that sexuality can be separated from conception, and therefore can be used to carry a personal message. That's a major reason why, even in our current culture, both may be called equally "shocking" or legally "obscene," a word whose Latin derivative means "dirty, containing filth." This gross condemnation of all sexuality that isn't harnessed to childbirth and marriage has been increased by the current backlash against women's progress. Out of fear that the whole patriarchal structure might be upset if women really had the autonomous power to decide our reproductive futures (that is, if we controlled the most basic means of production—the production of human beings), right-wing groups are not only denouncing pro-choice abortion literature as "pornographic," but are trying to stop the sending of all contraceptive information through the mails by invoking obscenity laws. . . .

Not surprisingly, this religious, visceral backlash has a secular, intellectual counterpart that relies heavily on applying the "natural" behavior of the animal world to humans. That application is questionable in itself, but these . . . studies make their political purpose even more clear in the particular animals they select and the habits they choose to emphasize. For example, some male primates (marmosets, titi monkeys, night monkeys) carry and/or generally "mother" their infants. [But these studies] prefer to discuss chimps and baboons, whose behavior is very "male chauvinist." The message is that females should accept their "destiny" of being sexually dependent and devote themselves to bearing and rearing their young.

Defending against such reaction in turn leads to another temptation: merely to reverse the terms, and declare that all nonprocreative sex is good. In fact, however, this human activity can be as constructive or destructive, moral or immoral, as any other. Sex as communication can send messages as different as life and death; even the origins of "erotica" and "pornography" reflect that fact. After all, "erotica" is rooted in "eros" or passionate love, and thus in the idea of positive choice, free will, the yearning for a particular person. (Interestingly, the definition of erotica leaves open the question of gender.) "Pornography" begins with a root "porno," meaning "prostitution" or "female captives," thus letting us know that the subject is not mutual love, or love at all, but domination and violence against women. (Though, of course, homosexual pornography may imitate this violence by putting a man in the "feminine" role of victim.) It ends with a root "graphos," meaning "writing about" or "description of," which puts still more distance between subject and object, and replaces a spontaneous yearning for closeness with objectification and voyeurism. The difference is clear in the words. It becomes even more so by example.

Look at any photo or film of people making love, really making love. The images may be diverse, but there is usually a sensuality and touch and warmth, an acceptance of bodies and nerve endings. There is always a spontaneous sense of people who are there because they want to be, out of shared pleasure.

Now look at any depiction of sex in which there is clear force, or an unequal power that spells coercion. It may be very blatant, with weapons of torture or bondage, wounds and bruises, some clear humiliation, or an adult's sexual power being used over a child. It may be much more subtle: a physical attitude of conqueror and victim, the use of race or class difference to imply the same thing, perhaps a very unequal nudity, with one person exposed and vulnerable while the other is clothed. In either case, there is no sense of equal choice or equal power.

The first is erotic: a mutually pleasurable, sexual expression between people who have enough power to be there by positive choice. It may or may not strike a sense-memory in the viewer, or be creative enough to make the unknown seem real; but it doesn't require us to identify with a conqueror or a victim. It is truly sensuous, and may give us a contagion of pleasure.

The second is pornographic: its message is violence, dominance, and conquest. It is sex being used to reinforce some inequality, or to create one, or to tell us that pain and humiliation (ours or someone else's) are really the same as pleasure. If we are to feel anything, we must identify with conqueror or victim. That means we can only experience pleasure through the adoption of some degree of sadism or masochism. It also means that we may feel diminished by the role of conqueror, or enraged, humiliated, and vengeful by sharing identity with the victim.

Perhaps one could simply say that erotica is about sexuality, but pornography is about power and sex-as-weapon—in the same way we have come to understand that rape is about violence, and not really about sexuality at all.

Yes, it's true that there are women who have been forced by violent families and dominating men to confuse love with pain, so much so that they have become masochists. (A fact that in no way excuses those who administer such

pain.) But the truth is that, for most women—and for men with enough humanity to imagine themselves in the predicament of women—pornography
could serve as aversion-conditioning toward sex.

Of course, there will always be personal differences about what is and is
not erotic, and there may be cultural differences for a long time to come.
Many women feel that sex makes them vulnerable and therefore may continue to need more sense of personal connection and safety than men do before allowing any erotic feelings. Men, on the other hand, may continue to
feel less vulnerable, and therefore more open to such potential danger as sex
with strangers. Women now frequently find competence and expertise erotic
in men, but that may pass as we develop those qualities in ourselves. As some
men replace the need for submission from childlike women with the pleasure
of cooperation from equals, they may find a partner's competence to be
erotic, too.

Such group changes plus individual differences will continue to be reflected in sexual love between people of the same gender, as well as between
women and men. The point is not to dictate sameness, but to discover ourselves and each other through a sexuality that is an exploring, pleasurable,
empathetic part of our lives; a human sexuality that is unchained both from
unwanted pregnancies and from violence.

But that is a hope, not a reality. At the moment, fear of change is increas-
ing both the indiscriminate repression of all nonprocreative sex in the religious and "conservative" male-dominated world, and the pornographic
vengeance against women's sexuality in the secular world of "liberal" or
"radical" men. It's almost futuristic to debate what is and is not truly erotic,
when many women are again being forced into compulsory motherhood,
and the number of pornographic murders, tortures, and women-hating images are on the increase in both popular culture and real life.

Together, both of the above forms of repression perpetuate that familiar
division: wife or whore; "good" woman who is constantly vulnerable to
pregnancy or "bad" woman who is unprotected from violence. Both roles
would be upset if we were to control our own sexuality. And that's exactly
what we must do.

In spite of all our atavistic suspicions and training for the "natural" role
of motherhood, we took up the complicated battle for reproductive freedom.
Our bodies had borne the health burden of endless births and poor abor-
tions, and we had a greater motive than men for separating sexuality and
conception.

Now we have to take up the equally complex burden of explaining that all
nonprocreative sex is not alike. We have a motive: our right to a uniquely
human sexuality, and sometimes even to survival. As it is, our bodies have too
rarely been enough our own to develop erotica in our own lives, much less
in art and literature. And our bodies have too often been the objects of pornography and the woman-hating, violent practice that it preaches. Consider

also our spirits that break a little each time we see ourselves in chains or full labial display for the conquering male viewer, bruised or on our knees, screaming a real or pretended pain to delight the sadist, pretending to enjoy what we don't enjoy, to be blind to the images of our sisters that really haunt us—humiliated often enough ourselves by the truly obscene idea that sex and the domination of women must be combined.

Sexuality is human, free, separate—and so are we.

But until we untangle the lethal confusion of sex with violence, there will be more pornography and less erotica. There will be little murders in our beds—and very little love.

HELEN E. LONGINO

Pornography, Oppression, and Freedom: A Closer Look

Helen E. Longino is professor of philosophy and women's studies at Rice University. One of the founding editors of Hypatia: A Journal of Feminist Philosophy, *she is the author of* Can There Be a Feminist Science? *(1986) and* Science as Social Knowledge: Values and Objectivity in Scientific Inquiry *(1990).*

I. Introduction

The much-touted sexual revolution of the 1960's and 1970's not only freed various modes of sexual behavior from the constraints of social disapproval, but also made possible a flood of pornographic material. According to figures provided by WAVPM (Women Against Violence in Pornography and Media), the number of pornographic magazines available at newsstands has grown from zero in 1953 to forty in 1977, while sales of pornographic films in Los Angeles alone have grown from $15 million in 1969 to $85 million in 1976.[1]

Traditionally, pornography was condemned as immoral because it presented sexually explicit material in a manner designed to appeal to "prurient interests" or a "morbid" interest in nudity and sexuality, material which furthermore lacked any redeeming social value and which exceeded "customary limits of candor." While these phrases, taken from a definition of "obscenity"

Source: From *Take Back the Night*, ed. Laura Lederer. New York: William Morrow & Co., 1980. Reprinted by permission of the author.

proposed in the 1954 American Law Institute's *Model Penal Code,*[2] require some criteria of application to eliminate vagueness, it seems that what is objectionable is the explicit description or representation of bodily parts or sexual behavior for the purpose of inducing sexual stimulation or pleasure on the part of the reader or viewer. This kind of objection is part of a sexual ethic that subordinates sex to procreation and condemns all sexual interactions outside of legitimated marriage. It is this code which was the primary target of the sexual revolutionaries in the 1960's, and which has given way in many areas to more open standards of sexual behavior.

One of the beneficial results of the sexual revolution has been a growing acceptance of the distinction between questions of sexual mores and questions of morality. This distinction underlies the old slogan, "Make love, not war," and takes harm to others as the defining characteristic of immorality. What is immoral is behavior which causes injury to or violation of another person or people. Such injury may be physical or it may be psychological. To cause pain to another, to lie to another, to hinder another in the exercise of her or his rights, to exploit another, to degrade another, to misrepresent and slander another are instances of immoral behavior. Masturbation or engaging voluntarily in sexual intercourse with another consenting adult of the same or the other sex, as long as neither injury nor violation of either individual or another is involved, is not immoral. Some sexual behavior is morally objectionable, but not because of its sexual character. Thus, adultery is immoral not because it involves sexual intercourse with someone to whom one is not legally married, but because it involves breaking a promise (of sexual and emotional fidelity to one's spouse). Sadistic, abusive, or forced sex is immoral because it injures and violates another.

The detachment of sexual chastity from moral virtue implies that we cannot condemn forms of sexual behavior merely because they strike us as distasteful or subversive of the Protestant work ethic, or because they depart from standards of behavior we have individually adopted. It has thus seemed to imply that no matter how offensive we might find pornography, we must tolerate it in the name of freedom from illegitimate repression. I wish to argue that this is not so, that pornography is immoral because it is harmful to people.

II. What Is Pornography?

I define pornography as *verbal or pictorial explicit representations of sexual behavior that,* in the words of the Commission on Obscenity and Pornography, *have as a distinguishing characteristic "the degrading and demeaning portrayal of the role and status of the human female . . . as a mere sexual object t be exploited and manipulated sexually."*[3] In pornographic books, magazin and films, women are represented as passive and as slavishly dependent u men. The role of female characters is limited to the provision of sexual services to men. To the extent that women's sexual pleasure is represented at all, it is subordinated to that of men and is never an end in itself as is the sexual pleasure of men. What pleases women is the use of their bodies to satisfy male desires. While the sexual objectification of women is common to all pornography, women are the recipients of even worse treatment in violent pornography, in which women characters are killed, tortured, gang-raped, mutilated, bound, and otherwise abused, as a means of providing sexual stimulation or pleasure to the male characters. It is this development which has attracted the attention of feminists and been the stimulus to an analysis of pornography in general.[4]

Not all sexually explicit material is pornography, nor is all material which contains representations of sexual abuse and degradation pornography.

A representation of a sexual encounter between adult persons which is characterized by mutual respect is, once we have disentangled sexuality and morality, not morally objectionable. Such a representation would be one in which the desires and experiences of each participant were regarded by the other participants as having a validity and a subjective importance equal to those of the individual's own desire and experiences. In such an encounter, each participant acknowledges the other participant's basic human dignity and personhood. Similarly, a representation of a nude human body (in whole or in part) in such a manner that the person shown maintains self-respect— e.g., is not portrayed in a degrading position—would not be morally objectionable. The educational films of the National Sex Forum, as well as a certain amount of erotic literature and art, fall into this category. While some erotic materials are beyond the standards of modesty held by some individuals, they are not for this reason immoral.

A representation of a sexual encounter which is not characterized by mutual respect, in which at least one of the parties is treated in a manner beneath her or his dignity as a human being, is no longer simple erotica. That a representation is of degrading behavior does not in itself, however, make it pornographic. Whether or not it is pornographic is a function of contextual features. Books and films may contain descriptions or representations of a rape in order to explore the consequences of such an assault upon its victim. What is being shown is abusive or degrading behavior which attempts to deny the humanity and dignity of the person assaulted, yet the context surrounding the representation, through its exploration of the consequences of the act, acknowledges and reaffirms her dignity. Such books and films, far from being pornographic, are (or can be) highly moral, and fall into the category of moral realism.

What makes a work a work of pornography, then, is not simply its representation of degrading and abusive sexual encounters, but its implicit, if not explicit, approval and recommendation of sexual behavior that is immoral, that physically or psychologically violates the personhood of one of the participants. Pornography, then, is verbal or pictorial material which represents or describes sexual behavior that is degrading or abusive to one or more of the participants in *such a way as to endorse the degradation*. The participants so treated in virtually all heterosexual pornography are women or children, so heterosexual pornography is, as a matter of fact, material which endorses sexual behavior that is degrading and/or abusive to women and children. As I use the term "sexual behavior," this includes sexual encounters between persons, behavior which produces sexual stimulation or pleasure for one of the participants, and behavior which is preparatory to or invites sexual activity. Behavior that is degrading or abusive includes physical harm or abuse, and physical or psychological coercion. In addition, behavior which ignores or devalues the real interests, desires, and experiences of one or more participants in any way is degrading. Finally, that a person has chosen or consented to be harmed, abused, or subjected to coercion does not alter the degrading character of such behavior.

Pornography communicates its endorsement of the behavior it represents by various features of the pornographic context: the degradation of the female characters is represented as providing pleasure to the participant males and, even worse, to the participant females, and there is no suggestion that this sort of treatment of others is inappropriate to their status as human beings. These two features are together sufficient to constitute endorsement of the represented behavior. The contextual features which make material pornographic are intrinsic to the material. In addition to these, extrinsic features, such as the purpose for which the material is presented—i.e., the sexual arousal/ pleasure/satisfaction of its (mostly) male consumers—or an accompanying text, may reinforce or make explicit the endorsement. Representations which in and of themselves do not show or endorse degrading behavior may be put into a pornographic context by juxtaposition with others that are degrading, or by a text which invites or recommends degrading behavior toward the subject represented. In such a case the whole complex—the series of representations or representations with text—is pornographic.

The distinction I have sketched is one that applies most clearly to sequential material—a verbal or pictorial (filmed) story—which represents an action and provides a temporal context for it. In showing the before and after, a narrator or film-maker has plenty of opportunity to acknowledge the dignity of the person violated or clearly to refuse to do so. It is somewhat more difficult to apply the distinction to single still representations. The contextual features cited above, however, are clearly present in still photographs or pictures that glamorize degradation and sexual violence. Phonograph album covers and advertisements offer some prime examples of such glamorization. Their representations of women in chains (the Ohio Players), or bound by ropes and black and blue (the Rolling Stones) are considered high-quality commercial "art" and glossily prettify the violence they represent. Since the standard function of prettification and glamorization is the communication of desirability, these albums and ads are communicating the desirability of violence against women. Representations of women bound or chained, particularly those of women bound in such a way as to make their breasts, or genital or anal areas vulnerable to any passerby, endorse the scene they represent by the absence of any indication that this treatment of women is in any way inappropriate.

To summarize: Pornography is not just the explicit representation or description of sexual behavior, nor even the explicit representation or description of sexual behavior which is degrading and/or abusive to women. Rather, it is material that explicitly represents or describes degrading and abusive sexual behavior so as to endorse and/or recommend the behavior as described. The contextual features, moreover, which communicate such endorsement are intrinsic to the material; that is, they are features whose removal or alteration would change the representation or description.

This account of pornography is underlined by the etymology and original meaning of the word "pornography." *The Oxford English Dictionary* defines pornography as "Description of the life, manners, etc. of prostitutes and their patrons [from πορνη (porne) meaning "harlot" and γραφειν (graphein) meaning "to write"]; hence the expression or suggestion of obscene or unchaste subjects in literature or art."[5]

Let us consider the first part of the definition for a moment. In the transactions between prostitutes and their clients, prostitutes are paid, directly or indirectly, for the use of their bodies by the client for sexual pleasure.* Traditionally males have obtained from female prostitutes what they could not or did not wish to get from their wives or women friends, who, because of the character of their relation to the male, must be accorded some measure of human respect. While there are limits to what treatment is seen as appropriate toward women as wives or women friends, the prostitute as prostitute exists to provide sexual pleasure to males. The female characters of contemporary pornography also exist to provide pleasure to males, but in the pornographic context no pretense is made to regard them as parties to a contractual arrangement. Rather, the anonymity of these characters makes each one Everywoman, thus suggesting not only that all women are appropriate subjects for the enactment of the most bizarre and demeaning male sexual fantasies, but also that this is their primary purpose. The recent escalation of violence in pornography—the presentation of scenes of bondage, rape, and torture of women for the sexual stimulation of the male characters or male viewers—while shocking in itself, is from this point of view merely a more vicious extension of a genre whose success depends on treating women in a manner beneath their dignity as human beings.

---

*In talking of prostitution here, I refer to the concept of, rather than the reality of, prostitution. The same is true of my remarks about relationships between women and their husbands or men friends.

III. *Pornography: Lies and Violence against Women*

What is wrong with pornography, then, is its degrading and dehumanizing portrayal of women (and *not* its sexual content). Pornography, by its very nature, requires that women be subordinate to men and mere instruments for the fulfillment of male fantasies. To accomplish this, pornography must lie. Pornography lies when it says that our sexual life is or ought to be subordinate to the service of men, that our pleasure consists in pleasing men and not ourselves, that we are depraved, that we are fit subjects for rape, bondage, torture, and murder. Pornography lies explicitly about women's sexuality, and through such lies fosters more lies about our humanity, our dignity, and our personhood.

Moreover, since nothing is alleged to justify the treatment of the female characters of pornography save their womanhood, pornography depicts all women as fit objects of violence by virtue of their sex alone. Because it is simply being female that, in the pornographic vision, justifies being violated, the lies of pornography are lies about all women. Each work of pornography is on its own libelous and defamatory, yet gains power through being reinforced by every other pornographic work. The sheer number of pornographic productions expands the moral issue to include not only assessing the morality or immorality of individual works, but also the meaning and force of the mass production of pornography.

The pornographic view of women is thoroughly entrenched in a booming portion of the publishing, film, and recording industries, reaching and affecting not only all who look to such sources for sexual stimulation, but also those of us who are forced into an awareness of it as we peruse magazines at newsstands and record albums in record stores, as we check the entertainment sections of city newspapers, or even as we approach a counter to pay for groceries. It is not necessary to spend a great deal of time reading or viewing pornographic material to absorb its male-centered definition of women. No longer confined within plain brown wrappers, it jumps out from billboards that proclaim "Live X-rated Girls!" or "Angels in Pain" or "Hot and Wild," and from magazine covers displaying a woman's genital area being spread open to the viewer by her own fingers.* Thus, even men who do not frequent pornographic shops and movie houses are supported in the sexist objectification of women by their environment. Women, too, are crippled by internalizing as self-images those that are presented to us by pornographers. Isolated from one another and with no source of support for an alternative view of female sexuality, we may not always find the strength to resist a message that dominates the common cultural media.

---

*This was a full-color magazine cover seen in a rack at the check-out counter of a corner delicatessen.

The entrenchment of pornography in our culture also gives it a signifi-cance quite beyond its explicit sexual messages. To suggest, as pornography does, that the primary purpose of women is to provide sexual pleasure to men is to deny that women are independently human or have a status equal to that of men. It is, moreover, to deny our equality at one of the most inti-mate levels of human experience. This denial is especially powerful in a hier-archical, class society such as ours, in which individuals feel good about themselves by feeling superior to others. Men in our society have a vested in-terest in maintaining their belief in the inferiority of the female sex, so that no matter how oppressed and exploited by the society in which they live and work, they can feel that they are at least superior to someone or some cat-egory of individuals—a woman or women. Pornography, by presenting women as wanton, depraved, and made for the sexual use of men, caters di-rectly to that interest.* The very intimate nature of sexuality which makes pornography so corrosive also protects it from explicit public discussion. The consequent lack of any explicit social disavowal of the pornographic image of women enables this image to continue fostering sexist attitudes even as the society publicly proclaims its (as yet timid) commitment to sexual equality.

In addition to finding a connection between the pornographic view of women and the denial to us of our full human rights, women are beginning to connect the consumption of pornography with committing rape and other acts of sexual violence against women. Contrary to the findings of the Com-mission on Obscenity and Pornography a growing body of research is docu-menting (1) a correlation between exposure to representations of violence and the committing of violent acts generally, and (2) a correlation between exposure to pornographic materials and the committing of sexually abusive or violent acts against women.[6] While more study is needed to establish pre-cisely what the causal relations are, clearly so-called hard-core pornography is not innocent.

From "snuff" films and miserable magazines in pornographic stores to *Hustler*, to phonograph album covers and advertisements, to *Vogue*, pornog-raphy has come to occupy its own niche in the communications and enter-tainment media and to acquire a quasi-institutional character (signaled by the use of diminutives such as "porn" or "porno" to refer to pornographic ma-terial, as though such familiar naming could take the hurt out). Its accep-tance by the mass media, whatever the motivation, means a cultural endorsement of its message. As much as the materials themselves, the social

---

*Pornography thus becomes another tool of capitalism. One feature of some contempo-rary pornography—the use of Black and Asian women in both still photographs and films—exploits the racism as well as the sexism of its white consumers. For a discussion of the interplay between racism and sexism under capitalism as it relates to violent crimes against women, see Angela Y. Davis, "Rape, Racism, and the Capitalist Setting," *The Black Scholar*, Vol. 9, No. 7, April 1978.

tolerance of these degrading and distorted images of women in such quantities is harmful to us, since it indicates a general willingness to see women in ways incompatible with our fundamental human dignity and thus to justify treating us in those ways.* The tolerance of pornographic representations of the rape, bondage, and torture of women helps to create and maintain a climate more tolerant of the actual physical abuse of women.† The tendency on the part of the legal system to view the victim of a rape as responsible for the crime against her is but one manifestation of this.

In sum, pornography is injurious to women in at least three distinct ways:

1. Pornography, especially violent pornography, is implicated in the committing of crimes of violence against women.

2. Pornography is the vehicle for the dissemination of a deep and vicious lie about women. It is defamatory and libelous.

3. The diffusion of such a distorted view of women's nature in our society as it exists today supports sexist (i.e., male-centered) attitudes, and thus reinforces the oppression and exploitation of women.

Society's tolerance of pornography, especially pornography on the contemporary massive scale, reinforces each of these modes of injury: By not disavowing the lie, it supports the male-centered myth that women are inferior and subordinate creatures. Thus, it contributes to the maintenance of a climate tolerant of both psychological and physical violence against women.

IV. Pornography and the Law

> Congress shall make no law respecting the establishment of religion, or prohibiting the free exercise thereof; or abridging the freedom of speech, or of the press; or the right of the people peaceably to assemble, and to petition the Government for a redress of grievances.
>
> —First Amendment, Bill of Rights of the United States Constitution

---

*This tolerance has a linguistic parallel in the growing acceptance and use of nonhuman nouns such as "chick," "bird," "filly," "fox," "doll," "babe," "skirt," etc., to refer to women, and of verbs of harm such as "fuck," "screw," "bang" to refer to sexual intercourse. See Robert Baker and Frederick Elliston. " 'Pricks' and 'Chicks': A Plea for Persons," *Philosophy and Sex* (Buffalo, N.Y.: Prometheus Books, 1975).

†This is supported by the fact that in Denmark the number of rapes committed has increased while the number of rapes reported to the authorities has decreased over the past twelve years. See *WAVPM Newspage,* Vol. 11, No. 5, June, 1978, quoting M. Harry, "Denmark Today—The Causes and Effects of Sexual Liberty" (paper presented to The Responsible Society, London, England, 1976). See also Eysenck and Nias, *Sex, Violence and the Media* (New York: St. Martin's Press, 1978), pp. 120–124.

Pornography is clearly a threat to women. Each of the modes of injury cited above offers sufficient reason at least to consider proposals for the social and legal control of pornography. The almost universal response from progressives to such proposals is that constitutional guarantees of freedom of speech and privacy preclude recourse to law.[7] While I am concerned about the erosion of constitutional rights and also think for many reasons that great caution must be exercised before undertaking a legal campaign against pornography, I find objections to such a campaign that are based on appeals to the First Amendment or to a right to privacy ultimately unconvincing.

Much of the defense of the pornographer's right to publish seems to assume that, while pornography may be tasteless and vulgar, it is basically an entertainment that harms no one but its consumers, who may at worst suffer from the debasement of their taste; and that therefore those who argue for its control are demanding an unjustifiable abridgment of the rights to freedom of speech of those who make and distribute pornographic materials and of the rights to privacy of their customers. The account of pornography given above shows that the assumptions of this position are false. Nevertheless, even some who acknowledge its harmful character feel that it is granted immunity from social control by the First Amendment, or that the harm that would ensue from its control outweighs the harm prevented by its control.

There are three ways of arguing that control of pornography is incompatible with adherence to constitutional rights. The first argument claims that regulating pornography involves an unjustifiable interference in the private lives of individuals. The second argument takes the First Amendment as a basic principle constitutive of our form of government, and claims that the production and distribution of pornographic material, as a form of speech, is an activity protected by that amendment. The third argument claims not that the pornographer's rights are violated, but that others' rights will be if controls against pornography are instituted.

The privacy argument is the easiest to dispose of. Since the open commerce in pornographic materials is an activity carried out in the public sphere, the publication and distribution of such materials, unlike their use by individuals, is not protected by rights to privacy. The distinction between the private consumption of pornographic material and the production and distribution of, or open commerce in, it is sometimes blurred by defenders of pornography. But I may entertain, in the privacy of my mind, defamatory opinions about another person, even though I may not broadcast them. So one might create without restraint—as long as no one were harmed in the course of preparing them—pornographic materials for one's personal use, but be restrained from reproducing and distributing them. In both cases what one is doing—in the privacy of one's mind or basement—may indeed be deplorable, but immune from legal proscription. Once the activity becomes public, however—i.e., once it involves others—it is no longer protected by the same rights that protect activities in the private sphere.*

In considering the second argument (that control of pornography, private or public, is wrong in principle), it seems important to determine whether we consider the right to freedom of speech to be absolute and unqualified. If it is, then obviously all speech, including pornography, is entitled to protection. But the right is, in the first place, not an unqualified right: There are several kinds of speech not protected by the First Amendment, including the incitement to violence in volatile circumstances, the solicitation of crimes, perjury and misrepresentation, slander, libel, and false advertising.† That there are forms of proscribed speech shows that we accept limitations on the right to freedom of speech if such speech, as do the forms listed, impinges on other rights. The manufacture and distribution of material which defames and threatens all members of a class by its recommendation of abusive and degrading behavior toward some members of that class simply in virtue of their membership in it seems a clear candidate for inclusion on the list. The right is therefore not an unqualified one.

Nor is it an absolute or fundamental right, underived from any other right: If it were there would not be exceptions or limitations. The first ten amendments were added to the Constitution as a way of guaranteeing the "blessings of liberty" mentioned in its preamble, to protect citizens against the unreasonable usurpation of power by the state. The specific rights mentioned in the First Amendment—those of religion, speech, assembly, press, petition—reflect the recent experiences of the makers of the Constitution under colonial government as well as a sense of what was and is required generally to secure liberty.

It may be objected that the right to freedom of speech is fundamental in that it is part of what we mean by liberty and not a right that is derivative from a right to liberty. In order to meet this objection, it is useful to consider a distinction explained by Ronald Dworkin in his book *Taking Rights Seriously*.[8] As Dworkin points out, the word "liberty" is used in two distinct, if related, senses: as "license," i.e., the freedom from legal constraints to do as one pleases, in some contexts; and as "independence," i.e., "the status of a person as independent and equal rather than subservient," in others. Failure

---

*Thus, the right to use such materials in the privacy of one's home, which has been upheld by the United States Supreme Court *(Stanley v. Georgia,* 394 U.S. 557), does not include the right to purchase them or to have them available in the commercial market. See also *Paris Adult Theater I v. Slaton,* 431 U.S. 49.

†The Supreme Court has also traditionally included obscenity in this category. As not everyone agrees it should be included, since as defined by statutes, it is a highly vague concept, and since the grounds accepted by the Court for including it miss the point, I prefer to omit it from this list.

to distinguish between these senses in discussions of rights and freedoms is fatal to clarity and understanding.

If the right to free speech is understood as a partial explanation of what is meant by liberty, then liberty is perceived as license: The right to do as one pleases includes a right to speak as one pleases. But license is surely not a condition the First Amendment is designed to protect. We not only tolerate but require legal constraints on liberty as license when we enact laws against rape, murder, assault, theft, etc. If everyone did exactly as she or he pleased at any given time, we would have chaos if not lives, as Hobbes put it, that are "nasty, brutish, and short." We accept government to escape, not to protect, this condition.

If, on the other hand, by liberty is meant independence, then freedom of speech is not necessarily a part of liberty; rather, it is a means to it. The right to freedom of speech is not a fundamental, absolute right, but one derivative from, possessed in virtue of, the more basic right to independence. Taking this view of liberty requires providing arguments showing that the more specific rights we claim are necessary to guarantee our status as persons "independent and equal rather than subservient." In the context of government, we understand independence to be the freedom of each individual to participate as an equal among equals in the determination of how she or he is to be governed. Freedom of speech in this context means that an individual may not only entertain beliefs concerning government privately, but may express them publicly. We express our opinions about taxes, disarmament, wars, social-welfare programs, the function of the police, civil rights, and so on. Our right to freedom of speech includes the right to criticize the government and to protest against various forms of injustice and the abuse of power. What we wish to protect is the free expression of ideas even when they are unpopular. What we do not always remember is that speech has functions other than the expression of ideas.

Regarding the relationship between a right to freedom of speech and the publication and distribution of pornographic materials, there are two points to be made. In the first place, the latter activity is hardly an exercise of the right to the free expression of ideas as understood above. In the second place, to the degree that the tolerance of material degrading to women supports and reinforces the attitude that women are not fit to participate as equals among equals in the political life of their communities, and that the prevalence of such an attitude effectively prevents women from so participating, the absolute and fundamental right of women to liberty (political independence) is violated.

This second argument against the suppression of pornographic material, then, rests on a premise that must be rejected, namely, that the right to freedom of speech is a right to utter anything one wants. It thus fails to show that the production and distribution of such material is an activity protected by the First Amendment. Furthermore, an examination of the issues involved leads to the conclusion that tolerance of this activity violates the rights of women to political independence.

The third argument (which expresses concern that curbs on pornography are the first step toward political censorship) runs into the same ambiguity that besets the arguments based on principle. These arguments generally have as an underlying assumption that the maximization of freedom is a worthy social goal. Control of pornography diminishes freedom—directly the freedom of pornographers, indirectly that of all of us. But again, what is meant by "freedom"? It cannot be that what is to be maximized is license— as the goal of a social group whose members probably have at least some incompatible interests, such a goal would be internally inconsistent. If, on the other hand, the maximization of political independence is the goal, then that is in no way enhanced by, and may be endangered by, the tolerance of pornography. To argue that the control of pornography would create a precedent for suppressing political speech is thus to confuse license with political independence. In addition, it ignores a crucial basis for the control of pornography, i.e., its character as libelous speech. The prohibition of such speech is justified by the need for protection from the injury (psychological as well as physical or economic) that results from libel. A very different kind of argument would be required to justify curtailing the right to speak our minds about the institutions which govern us. As long as such distinctions are insisted upon, there is little danger of the government's using the control of pornography as precedent for curtailing political speech.

In summary, neither as a matter of principle nor in the interests of maximizing liberty can it be supposed that there is an intrinsic right to manufacture and distribute pornographic material.

The only other conceivable source of protection for pornography would be a general right to do what we please as long as the rights of others are respected. Since the production and distribution of pornography violates the rights of women—to respect and to freedom from defamation, among others—this protection is not available.

V. Conclusion

I have defined pornography in such a way as to distinguish it from erotica and from moral realism, and have argued that it is defamatory and libelous toward women, that it condones crimes against women, and that it invites tolerance of the social, economic, and cultural oppression of women. The production and distribution of pornographic material is thus a social and moral wrong. Contrasting both the current volume of pornographic production and its growing infiltration of the communications media with the status of women in this culture makes clear the necessity for its control. Since the goal of controlling pornography does not conflict with constitutional rights, a common obstacle to action is removed.

Appeals for action against pornography are sometimes brushed aside with the claim that such action is a diversion from the primary task of feminists— the elimination of sexism and of sexual inequality. This approach focuses on the enjoyment rather than the manufacture of pornography, and sees it as merely a product of sexism which will disappear when the latter has been overcome and the sexes are socially and economically equal. Pornography cannot be separated from sexism in this way: Sexism is not just a set of attitudes regarding the inferiority of women but the behaviors and social and economic rules that manifest such attitudes. Both the manufacture and distribution of pornography and the enjoyment of it are instances of sexist behavior. The enjoyment of pornography on the part of individuals will presumably decline as such individuals begin to accord women their status as fully human. A cultural climate which tolerates the degrading representation of women is not a climate which facilitates the development of respect for women. Furthermore, the demand for pornography is stimulated not just by the sexism of individuals but by the pornography industry itself. Thus, both as a social phenomenon and in its effect on individuals, pornography, far from being a mere product, nourishes sexism. The campaign against it is an essential component of women's struggle for legal, economic, and social equality, one which requires the support of all feminists.

NOTES

1. *Women Against Violence in Pornography and Media Newspage,* Vol. II, No. 5, June 1978; and Judith Reisman in *Women Against Violence in Pornography and Media Proposal.* [Editor's note: More recent estimates put the size of the U.S. pornography business at $7 billion–$8 billion. See Joseph L. Galloway and Jeannye Thornton, "Crackdown on Pornography—A No-Win Battle," *U.S. News and World Report,* 4, June 1984, p. 84. Compare: precious metal and costume jewelry—$3.7 billion; household appliances—$12.2 billion.]

2. American Law Institute *Model Penal Code,* sec. 251.4.

3. *Report of the Commission on Obscenity and Pornography* (New York: Bantam Books, 1979), p. 239. The Commission, of course, concluded that the demeaning content of pornography did not adversely affect male attitudes toward women.

4. Among recent feminist discussions are Diana Russell, "Pornography: A Feminist Perspective" and Susan Griffin, "On Pornography," *Chrysalis,* Vol. I, No. 4, 1978; and Ann Garry, "Pornography and Respect for Women," *Social Theory and Practice,* Vol. 4, Spring 1978, pp. 395–421.

5. *The Oxford English Dictionary,* Compact Edition (London: Oxford University Press, 1971), p. 2242.

6. Urie Bronfenbrenner, *Two Worlds of Childhood* (New York: Russell Sage Foundation, 1970); H. J. Eysenck and D. K. B. Nias, *Sex, Violence and the Media* (New York: St. Martin's Press, 1978); and Michael Goldstein, Harold Kant, and John Hartman, *Pornography and Sexual Deviance* (Berkeley: University of California Press, 1973). . . . [Editor's note: Longino is referring here to the 1970 Report of the Commission on Obscenity and Pornography. The findings of the Attorney General's Commission on Pornography (The Meese Commission, 1986) were substantially different. However, a considerable controversy arose over the composition of that committee and over the use it made of empirical work on pornography. See, for example, Daniel G. Linz, Edward Donnerstein, and Steven Penrod, "The Findings and Recommendations of the Attorney General's Commission on Pornography: Do the Psychological 'Facts' Fit the Political Fury?" *American Psychologist* 42 (1987): 946–953.]

7. Cf. Marshall Cohen, "The Case Against Censorship," *The Public Interest,* No. 22, Winter 1971, reprinted in John R. Burr and Milton Goldinger, *Philosophy and Contemporary Issues* (New York: Macmillan 1976), and Justice William Brennan's dissenting opinion in *Paris Adult Theater I* v. *Slaton,* 431 U.S. 49.

8. Ronald Dworkin, *Taking Rights Seriously* (Cambridge: Harvard University Press, 1977), p. 262.

A N D R E A   D W O R K I N

Power

Andrea Dworkin is a feminist activist, speaker, and writer.
Among her works of fiction and theory are Right-Wing Women
(1983), Fire and Ice *(1986),* Intercourse *(1987), and* Mercy
(1991).

. . . The major theme of pornography as a genre is male power, its nature, its magnitude, its use, its meaning. Male power, as expressed in and through pornography, is discernible in discrete but interwoven, reinforcing strains: the power of self, physical power over and against others, the power of terror, the power of naming, the power of owning, the power of money, and the power of sex. These strains of male power are intrinsic to both the substance and production of pornography; and the ways and means of pornography are the ways and means of male power. The harmony and coherence of hateful values, perceived by men as normal and neutral values when applied to women, distinguish pornography as message, thing, and experience. The strains of male power are embodied in pornography's form and content, in economic control of and distribution of wealth within the industry, in the picture or story as thing, in the photographer or writer as aggressor, in the critic or intellectual who through naming assigns value, in the actual use of models, in the application of the material in what is called real life (which

---

48

women are commanded to regard as distinct from fantasy). A saber penetrating a vagina is a weapon; so is the camera or pen that renders it; so is the penis for which it substitutes (*vagina* literally means "sheath"). The persons who produce the image are also weapons as men deployed in war become in their persons weapons. Those who defend or protect the image are, in this same sense, weapons. The values in the pornographic work are also manifest in everything surrounding the work. The valuation of women in pornography is a secondary theme in that the degradation of women exists in order to postulate, exercise, and celebrate male power. Male power, in degrading women, is first concerned with itself, its perpetuation, expansion, intensification, and elevation. In her essay on the Marquis de Sade, Simone de Beauvoir describes Sade's sexuality as autistic. Her use of the word is figurative, since an autistic child does not require an object of violence outside of himself (most autistic children are male). Male power expressed in pornography is autistic as de Beauvoir uses the word in reference to Sade: it is violent and self-obsessed; no perception of another being ever modifies its behavior or persuades it to abandon violence as a form of self-pleasuring. Male power is the raison d'être of pornography; the degradation of the female is the means of achieving this power.

The photograph is captioned "BEAVER HUNTERS." Two white men, dressed as hunters, sit in a black Jeep. The Jeep occupies almost the whole frame of the picture. The two men carry rifles. The rifles extend above the frame of the photograph into the white space surrounding it. The men and the Jeep face into the camera. Tied onto the hood of the black Jeep is a white woman. She is tied with thick rope. She is spread-eagle. Her pubic hair and crotch are the dead center of the car hood and the photograph. Her head is turned to one side, tied down by rope that is pulled taut across her neck, extended to and wrapped several times around her wrists, tied around the rearview mirrors of the Jeep, brought back around her arms, crisscrossed under her breasts and over her thighs, drawn down and wrapped around the bumper of the Jeep, tied around her ankles. Between her feet on the car bumper, in orange with black print, is a sticker that reads: I brake for Billy Carter. The text under the photograph reads: "Western sportsmen report beaver hunting was particularly good throughout the Rocky Mountain region during the past season. These two hunters easily bagged their limit in the high country. They told *Hustler* that they stuffed and mounted their trophy as soon as they got her home."

The men in the photograph are self-possessed; that is, they possess the power of self. This power radiates from the photograph. They are armed: first, in the sense that they are fully clothed; second, because they carry rifles, which are made more prominent, suggesting erection, by extending outside the frame of the photograph; third, because they are shielded by being inside the vehicle, framed by the windshield; fourth, because only the top parts of their bodies are shown. The woman is possessed; that is, she has no self. A captured animal, she is naked, bound, exposed on the hood of the car out-doors, her features not distinguishable because of the way her head is twisted and tied down. The men sit, supremely still and confident, displaying the captured prey for the camera. The stillness of the woman is like the stillness of death, underlined by the evocation of taxidermy in the caption. He is, he takes; she is not, she is taken.

The photograph celebrates the physical power of men over women. They are hunters, use guns. They have captured and bound a woman. They will stuff and mount her. She is a trophy. While one could argue that the victory of two armed men over a woman is no evidence of physical superiority, the argument is impossible as one experiences (or remembers) the photograph. The superior strength of men is irrefutably established by the fact of the pho-tograph and the knowledge that one brings to it: that it expresses an authen-tic and commonplace relationship of the male strong to the female weak, wherein the hunt—the targeting, tracking down, pursuing, the chase, the overpowering of, the immobilizing of, even the wounding of—is common practice, whether called sexual pursuit, seduction, or romance. The photo-graph exists in an immediate context that supports the assertion of this physi-cal power; and in the society that is the larger context, there is no viable and meaningful reality to contradict the physical power of male over female ex-pressed in the photograph.

In the photograph, the power of terror is basic. The men are hunters with guns. Their prey is women. They have caught a woman and tied her onto the hood of a car. The terror is implicit in the content of the photograph, but beyond that the photograph strikes the female viewer dumb with fear. One perceives that the bound woman must be in pain. The very power to make the photograph (to use the model, to tie her in that way) and the fact of the photograph (the fact that someone did use the model, did tie her in that way, that the photograph is published in a magazine and seen by millions of men who buy it specifically to see such photographs) evoke fear in the female ob-server unless she entirely dissociates herself from the photograph: refuses to believe or understand that real persons posed for it, refuses to see the bound person as a woman like herself. Terror is finally the content of the photo-graph, and it is also its effect on the female observer. That men have the power and desire to make, publish, and profit from the photograph engen-ders fear. That millions more men enjoy the photograph makes the fear pal-pable. That men who in general champion civil rights defend the photograph without experiencing it as an assault on women intensifies the fear, because if the horror of the photograph does not resonate with these men, that horror is not validated as horror in male culture, and women are left without appar-ent recourse. . . .

The threat in the language accompanying the photograph is also fierce and frightening. She is an animal, think of deer fleeing the hunter, think of seals clubbed to death, think of species nearly extinct. The men will stuff and mount her as a trophy: think of killing displayed proudly as triumph.

Here is the power of naming. Here she is named beaver. In the naming she is diminished to the point of annihilation; her humanity is canceled out. Instead of turning to the American Civil Liberties Union for help, she should perhaps turn to a group that tries to prevent cruelty to animals—beaver, bird, chick, bitch, dog, pussy, and so forth. The words that transform her into an animal have permanence: the male has done the naming. The power of naming includes the freedom to joke. The hunters will brake for Billy Carter. The ridicule is not deadly; they will let him live. The real target of the ridicule is the fool who brakes for animals, here equated with women. The language on the bumper sticker suggests the idea of the car in motion, which would otherwise be lacking. The car becomes a weapon, a source of death, its actual character as males use it. One is reminded of the animal run over on the road, a haunting image of blood and death. One visualizes the car, with the woman tied onto its hood, in motion crashing into something or someone.

Owning is expressed in every aspect of the photograph. These hunters are sportsmen, wealth suggested in hunting as a leisure-time pursuit of pleasure. They are equipped and outfitted. Their car shines. They have weapons: guns, a car. They have a woman, bound and powerless, to do with as they like. They will stuff and mount her. Their possession of her extends over time, even into (her) death. She is owned as a thing, a trophy, or as something dead, a dead bird, a dead deer; she is dead beaver. The camera and the photographer behind it also own the woman. The camera uses and keeps her. The photographer uses her and keeps the image of her. The publisher of the photograph can also claim her as a trophy. He has already mounted her and put her on display. Hunting as a sport suggests that these hunters have hunted before and will hunt again, that each captured woman will be used and owned, stuffed and mounted, that this right to own inheres in man's relationship to nature, that this right to own is so natural and basic that it can be taken entirely for granted, that is, expressed as play or sport.

Wealth is implicit in owning. The woman is likened to food (a dead animal), the hunter's most immediate form of wealth. As a trophy, she is wealth displayed. She is a commodity, part of the measure of male wealth. Man as hunter owns the earth, the things of it, its natural resources. She is part of the wildlife to be plundered for profit and pleasure, collected, used. That they "bagged their limit," then used what they had caught, is congruent with the idea of economy as a sign of mature masculinity.

The fact of the photograph signifies the wealth of men as a class. One class simply does not so use another class unless that usage is maintained in the distribution of wealth. The female model's job is the job of one who is economically imperiled, a sign of economic degradation. The relationship of the men to the woman in the photograph is not fantasy; it is symbol, meaningful because it is rooted in reality. The photograph shows a relationship of rich to poor that is actual in the larger society. The fact of the photograph in relation to its context—an industry that generates wealth by producing images of women abjectly used, a society in which women cannot adequately earn money because women are valued precisely as the woman in the photograph is valued—both proves and perpetuates the real connection between masculinity and wealth. The sexual-economic significance of the photograph is so simple that it is easily overlooked: the photograph could not exist as a type of photograph that produces wealth without the wealth of men to produce and consume it.

Sex as power is the most explicit meaning of the photograph. The power of sex unambiguously resides in the male, though the characterization of the female as a wild animal suggests that the sexuality of the untamed female is dangerous to men. But the triumph of the hunters is the nearly universal triumph of men over women, a triumph ultimately expressed in the stuffing and mounting. The hunters are figures of virility. Their penises are hidden but their guns are emphasized. The car, beloved ally of men in the larger culture, also indicates virility, especially when a woman is tied to it naked instead of draped over it wearing an evening gown. The pornographic image explicates the advertising image, and the advertising image echoes the pornographic image.

The power of sex is ultimately defined as the power of conquest. They hunted her down, captured, tied, stuffed, and mounted her. The excitement is precisely in the nonconsensual character of the event. The hunt, the ropes, the guns, show that anything done to her was or will be done against her will. Here again, the valuation of conquest as being natural—of nature, of man in nature, of natural man—is implicit in the visual and linguistic imagery.

The power of sex, in male terms, is also funereal. Death permeates it. The male erotic trinity—sex, violence, and death—reigns supreme. She will be or is dead. They did or will kill her. Everything that they do to or with her is violence. Especially evocative is the phrase "stuffed and mounted her," suggesting as it does both sexual violation and embalming.

CATHARINE A. MACKINNON

Francis Biddle's Sister: Pornography, Civil Rights, and Speech

Catharine A. MacKinnon is professor of law at the University of Michigan. She is the author of Toward a Feminist Theory of the State *(1989) and, most recently, of* Only Words *(1993). Several of her papers and speeches are collected in* Feminism Unmodified: Discourses on Life and Law *(1987).*

. . . I will first situate a critique of pornography within a feminist analysis of the condition of women. I will speak of what pornography means for the social status and treatment of women. I will briefly contrast that with the obscenity approach, the closest this government has come to addressing pornography. Next I will outline an argument for the constitutionality of the ordinance Andrea Dworkin and I conceived, in which we define pornography as a civil rights violation.[1] Here I will address what pornography *does* as a practice of sex discrimination, and the vision of the First Amendment with which our law is consistent. Evidence, much of it drawn from hearings on the ordinance in Minneapolis,[2] supports this argument. The Supreme Court has never considered this legal injury before, nor the factual support we bring to it. They have allowed the recognition of similar injuries to other people, consistent with their interpretation of the First Amendment. More drastic steps

53

have been taken on a showing of a great deal less harm, and the courts have allowed it. The question is: Will they do it for women?

. . . My formal agenda has three parts. The first treats pornography by connecting epistemology—which I understand to be about theories of knowing—with politics—which I will take to be about theories of power.[3] For instance, Justice Stewart said of obscenity, "I know it when I see it."[4] I see this as a statement connecting epistemology—what he knows through his way of knowing, in this case, seeing—with the fact that his seeing determines what obscenity *is* in terms of what he sees it to be, because of his position of power. To wonder if he and I know the same things from what we see, given what's on the newsstand, is not a personal query about him.

Another example of the same conceptual connection is this. Having power means, among other things, that when someone says, "This is how it is," it is taken as being that way. When this happens in law, such a person is accorded what is called credibility. When that person is believed over another speaker, what was said becomes proof. Speaking socially, the beliefs of the powerful become proof, in part because the world actually arranges itself to affirm what the powerful want to see. If you perceive this as a process, you might call it force, or at least pressure or socialization or what money can buy. If it is imperceptible as a process, you may consider it voluntary or consensual or free will or human nature, or just the way things are. Beneath this, though, the world is not entirely the way the powerful say it is or want to believe it is. If it appears to be, it is because power constructs the appearance of reality by silencing the voices of the powerless, by excluding them from access to authoritative discourse. Powerlessness means that when you say "This is how it is," it is *not* taken as being that way. This makes articulating silence, perceiving the presence of absence, believing those who have been socially stripped of credibility, critically contextualizing what passes for simple fact, necessary to the epistemology of a politics of the powerless.

My second thematic concern is jurisprudential. It is directed toward identifying, in order to change, one dimension of liberalism as it is embodied in law: the definition of justice as neutrality between abstract categories. The liberal view is that abstract categories—like speech or equality—define systems. Every time you strengthen free speech in one place, you strengthen it everywhere. Strengthening the free speech of the Klan strengthens the free speech of Blacks. Getting things for men strengthens equality for women. Getting men access to women's schools strengthens women's access to education. What I will be exploring is the way in which substantive systems, made up of real people with social labels attached, are *also systems*. You can reverse racism abstractly, but white supremacy is unfudgeably substantive. Sexism can be an equal abstraction, but male supremacy says who is where. Substantive systems like white supremacy do substantively different things to people of color than they do to white people. To say they are *also systems* is to say that every time you score one for white supremacy in one place, it is strengthened every place else.

In this view, the problem with neutrality as the definition of principle in constitutional adjudication[5] is that it equates substantive powerlessness with substantive power and calls treating these the same, "equality." The neutrality approach understands that abstract systems are systems, but it seems not to understand that substantive systems are also systems. . . .

The *Lochner* line of cases[6] created concern about the evils of their substance, which . . . came to stand for the evils of substantivity *as such*. There has been correspondingly little discussion, with the partial exception of the debate on affirmative action,[7] on the drawbacks of abstraction as such. Granted, trying to do anything on a substantive basis is a real problem in a legal system that immediately turns everything into an abstraction. I do hope to identify this as something of a syndrome, as a risk of abuse. Considering it the definition of principle itself ensures that nothing will ever basically change, at least not by law.

When these two frames converge—epistemology and politics on the one hand with the critique of neutrality on the other—they form a third frame: one of political philosophy. Here is how they converge. Once power constructs social reality, as I will show pornography constructs the social reality of gender, the force behind sexism, the subordination in gender inequality, is made invisible; dissent from it becomes inaudible as well as rare. What a woman is, is defined in pornographic terms; this is what pornography *does*. If the law then looks neutrally on the reality of gender so produced, the harm that has been done *will not be perceptible as harm*. It becomes just the way things are. Refusing to look at what has been done substantively institutionalizes inequality in law and makes it look just like principle.

In the philosophical terms of classical liberalism, an equality–freedom dilemma is produced: freedom to make or consume pornography weighs against the equality of the sexes. Some people's freedom hurts other people's equality. There is something to this, but my formulation, as you might guess, comes out a little differently. If one asks whose freedom pornography represents, a tension emerges that is not a dilemma among abstractions so much as it is a conflict between groups. Substantive interests are at stake on *both* sides of the abstract issues, and women are allowed to matter in neither. If women's freedom is as incompatible with pornography's construction of our freedom as our equality is incompatible with pornography's construction of our equality, we get neither freedom nor equality under the liberal calculus. Equality for women is incompatible with a definition of men's freedom that is at our expense. What can freedom for women mean, so long as we remain unequal? Why should men's freedom to use us in this way be purchased with our second-class civil status?

Substantively considered, the situation of women is *not really like anything else*. Its specificity is not just the result of our numbers—we are half the human race—and our diversity, which at times has obscured that we are a group with an interest at all. It is, in part, that our status as a group relative to men has almost never, if ever, been much changed from what it is. Women's roles do vary enough that gender, the social form sex takes, cannot be said to be biologically determined. Different things are valued in different cultures, but whatever is valued, women are not that. If bottom is bottom, look across time and space, and women are who you will find there. Together with this, you will find, in as varied forms as there are cultures, the belief that women's social inferiority to men is not that at all but is merely the sex difference.

Doing something legal about a situation that is not really like anything else is hard enough in a legal system that prides itself methodologically on reasoning by analogy. Add to this the specific exclusion or absence of women and women's concerns from the definition and design of this legal system since its founding, combined with its determined adherence to precedent, and you have a problem of systemic dimension. The best attempt at grasping women's situation in order to change it by law has centered on an analogy between sex and race in the discrimination context. This gets a lot, since inequalities are alike on some levels, but it also misses a lot. It gets the stigmatization and exploitation and denigration of a group of people on the basis of a condition of birth. It gets that difference, made an issue of, is an excuse for dominance, and that if forced separation is allowed to mean equality in a society where the line of separation also divides top from bottom in a hierarchy, the harm of that separation is thereby made invisible. It also gets that defining neutrality as principle, when reality is not neutral, prevents change in the guise of promoting it. But segregation is not the central practice of the inequality of the sexes. Women are as often forcibly integrated with men, if not on an equal basis. And it did help the struggle against white supremacy that Blacks had not always been in bondage to white people.

Most important, I think it never was a central part of the ideology of racism that the system of chattel slavery of Africans really was designed for their enjoyment and benefit. The system *was* defended as an expression of their true nature and worth. They *were* told to be grateful for good treatment and kind masters. Their successful struggle to organize resistance and avoid complicity while still surviving is instructive to all of us. But although racism *has* been defended by institutionalizing it in law, and then calling that legal; although it *has* been cherished not just as a system of exploitation of labor but as a way of life; and although it *is* based on force, changes in its practices are opposed by implying that they are really only a matter of choice of personal values. For instance: "You can't legislate morality."[8] And slave owners *did* say they couldn't be racist—they loved their slaves. Nonetheless, few people pretended that the entire system existed *because* of its basis in love and mutual respect and veneration, that white supremacy really treated Blacks in many cases *better* than whites, and that the primary intent and effect of their special status was and is their protection, pleasure, fulfillment, and liberation. Crucially, many have believed, and some actually still do, that Black people were not the equals of whites. But at least since *Brown v. Board of Education,*[9] few have pretended, much less authoritatively, that the social system, as it was, *was equality for them*.

There is a belief that this is a society in which women and men are basically equals. Room for marginal corrections is conceded, flaws are known to exist, attempts are made to correct what are conceived as occasional lapses from the basic condition of sex equality. Sex discrimination law has concentrated most of its focus on these occasional lapses. It is difficult to overestimate the extent to which this belief in equality is an article of faith for most people, including most women, who wish to live in self-respect in an internal universe, even (perhaps especially) if not in the world. It is also partly an expression of natural law thinking: if we are inalienably equal, we can't "really" be degraded.

This is a world in which it is worth trying. In this world of presumptive equality, people make money based on their training or abilities or diligence or qualifications. They are employed and advanced on the basis of merit. In this world of just deserts, if someone is abused, it is thought to violate the basic rules of the community. If it doesn't, victims are seen to have done something they could have chosen to do differently, by exercise of will or better judgment. Maybe such people have placed themselves in a situation of vulnerability to physical abuse. Maybe they have done something provocative. Or maybe they were just unusually unlucky. In such a world, if such a person has an experience, there are words for it. When they speak and say it, they are listened to. If they write about it, they will be published. If certain experiences are never spoken about, if certain people or issues are seldom heard from, it is supposed that silence has been chosen. The law, including much of the law of sex discrimination and the First Amendment, operates largely within the realm of these beliefs.

Feminism is the discovery that women do not live in this world, that the person occupying this realm is a man, so much more a man if he is white and wealthy. This world of potential credibility, authority, security, and just rewards, recognition of one's identity and capacity, is a world that some people do inhabit as a condition of birth, with variations among them. It is not a basic condition accorded humanity in this society, but a prerogative of status, a privilege, among other things, of gender.

I call this a discovery because it has not been an assumption. Feminism is the first theory, the first practice, the first movement, to take seriously the situation of all women from the point of view of all women, both on our situation and on social life as a whole. The discovery has therefore been made that the implicit social content of humanism, as well as the standpoint from which legal method has been designed and injuries have been defined, has not been women's standpoint. Defining feminism in a way that connects epistemology with power as the politics of women's point of view, this discovery can be summed up by saying that women live in another world: specifically, a world of *not* equality, a world of inequality.

Looking at the world from this point of view, a whole shadow world of previously invisible silent abuse has been discerned. Rape, battery, sexual harassment, forced prostitution, and the sexual abuse of children emerge as common and systematic.[10] We find that rape happens to women in all contexts, from the family, including rape of girls and babies, to students and women in the workplace, on the streets, at home, in their own bedrooms by men they do not know and by men they do know, by men they are married to, men they have had a social conversation with, and, least often, men they have never seen before. Overwhelmingly, rape is something that men do or attempt to do to women (44 percent of American women according to a recent study)[11] at some point in our lives. Sexual harassment of women by men is common in workplaces and educational institutions. Based on reports in one study of the federal workforce, up to 85 percent of women will experience it, many in physical forms.[12] Between a quarter and a third of women are battered in their homes by men. Thirty-eight percent of little girls are sexually molested inside or outside the family. Until women listened to women, this world of sexual abuse was *not spoken* of. It was the unspeakable. What I am saying is, if you *are* the tree falling in the epistemological forest, your demise doesn't make a sound if no one is listening. Women did not "report" these events, and overwhelmingly do not today, because no one is listening, because no one believes us. This silence does not mean nothing happened, and it does not mean consent. It is the silence of women of which Adrienne Rich has written, "Do not confuse it with any kind of absence."[13] . . .

. . . People don't really believe that the things I have just said are true, though there really is little question about their empirical accuracy. The data are extremely simple, like women's pay figure of fifty-nine cents on the dollar.[14] People don't really seem to believe that either. Yet there is no question of its empirical validity. This is the workplace story: what women do is seen as not worth much, or what is not worth much is seen as something for women to do. *Women* are seen as not worth much, is the thing. Now why are these basic realities of the subordination of women to men, for example, that only 7.8 percent of women have never been sexually assaulted,[15] not effectively believed, not perceived as real in the face of all this evidence? Why don't *women* believe our own experiences? In the face of all this evidence, especially of systematic sexual abuse—subjection to violence with impunity is one extreme expression, although not the only expression, of a degraded status—the view that basically the sexes are equal in this society remains unchallenged and unchanged. The day I got this was the day I understood its real message, its real coherence: *This is equality for us.*

I could describe this, but I couldn't explain it until I started studying a lot of pornography. In pornography, there it is, in one place, all of the abuses that women had to struggle so long even to begin to articulate, all the *unspeakable* abuse: the rape, the battery, the sexual harassment, the prostitution, and the sexual abuse of children. Only in the pornography it is called something else: sex, sex, sex, sex, and sex, respectively. Pornography sexualizes rape, battery, sexual harassment, prostitution, and child sexual abuse; it thereby celebrates, promotes, authorizes, and legitimizes them. More generally, it eroticizes the dominance and submission that is the dynamic common to them all. It makes hierarchy sexy and calls that "the truth about sex"[16] or just a mirror of reality. Through this process pornography constructs what a woman is as what men want from sex. This is what the pornography means.

Pornography constructs what a woman is in terms of its view of what men want sexually, such that acts of rape, battery, sexual harassment, prostitution, and sexual abuse of children become acts of sexual equality. Pornography's world of equality is a harmonious and balanced place.[17] Men and women are perfectly complementary and perfectly bipolar. Women's desire to be fucked by men is equal to men's desire to fuck women. All the ways men love to take and violate women, women love to be taken and violated. The women who most love this are most men's equals, the most liberated; the most participatory child is the most grown-up, the most equal to an adult. Their consent merely expresses or ratifies these preexisting facts.

The content of pornography is one thing. There, women substantively desire dispossession and cruelty. We desperately want to be bound, battered, tortured, humiliated, and killed. Or, to be fair to the soft core, merely taken and used. This is erotic to the male point of view. Subjection itself, with self-determination ecstatically relinquished, is the content of women's sexual desire and desirability. Women are there to be violated and possessed, men to violate and possess us, either on screen or by camera or pen on behalf of the consumer. On a simple descriptive level, the inequality of hierarchy, of which gender is the primary one, seems necessary for sexual arousal to work. Other added inequalities identify various pornographic genres or subthemes, although they are always added through gender: age, disability, homosexuality, animals, objects, race (including anti-Semitism), and so on. Gender is never irrelevant.

What pornography *does* goes beyond its content: it eroticizes hierarchy, it sexualizes inequality. It makes dominance and submission into sex. Inequality is its central dynamic; the illusion of freedom coming together with the reality of force is central to its working. Perhaps because this is a bourgeois culture, the victim must look free, appear to be freely acting. Choice is how she got there. Willing is what she is when she is being equal. It seems equally important that then and there she actually be forced and that forcing be communicated on some level, even if only through still photos of her in postures of receptivity and access, available for penetration. Pornography in this view is a form of forced sex, a practice of sexual politics, an institution of gender inequality.

From this perspective, pornography is neither harmless fantasy nor a corrupt and confused misrepresentation of an otherwise natural and healthy sexual situation. It institutionalizes the sexuality of male supremacy, fusing the erotization of dominance and submission with the social construction of male and female. To the extent that gender is sexual, pornography is part of constituting the meaning of that sexuality. Men treat women as who they see women as being. Pornography constructs who that is. Men's power over women means that the way men see women defines who women can be. Pornography is that way. Pornography is not imagery in some relation to a reality elsewhere constructed. It is not a distortion, reflection, projection, expression, fantasy, representation, or symbol either. It is a sexual reality.

In Andrea Dworkin's definitive work, *Pornography: Men Possessing Women,*[18] sexuality itself is a social construct gendered to the ground. Male dominance here is not an artificial overlay upon an underlying inalterable substratum of uncorrupted essential sexual being. Dworkin presents a sexual theory of gender inequality of which pornography is a constitutive practice. The way pornography produces its meaning constructs and defines men and women as such. Gender has no basis in anything other than the social reality its hegemony constructs. Gender is what gender means. The process that gives sexuality its male supremacist meaning is the same process through which gender inequality becomes socially real.

In this approach, the experience of the (overwhelmingly) male audiences who consume pornography is therefore not fantasy or simulation or catharsis but sexual reality, the level of reality on which sex itself largely operates. Understanding this dimension of the problem does not require noticing that pornography models are real women to whom, in most cases, something real is being done; nor does it even require inquiring into the systematic infliction of pornography and its sexuality upon women, although it helps. What matters is the way in which the pornography itself provides what those who consume it want. Pornography *participates* in its audience's eroticism through creating an accessible sexual object, the possession and consumption of which *is* male sexuality, as socially constructed; to be consumed and possessed as which, *is* female sexuality, as socially constructed; pornography is a process that constructs it that way.

The object world is constructed according to how it looks with respect to its possible uses. Pornography defines women by how we look according to how we can be sexually used. Pornography codes how to look at women, so you know what you can do with one when you see one. Gender is an assignment made visually, both originally and in everyday life. A sex object is defined on the basis of its looks, in terms of its usability for sexual pleasure, such that both the looking—the quality of the gaze, including its point of view—and the definition according to use become eroticized as part of the sex itself. This is what the feminist concept "sex object" means. In this sense, sex in life is no less mediated than it is in art. Men have sex with their image of a woman. It is not that life and art imitate each other; in this sexuality, they *are* each other.

. . . To defend pornography as consistent with the equality of the sexes is to defend the subordination of women to men as sexual equality. What in the pornographic view is love and romance looks a great deal like hatred and torture to the feminist. Pleasure and eroticism become violation. Desire appears as lust for dominance and submission. The vulnerability of women's projected sexual availability, that acting we are allowed (that is, asking to be acted upon), is victimization. Play conforms to scripted roles. Fantasy expresses ideology, is not exempt from it. Admiration of natural physical beauty becomes objectification. Harmlessness becomes harm. Pornography is a harm of male supremacy made difficult to see because of its pervasiveness, potency, and, principally, because of its success in making the world a pornographic place. Specifically, its harm cannot be discerned, and will not be addressed, if viewed and approached neutrally, because it *is* so much of "what is." In other words, to the extent pornography succeeds in constructing social reality, it becomes invisible as harm. If we live in a world that pornography creates through the power of men in a male-dominated situation, the issue is not what the harm of pornography is, but how that harm is to become visible.

Obscenity law provides a very different analysis and conception of the problem of pornography. In 1973 the legal definition of obscenity became that which the average person, applying contemporary community standards, would find that, taken as a whole, appeals to the prurient interest; that which depicts or describes in a patently offensive way—you feel like you're a cop reading someone's *Miranda* rights—sexual conduct specifically defined by the applicable state law; and that which, taken as a whole, lacks serious literary, artistic, political or scientific value.[19] Feminism doubts whether the average person gender-neutral exists; has more questions about the content and process of defining what community standards are than it does about deviations from them; wonders why prurience counts but powerlessness does not and why sensibilities are better protected from offense than women are from exploitation; defines sexuality, and thus its violation and expropriation, more broadly than does state law; and questions why a body of law that has not in practice been able to tell rape from intercourse should, without further guidance, be entrusted with telling pornography from anything less. Taking the work "as a whole" ignores that which the victims of pornography have long known: legitimate settings diminish the perception of injury done to those whose trivialization and objectification they contextualize. Besides, and this is a heavy one, if a woman is subjected, why should it matter that the work has other value? Maybe what redeems the work's value is what enhances its injury to women, not to mention that existing standards of literature, art, science, and politics, examined in a feminist light, are remarkably consonant with pornography's mode, meaning, and message. And finally—first and foremost, actually—although the subject of these materials is overwhelm-ingly women, their contents almost entirely made up of women's bodies, our invisibility has been such, our equation as a sex *with* sex has been such, that the law of obscenity has never even considered pornography a women's issue.

Obscenity, in this light, is a moral idea, an idea about judgments of good and bad. Pornography, by contrast, is a political practice, a practice of power and powerlessness. Obscenity is ideational and abstract; pornography is con-crete and substantive. The two concepts represent two entirely different things. Nudity, excess of candor, arousal or excitement, prurient appeal, ille-gality of the acts depicted, and unnaturalness or perversion are all qualities that bother obscenity law when sex is depicted or portrayed. Sex forced on real women so that it can be sold at a profit and forced on other real women; women's bodies trussed and maimed and raped and made into things to be hurt and obtained and accessed, and this presented as the nature of women in a way that is acted on and acted out, over and over; the coercion that is vis-ible and the coercion that has become invisible—this and more bothers femi-nists about pornography. Obscenity as such probably does little harm. Pornography is integral to attitudes and behaviors of violence and discrimi-nation that define the treatment and status of half the population.

At the request of the city of Minneapolis, Andrea Dworkin and I conceived and designed a local human rights ordinance in accordance with our ap-proach to the pornography issue. We define pornography as a practice of sex discrimination, a violation of women's civil rights, the opposite of sexual equality. Its point is to hold those who profit from and benefit from that in-jury accountable to those who are injured. It means that women's injury—our damage, our pain, our enforced inferiority—should outweigh their pleasure and their profits, or sex equality is meaningless.

We define pornography as the graphic sexually explicit subordination of women through pictures or words that also includes women dehumanized as sexual objects, things, or commodities; enjoying pain or humiliation or rape; being tied up, cut up, mutilated, bruised, or physically hurt; in postures of sexual submission or servility or display; reduced to body parts, penetrated by objects or animals, or presented in scenarios of degradation, injury, torture; shown as filthy or inferior; bleeding, bruised, or hurt in a context that makes these conditions sexual. Erotica, defined by distinction as not this, might be sexually explicit materials premised on equality.[21] We also provide that the use of men, children, or transsexuals in the place of women is pornography. The definition is substantive in that it is sex-specific, but it covers everyone in a sex-specific way, so is gender neutral in overall design. . . .

To define pornography as a practice of sex discrimination combines a mode of portrayal that has a legal history—the sexually explicit—with an ac-tive term that is central to the inequality of the sexes—subordination. Among other things, subordination means to be in a position of inferiority or loss of power, or to be demeaned or denigrated.[22] To be someone's subordinate is the opposite of being their equal. The definition does not include all sexually explicit depictions *of* the subordination of women. That is not what it says. It says, this which *does* that: the sexually explicit that subordinates women. To these active terms to capture what the pornography *does,* the definition adds a list of what it must also contain. This list, from our analysis, is an exhaustive description of what must be in the pornography for it to do what it does behaviorally. Each item in the definition is supported by experimental, testimonial, social, and clinical evidence. We made a legislative choice to be exhaustive and specific and concrete rather than conceptual and general, to minimize problems of chilling effect, making it hard to guess wrong, thus making self-censorship less likely, but encouraging (to use a phrase from discrimination law) voluntary compliance, knowing that if something turns up that is not on the list, the law will not be expansively interpreted.

The list in the definition, by itself, would be a content regulation. But together with the first part, the definition is not simply a content regulation. It is a medium–message combination that resembles many other such exceptions to First Amendment guarantees. . . .

This law aspires to guarantee women's rights consistent with the First Amendment by making visible a conflict of rights between the equality guaranteed to all women and what, in some legal sense, is now the freedom of the pornographers to make and sell, and their consumers to have access to, the materials this ordinance defines. Judicial resolution of this conflict, if the judges do for women what they have done for others, is likely to entail a balancing of the rights of women arguing that our lives and opportunities, including our freedom of speech and action, are constrained by—and in many cases flatly precluded by, in, and through—pornography, against those who argue that the pornography is harmless, or harmful only in part but not in the whole of the definition; or that it is more important to preserve the pornography than it is to prevent or remedy whatever harm it does.

. . . This ordinance enunciates a new form of the previously recognized governmental interest in sex equality. Many laws make sex equality a governmental interest.[23] Our law is designed to further the equality of the sexes, to help make sex equality real. Pornography is a practice of discrimination on the basis of sex, on one level because of its role in creating and maintaining sex as a basis for discrimination. It harms many women one at a time and helps keep all women in an inferior status by defining our subordination as our sexuality and equating that with our gender. It is also sex discrimination because its victims, including men, are selected for victimization on the basis of their gender. But for their sex, they would not be so treated.

The harm of pornography, broadly speaking, is the harm of the civil inequality of the sexes made invisible as harm because it has become accepted as the sex difference. Consider this analogy with race: if you see Black people as different, there is no harm to segregation; it is merely a recognition of that difference. To neutral principles, separate but equal was equal. The injury of racial separation to Blacks arises "solely because [they] choose to put that construction upon it."[24] Epistemologically translated: how you see it is not the way it is. Similarly, if you see women as just different, even or especially if you don't know that you do, subordination will not look like subordination at all, much less like harm. It will merely look like an appropriate recognition of the sex difference.

　　Pornography does treat the sexes differently, so the case for sex differentiation can be made here. But men as a group do not tend to be (although some individuals may be) treated the way women are treated in pornography. As a social group, men are not hurt by pornography the way women as a social group are. Their social status is not defined as *less* by it. So the major argument does not turn on mistaken differentiation, particularly since the treatment of women according to pornography's dictates makes it all too often accurate. The salient quality of a distinction between the top and the bottom in a hierarchy is not difference, although top is certainly different from bottom; it is power. So the major argument is: subordinate but equal is not equal. . . .

N O T E S

1. Editor's note: See Legal Appendix for the definitions of pornography employed in the Minneapolis and Indianapolis ordinances.

2. *See Public Hearings on Ordinances to Add Pornography as Discrimination Against Women,* Committee on Government Operations, City Council, Minneapolis, Minn. (Dec. 12–13, 1983). . . . All those who testified in these hearings were fully identified to the City Council. . . .

3. I treat these themes more fully in "Feminism, Marxism, Method and the State: Toward Feminist Jurisprudence," 8 *Signs: Journal of Women in Culture and Society* 635 (1983); "Feminism, Marxism, Method and the State: An Agenda for Theory," 7 *Signs: Journal of Women in Culture and Society* 515 (1982).

4. *Jacobellis v. Ohio,* 378 U.S. 184, 197 (1964) (Stewart, J., concurring).

5. The classic enunciation of the meaning of neutrality as the principled approach to constitutional adjudication is Herbert Wechsler, "Toward Neutral Principles of Constitutional Law," 73 *Harvard Law Review* 1 (1959). The doctrine of gender neutrality applies this approach to the area of sex, which goes far toward explaining the predominance of male plaintiffs in the Supreme Court's leading gender discrimination cases, especially among successful plaintiffs. *See* cases collected at David Cole, "Strategies of Difference: Litigating for Women's Rights in a Man's World," 2 *Law & Inequality: Journal of Theory and Practice* 33 n.4 (1984) ("The only area in which male plaintiffs do not dominate constitutional gender discrimination cases involves treatment of pregnancy").

6. *See Lochner v. New York,* 198 U.S. 45 (1905); *Allgeyer v. Louisiana,* 165 U.S. 578 (1897) (invalidating maximum hours restrictions on the ground of liberty to freely contract). . . .

7. *See, e.g., Regents of the University of California v. Bakke,* 438 U.S. 265 (1978); John Ely, *Democracy and Distrust: A Theory of Judicial Review* 54–55 (1981). *But see* Laurence Tribe, "Speech as Power: Swastikas, Spending, and the Mask of Neutral Principles," in *Constitutional Choices* (1985).

8. *See, e.g.,* Derrick Bell, *Race, Racism and American Law* 1–85 (1972).

9. 347 U.S. 483 (1954).

10. Editor's note: Many of MacKinnon's references will be found in the Bibliography, VII: Violence against Women.

11. *See* Diana Russell, "The Prevalence of Rape in United States Revisited," 8 *Signs: Journal of Women in Culture and Society* 689 (1983).

12. U.S. Merit Systems Protection Board, *Sexual Harassment in the Federal Workplace: Is It a Problem?* Washington, D.C.: U.S. Government Printing Office, 1981.

13. Adrienne Rich, "Cartographies of Silence," in *The Dream of a Common Language* 16, 17 (1978).

14. *See* Employment Standards Administration, U.S. Department of Labor, *Handbook on Women Workers* (1975); U.S. Department of Labor, *Women's Bureau Bulletin* 297 (1975 and 1982 update).

15. Diana Russell produced this figure at my request from the random sample data base of 930 San Francisco households discussed in her *The Secret Trauma: Incest in the Lives of Girls and Women* 20–37 (1986) and *Rape in Marriage* 27–41 (1982). The figure includes all the forms of rape or other sexual abuse or harassment surveyed, non-contact as well as contact, from gang rape by strangers to obscene phone calls, unwanted sexual advances on the street, unwelcome requests to pose for pornography, and subjection to peeping Toms and sexual exhibitionists (flashers).

16. Foucault, "The West and the Truth of Sex," 20 *Sub-Stance* 5 (1978).

17. This became a lot clearer to me after reading Margaret Baldwin, "The Sexuality of Inequality: The Minneapolis Pornography Ordinance," 2 *Law and Inequality: Journal of Theory and Practice* 629 (1984). This paragraph is directly indebted to her insight and language there.

18. Andrea Dworkin, *Pornography: Men Possessing Women* (1981).

19. *Miller v. California,* 413 U.S. 15, 24 (1973).

20. *See The Report of the Presidential Commission on Obscenity and Pornography* (1970).

21. *See, e.g.,* Gloria Steinem, "Erotica v. Pornography," in *Outrageous Acts and Everyday Rebellions* 219 (1983).

22. For a lucid discussion of subordination, *see* Andrea Dworkin, "Against the Male Flood: Censorship, Pornography, and Equality," 8 *Harvard Women's Law Journal* 1 (1985).

23. *See, e.g.,* Title IX of the Educ. Amends. of 1972, 20 U.S.C. §§ 1681–1686 (1972); Equal Pay Act, 29 U.S.C. § 206(d) (1963); Title VII of the Civil Rights

Act of 1964, 42 U.S.C. §§ 2000e to 2000e–17 (1976). Many states have equal rights amendments to their constitutions, *see* Barbara Brown and Ann Freedman, "Equal Rights Amendment: Growing Impact on the States," 1 *Women's Rights Law Reporter* 1.63, 1.63–1.64 (1974); many states and cities, including Minneapolis and Indianapolis, prohibit discrimination on the basis of sex. *See also Roberts v. United States Jaycees,* 468 U.S. 609 (1984) (recently recognizing that sex equality is a compelling state interest); *Frontiero v. Richardson,* 411 U.S. 677 (1973); *Reed v. Reed,* 404 U.S. 71 (1971); U.S. Const. amend. XIV.

24. *See Plessy v. Ferguson,* 163 U.S. at 551.

PART TWO

Rights, Equality, and Free Speech

We North Americans make a lot of noise about our rights. It seems we know when one of them is being threatened. But the appeal to rights is often made unreflectively. That is, we may be sure that we have this right or that right, but we don't know why. This is especially true of our right to free speech (or, more vaguely, to freedom of expression). It is important, however, to know why we have that right; otherwise, we will not know what to say in defense of it when it is threatened. It will do no good simply to argue that you have a right to free speech because the Constitution or the Charter of Rights says you do. The justificatory question remains: Why is that right stated in these documents? Why would we think it amiss if the right to free speech were not recognized and protected in these documents?

Another equally important question to ask about our rights concerns their scope. For example, is the right to free speech unlimited? Or, as it is sometimes put, is that right absolute? To claim that a right is absolute is to say that it cannot ever be permissibly infringed. If the right to free speech is absolute, then no matter what the consequences are, it would be wrong to restrict or censor any speech. Your intuition probably tells you that very few, if any, of your rights are absolute in this sense. (For instance, we think it is sometimes permissible to violate another person's right to life—such as killing an attacker in self-defense.) But even if rights are not absolute, some rights may be very strong. That is, some rights may be so important to us that we are prepared to tolerate quite a lot of bad consequences rather than see these rights infringed. To put the point slightly differently: a particular right might be so important to us that its infringement on a particular occasion could be justified only on the grounds that a great deal of good would come from infringing it. Perhaps this is how we think (or ought to think) of our right to free speech.

These two issues—namely, the justification of the right to free speech and the scope of that right—have been and continue to be at the center of debates concerning pornography. Any suggestion that some or all pornography should be banned or restricted is quickly met by counterclaims that invoke the right to free speech. However, parties on both sides of this dispute need to supplement their suggestions and claims with arguments. People who want to curtail or eliminate pornography must say why pornography is problematic. Proponents of free speech must say why free speech is important and how important it is. In the terms of the previous paragraph, we need to be told what the bad consequences of pornography are and whether they are bad enough to warrant infringing some people's right to free speech. The papers in Part One represent several ways of arguing that pornography is problematic; the papers in this part focus more on the right to free speech.

North Americans also care about equality. Again this notion is easily invoked—"We're all equal"—but usually not reflectively. What does it mean to say that we are all equal? Equal with respect to what? Factually, we differ in many ways: some of us are short, some are tall; many of us are poor, some are wealthy; some of us are smart, others are not so smart. In general, what people have in mind when they talk about equality is that persons ought to be treated equally, despite their obvious differences—in particular, despite their race, gender, and class differences. Sometimes this idea, too, is phrased in terms of a certain right—the right to be treated as an equal. Or, as Ronald Dworkin puts it elsewhere,[1] we have the right to be treated with equal concern and respect. (We will return to this notion later.)

It should be clear where equality enters the debate on pornography. Each of the papers in Part One, either directly or indirectly, argues that pornography poses a threat to women's equality. It might be further argued that this consequence is bad enough to limit some people's freedom of expression. That is, the right to free speech is very strong, but it must yield when its exercise violates others' right to equality. In order to assess this claim, however,

---

[1]See Ronald Dworkin, "What Rights Do We Have?" in *Taking Rights Seriously* (Cambridge, Mass.: Harvard University Press, 1977).

we need to return to our first question: How can the right to free speech be justified? Only then will we be in a position to assess properly the situations in which this right apparently conflicts with other values.

A traditional argument against state restriction of speech, and arguably the historical rationale behind the First Amendment, is that free speech and especially freedom of the press are necessary for the full and equal participation of citizens in the political process. People must have the chance to influence opinion and access to information about what their elected officials are doing. But this sort of argument will not apply in the case of pornography. As Ronald Dworkin points out very early in "Do We Have a Right to Pornography?" it is silly to suggest that access to pornographic material is essential to participation in the political process.[2] Hence, one must formulate a more general defense of free speech to protect pornography in its name.

Dworkin distinguishes between what he calls the "goal-based" strategy and the "rights-based" strategy for justifying free speech. Simply put, a goal-based argument for free speech assumes some goal or ideal—for instance, the attainment of truth—and contends that that ideal will be best achieved if we allow people to say and think what they want. Put negatively, the goal-based argument says that the long-term consequences of restricting speech are likely to be worse than the consequences of allowing some particular speech (for example, pornography) to flourish. On the other hand, the rights-based strategy asks, "Do people have moral or political rights such that it would be wrong to prohibit them from either publishing or reading or contemplating dirty books or pictures or films even if the community would be better off . . . if they did not?" The rights-based argument is stronger than the goal-based argument, because it does not derive its force from a guess about what would be best for the community in the long run. (In his paper in this part, Stanley Fish also rejects the goal-based argument, but for very different reasons.) What sort of right could play this role—that is, the role of rendering impermissible a policy that would in some sense be in the best interests of the community as a whole? A person

---

[2]Turning this justification for free speech on its head, we can ask, as some feminists do: Does the wide availability of pornography *hinder* some people's ability to participate in the political process? That is, we might want to think about whether pornography plays a part in establishing and maintaining attitudes about women that make it difficult for them to be taken seriously in political life. This issue is addressed later and in Ronald Dworkin's paper, "Liberty and Pornography," and in Jennifer Hornsby's contribution to Part Four, entitled "Speech Acts and Pornography."

who is trying to defend the right to pornography needs to identify and justify this right.

It is important to understand Dworkin's general proposal concerning what rights we have. He says, "Rights . . . are best understood as trumps over some background justification for political decisions that states a goal for the community as a whole." This means that the state would be wrong to act in a way pursuant to some goal that requires violating that right. So, to say that we have a right to free speech is to say that the state would be wrong to violate that right, even though the community would be better off in the long run if the state were to do so.

In particular, Dworkin contends that we have a "right to moral independence"—the right not to suffer disadvantage just because the state or our fellow citizens think that "[our] opinions about the right way . . . to lead [our] own lives are ignoble or wrong." Here we return to Dworkin's concept of equality, because the right to moral independence is grounded in considerations of equality. As Rae Langton expresses it, the right to be treated as an equal is "the right to have one's interests treated as fully and as sympathetically as the interests of anyone else," and one's conception of the good life should be treated with as much respect as anyone else's. The state would violate this right if, for example, it were to make decisions about the distribution of resources or opportunities on the grounds that some group's conception of the good life is superior to another's, or on the grounds that some people are worthy of more concern than others. Hence, the right to be treated as an equal, and thus the right to moral independence, constrains how the government may act towards its citizens.

Therefore, when we consider what to do about pornography, we must ask whether a policy that restricts or bans pornography would compromise some citizens' right to moral independence. This is a very complex question. Both Ronald Dworkin and Rae Langton tackle it in considerable detail, although ultimately they reach very different conclusions about what ought to be done about pornography.

Democratic policy making is, by and large, utilitarian. This means, as Dworkin says, that "a political decision is justified if it promises to make citizens happier, or to fulfill more of their preferences, on average, than any other decision could." Now, suppose that a policy that bans pornography has this effect. Dworkin argues that in order to see whether this policy violates anyone's right to moral independence—that is, whether it fails to treat them with equal concern and respect—we need to examine the nature of the preferences it seeks to fulfill. In particular, we need to investigate the moral convictions underlying the policy in question.

Dworkin elsewhere[3] draws a distinction between "personal" and "external" preferences. Roughly, your personal preferences concern how you would like goods and opportunities to be assigned to you; your external preferences concern how you would like goods and opportunities to be assigned to other people. Our external preferences are often the result of what we think about other people's characters and the way they lead their lives. If these preferences are taken into account in determining whether a particular policy ought to be adopted, then unfairness will result. As Langton summarizes it, "Consider . . . a group of citizens who believe that blacks are simply worth less concern than whites, and whose preferences manifest this prejudice. They prefer, say, that the preferences of blacks be worth half those of whites in the utilitarian calculus. If such racist preferences are taken into account . . . the utilitarian calculus will be distorted, and blacks will suffer unjustly as a result." In general, then, we must be wary of any proposed policy whose support depends upon such external preferences.

In practice, it is, of course, difficult to separate purely personal preferences from external ones. But it is not impossible to identify cases in which both sorts of preferences are at work, or where people's preferences are mixed. In these cases, Dworkin argues, we need to assess whether anyone would "suffer *serious* damage through legal restraint when this [restraint] can only be justified by the fact that what he proposes to do will frustrate or defeat preferences of others we have reason to believe are mixed with or are consequences of the conviction that people who act in that way are people of bad character." It is arguable, when it comes to thinking about pornography, that our preferences are mixed. Those who are anti-pornography often harbor views about the inherently degrading nature of certain sexual practices (for example, masturbation) or about the unwholesomeness of "some people's conception of what sexual experience should be like, and of what part fantasy should play in that experience, and of what the character of that fantasy should be. . . ." Thus, with respect to a policy that would restrict or ban pornography, we must ask what effects this policy is likely to have on those who will be denied access to pornography. A massively restrictive policy on pornography based on mixed preferences will violate some citizens' right

---

[3]Ronald Dworkin, "What Rights Do We Have?" in *Taking Rights Seriously.* Langton also discusses the distinction in her paper in this part.

to moral independence and thus would not be justified. This does not mean, however, that some less restrictive policy could not be justified. Indeed, Dworkin argues that certain zoning policies might be perfectly consistent with the right to moral independence.

Rae Langton adopts this general Dworkinian strategy for the assessment of the justifiability of public policy and turns it on its head. Drawing on the work of MacKinnon (see Part One), Langton investigates what happens if we embed Dworkin's style of argument in the context of feminist observations about pornography. Just as Dworkin examines what can be said in favor of a restrictive policy on pornography, Langton examines what can be said about a permissive policy. The crucial step in her argument concerns the preferences that might be thought to underpin such a policy. Langton argues that we have good reason to think that the preferences of those who wish to consume pornography are mixed. Such people may express what appear to be purely personal preferences: "I like pornography and I want to be able to look at it." But given the content of violent pornography, we might imagine that such people's desire for pornography is in part determined by their views concerning the worth of women and the respect that women are due or not due. Therefore, a permissive policy on pornography would violate women's right to moral independence and would for that reason not be justified.

If Langton's argument is compelling, it raises very interesting questions about the relationship between liberalism (of which Ronald Dworkin is a representative) and feminism. By and large, liberals argue against censorship. But if Langton is right, then perhaps liberals are mistaken in not supporting the anti-pornography measures that feminists such as MacKinnon and Andrea Dworkin recommend. However, as Ronald Dworkin's second essay in this part shows, the relationship of liberalism to feminism on the subject of pornography is rather complex.

In "Liberty and Pornography," Ronald Dworkin addresses some feminist anti-pornography arguments in the context of Isaiah Berlin's distinction between negative liberty and positive liberty. "Negative liberty . . . means not being obstructed by others in doing what one might wish to do." Thus, "the freedom to speak our minds without censorship" is an example of a negative liberty. Positive liberty refers to our ability to play a role in the political life of our community; for example, the right to vote is one of our positive liberties. Berlin argued that positive and negative liberties may collide. Moreover, liberty of either sorts often competes with other substantive values such as justice and happiness. There are two things to bear in mind here. First, we must tread carefully when we invoke the idea of liberty. We must be clear about what sort of liberty we have in mind and about why we value that liberty. This is essential, for example, if there are occasions when the negative liberty of free speech collides with the positive liberty to participate in the political process. Second, we must recognize the complexity of political value. In particular, if Berlin was right to say that not all political virtues can be simultaneously realized, then collectively we will have to choose which of them we value most.

As Ronald Dworkin points out, certain feminist arguments against pornography can be recast in terms of the distinction between positive liberty and negative liberty. As we have already seen in Part One, some feminists argue that the prevalence of pornography in our society contributes to an atmosphere in which women are not taken seriously as persons. If this is right, then arguably pornography is politically damaging for women. If as Dworkin puts it, pornography "produces a climate . . . in which women cannot have genuine political power or authority because they are perceived and understood inauthentically—that is, they are made over by male fantasy into people very different from, and of much less consequence than, the people they really are," then it looks as if we have an instance of the collision between negative liberty and positive liberty. In other words, it seems that pornographers' negative liberty to produce their material is in conflict with women's positive liberty to have equitable access to the political process.

Dworkin is skeptical of these claims about pornography's effects. He suggests that mainstream advertising is a far more powerful, pervasive, and negative influence on attitudes about women's abilities. But his real response to this argument is to reaffirm that "the point of free speech is precisely to allow ideas to have whatever consequences follow from their dissemination, including undesirable consequences for positive liberty." This is borne out by the commitment to the negative liberty of free speech that is embedded in both the U.S. Constitution and the Canadian Charter of Rights and Freedoms. In Berlin's terms, these modern democratic states have chosen this liberty to be at the center of their respective constellations of political virtues. Thus, even if pornography poses a threat to women's positive liberty, this threat is not sufficient grounds on which to censor or restrict pornography. Whatever our response to pornography is, it must be consistent with our primary adherence to free speech.

In light of this, we might imagine that a more powerful anti-pornography argument could be made. Suppose that our primary political value *is* the negative liberty of free speech. A strong anti-pornography argument might then take the form of showing that pornography poses a threat to women's negative liberty. Such an argument has in fact been made by Frank Michelman.[4] He claims that pornography affects everyone's perceptions about women; it promulgates a fallacious view about what women are like, what women want, and what women are capable of. In doing this, it is just as effective in silencing women as heckling is in silencing a public speaker. To be sure, when we worry about restrictions on free speech—when we invoke our negative liberty—we usually have in mind curtailing the activity of the state. Michelman's argument depends on extending this caution to the activities of private citizens. It is not the state but other citizens who produce and circulate pornography.

Dworkin remains skeptical about this argument too. He emphasizes that there is a difference between ideas being misunderstood or not receiving due consideration and people being physically prevented from expressing ideas. Pornography might work to achieve the former, but Dworkin does not think that it achieves the latter. Therefore, he concludes that even this initially promising anti-pornography argument fails.[5]

In contrast with Ronald Dworkin, who clearly gives a prominent place to freedom of expression, Stanley Fish argues for the somewhat surprising conclusion that there is no such thing as free speech. What Fish means by this is that free speech is not something we value (or ought to value) just for itself. When we talk about free speech, we are not simply talking about the liberty to make sounds. Rather we are asserting our right to say something (that is, to utter intelligible speech). But when we say something—put forward a particular political view, for example—we are necessarily *not* saying something else. As Fish says, "Without restriction, without an in-built sense of what it would be meaningless to say or wrong to say, there could be no assertion and no reason for asserting it." So meaningful speech depends on excluding other speech. Thus there is no *free* speech, per se.

This is not, of course, to say that meaningful speech lacks value. Rather, what Fish argues is that we must understand the value of speech in the context of the community in which it is asserted. We claim that speech ought to

---

[4]Frank Michelman, "Conceptions of Democracy in American Constitutional Argument: The Case of Pornography Regulation," *Tennessee Law Review* 56 (1989): 291–319.

[5]Jennifer Hornsby's paper in Part Four, "Speech Acts and Pornography," provides a counterpoint to Dworkin's argument here.

be protected, because we think that only in this way are *other* things we value protected. Thus, speech derives whatever value it has from what it protects. And we determine which speech is to be protected and which not by asking Milton's question, which Fish expresses as: "Would this form of speech or advocacy, if permitted to flourish, tend to undermine the very purpose for which our society is constituted?" In other words, whenever we consider the question of whether some speech (for example, racist speech or pornography) ought to be protected or restricted, we already have in mind a particular conception of the good. If we value equality, for example, we will want to know whether allowing some type of speech would uphold and maintain that value or whether it would undermine it. Fish draws our attention to a recent hate propaganda case in Canada—the *Keegstra* case.[6] In its decision about the constitutionality of the hate propaganda provisions of the Criminal Code, the Canadian Supreme Court appeared to argue in just the way Milton recommends. Emphasizing the value of equality, it held that insofar as hate speech constitutes a threat to equality, it is not to be protected.

This highlights a very interesting distinction between Canada and the United States. Section 1 of the Canadian Charter of Rights and Freedoms reads, "The Canadian Charter of Rights and Freedoms guarantees the rights and freedoms set out in it subject to reasonable limits prescribed by law as can be demonstrably justified in a free and democratic society." So the idea that free speech is to be balanced in the scales along with other political values is made explicit in Canadian law. This is not, however, the case in the United States. The U.S. Supreme Court has, of course, sometimes ruled that certain speech is not protected by the First Amendment. But on several of these occasions it has resorted to drawing a distinction between speech and action. For example, in *Chaplinsky v. New Hampshire*,[7] the Court ruled that "fighting words" are not protected speech, on the grounds that such words are not really speech at all but a kind of action—namely, the incitement to violence. Fish argues that this distinction makes no sense, for it assumes that we can separate speech that has consequences from speech that does not. Moreover, it appears to entail that the First Amendment protects only speech

---

[6]*R. v. Keegstra* [1990] 3 S.C.R. 697. The Canadian Supreme Court engaged in similar, but not identical, reasoning in *R. v. Butler* [1992] 1 S.C.R. 452. In that case the court ruled that while the obscenity provisions of the Canadian Criminal Code do infringe on the right to free speech guaranteed in the Charter, such an infringement is justifiable in a "free and democratic society." (See the Legal Appendix.)

[7]315 U.S. 568 (1942).

that does not have consequences. But as Fish contends throughout his paper, we speak for a reason. Our purpose in saying something is to effect some change in the world; we want to convey information, persuade someone, defend a particular view, and so on. All meaningful speech is consequential. Hence, if the First Amendment really were to protect only nonconsequential speech, it would protect only meaningless noise. This ought to strike us as absurd.

Fish denies that abstract principles such as the First Amendment can help us in making decisions on what speech to allow and what speech not to allow. Such decisions are always contextual; they are always political. We must choose on the basis of what we think best for us here and now, given the things we value here and now. In defending this view against the charge that it is too instrumentalistic, Fish argues against the goal-based justification of free speech, which says that we must allow freedom of expression, because we do not know what will be best for us in the long run. If our ultimate goal is the attainment of truth, we must give every idea an airing. But Fish argues, in the context of a racist and sexist society, this sort of view is of little comfort. Indeed, it appears to require that we refrain from prohibiting hurtful speech without being told precisely what is the good outcome of doing so. It is our ignorance about what is best for us in the long run that lies at the base of the goal-based argument. However, we are *not* ignorant of some very bad things that currently exist in our society. A yet-unspecified good future can pale in significance in the face of current injustice.

Fish's conclusion is not that we ought to restrict whatever we like. Rather he emphasizes that we must be aware that our decisions about free speech have a lot to do with power and politics, and that we must make these decisions responsibly, taking into account as much as possible the consequences of both allowing and restricting certain forms of speech.

RONALD DWORKIN

Do We Have a Right to Pornography?

Ronald Dworkin is professor of jurisprudence at Oxford
University and professor of law at New York University. He is
the author of many books and articles, including Taking Rights
Seriously *(1977),* A Matter of Principle *(1985),* Law's Empire
(1986), and, most recently, Life's Dominion: An Argument
about Abortion, Euthanasia, and Individual Freedom *(1993).*
He also writes regularly for The New York Review of Books.

It is an old problem for liberal theory how far people should have the right to do the wrong thing. Liberals insist that people have the legal right to say what they wish on matters of political or social controversy. But should they be free to incite racial hatred, for example? British and American law now give different answers to that specific question. The United Kingdom Race Relations law makes it a crime to advocate racial prejudice, but the First Amendment to the United States Constitution forbids Congress or any of the states from adopting any such law.

Pornography in its various forms presents another instance of the same issue. The majority of people in both countries would prefer (or so it seems)

[Editor's note: This reading is an excerpt from a longer paper of the same title, in which Dworkin critically discusses the Williams Report (1977).]

Source: *Oxford Journal of Legal Studies,* Vol. 1 (Summer 1981), pp. 177–212. Reprinted by permission of Oxford University Press.

substantial censorship, if not outright prohibition, of "sexually explicit" books, magazines, photographs, and films, and this majority includes a considerable number of those who are themselves consumers of whatever pornography is on offer (It is part of the complex psychology of sex that many of those with a fixed taste for the obscene would strongly prefer that their children, for example, not follow them in that taste.) If we assume that the majority is correct, and that people who publish and consume pornography do the wrong thing, or at least display the wrong sort of character, should they nevertheless have the legal right to do so?

Some lawyers and political philosophers consider the problem of pornography to be only an instance of the first problem I mentioned, the problem of freedom to speak unpopular or wicked thoughts. But we should be suspicious of that claim, because the strongest arguments in favor of allowing *Mein Kampf* to be published hardly seem to apply in favor of the novel *Whips Incorporated* or the film *Sex Kittens*. No one, I think, is denied an equal voice in the political process, however broadly conceived, when he is forbidden to circulate photographs of genitals to the public at large, or denied his right to listen to argument when he is forbidden to consider these photographs at his leisure. If we believe it wrong to censor these forms of pornography, then we should try to find the justification for that opinion elsewhere than in the literature celebrating freedom of speech and press.

We should consider two rather different strategies that might be thought to justify a permissive attitude. The first argues that even if the publication and consumption of pornography is bad for the community as a whole, just considered in itself, the consequences of trying to censor or otherwise suppress pornography would be, in the long run, even worse. I shall call this the "goal-based" strategy. The second argues that even if pornography makes the community worse off, even in the very long run, it is nevertheless wrong to censor or restrict it because this violates the individual moral or political rights of citizens who resent the censorship. I shall call this the "rights-based" strategy. . . .

. . . Most of us feel, for reasons we perhaps cannot fully formulate, that it would be wrong to prevent Communists from defending the Russian invasion of Afghanistan on Hyde Park soapboxes, or neo-Nazis from publishing tracts celebrating Hitler. The goal-based justification of these convictions proposes that even though we might be worse off in the short run by tolerating distasteful political speech, because it distresses us and because there is always some chance that it will prove persuasive to others, there are reasons why we shall nevertheless be better off in the long run—come nearer to fulfilling the goals we ought to set for ourselves—if we do tolerate that speech. This argument has the weakness of providing contingent reasons for convictions that we do not hold contingently. For the story usually told about why free speech is in our long-term interests is not drawn from any deep physical necessity like the laws of motion, or even deep facts about the genetic structure or psychic constitution of human beings; the argument is highly problematical, speculative and in any case marginal. If the story is true, we might say, it is only just true, and no one can have any overwhelming ground for accepting it. But our convictions about free speech are not tentative or half-hearted or marginal. They are not just barely convictions. We can easily construct a goal-based *explanation* of why people like us would develop convictions we thought deep and lasting, even though the advantages to us of having these convictions were both temporary and contingent. But that is beside the present point, which is rather that these explanations do not provide a *justification* of the meaning these convictions have for us.

This problem in all goal-based justifications of fundamental political convictions is aggravated, in the case of liberal convictions about pornography, because the goal-based story seems not only speculative and marginal, but implausible as well. In the case of free political speech, we might well concede, to the goal-based theory, that each person has an important interest in developing his own independent political convictions, because that is an essential part of his personality, and because his political convictions will be more authentically his own, more the product of his own personality, the more varied the opinions of others he encounters. We might also concede that political activity in a community is made more vigorous by variety, even by the entry, that is, of wholly despicable points of view. These are decent arguments why both individuals and the community as a whole are at least in certain respects better off when the Nazi has spoken his piece; they are arguments not only for liberty of political expression but also for more political speech rather than less. But the parallel arguments in the case of most pornography seem silly, and very few of those who defend peoples' right to read pornography in private would actually claim that the community or any individual is better off with more pornography rather than less. So a goal-based argument for pornography must do without what seem the strongest (though still contingent) strands in the goal-based argument for free speech. . . .

I want to consider what sort of an argument might be found in the other kind of strategy I mentioned at the outset, the rights-based strategy. Do people have moral or political rights such that it would be wrong to prohibit them from either publishing or reading or contemplating dirty books or pictures or films even if the community would be better off—provide more suitable conditions within which its members might develop—if they did not? . . .

Rights

Consider the following suggestion. People have the right not to suffer disadvantage in the distribution of social goods and opportunities, including disadvantage in the liberties permitted to them by the criminal law, just on the ground that their officials or fellow-citizens think that their opinions about the right way for them to lead their own lives are ignoble or wrong. I shall call this (putative) right the right to moral independence, and in this part I shall consider what force this right would have on the law of pornography if it were recognized. In the next part I shall consider what grounds we might have to recognize it.

The right to moral independence is a very abstract right (or, if you prefer, the statement of the right I gave is a very abstract statement of the right) because this statement takes no account of the impact of competing rights. It does not attempt to decide whether the right can always be jointly satisfied for everyone, or how conflicts with other rights, if they arise, are to be settled. These further questions, along with other related questions, are left for more concrete statements of the right. Or (what comes to the same thing) for statements of the more concrete rights that people have in virtue of the abstract right. Nevertheless, the questions I wish to put may usefully be asked even about the abstract statement or the abstract right.

Someone who appeals to the right of moral independence in order to justify a permissive legal regime of obscenity does not suppose that the community will be better off in the long run (according to some description of what makes a community better off . . .) if people are free to look at obscene pictures in private. He does not deny this. His argument is in the conditional mood: even if conditions will not then be so suitable for human flourishing as they might be, for example, nevertheless the right must be respected. But what force does the right then have? When does the government violate that right?

It violates the right, we may say, at least in this case: when the only apparent or plausible justification for a scheme of regulation of pornography includes the hypothesis that the attitudes about sex displayed or nurtured in pornography are demeaning or bestial or otherwise unsuitable to human beings of the best sort, even though this hypothesis may be true. It also violates that right when that justification includes the proposition that most people in the society accept that hypothesis and are therefore pained or disgusted when other members of their own community, for whose lives they understandably feel special responsibility, do read dirty books or look at dirty pictures. The right is therefore a powerful constraint on the regulation of pornography, or at least so it seems, because it prohibits giving weight to exactly the arguments most people think are the best arguments for even a mild and enlightened policy of restriction of obscenity. What room is left, by the apparently powerful right, for the government to do anything at all about pornography?

Suppose it is discovered that the private consumption of pornography does significantly increase the danger of crimes of violence, either generally or specifically crimes of sexual violence. Or suppose that private consumption has some special and deleterious effect on the general economy, by causing great absenteeism from work, for example, as drink or breakfast television is sometimes said to do. Then government would have, in these facts, a justification for the restraint and perhaps even for the prohibition of pornography that does not include the offending hypothesis either directly, by the assumption that the hypothesis is true, or indirectly, in the proposition that many people think it true. After all (as is often pointed out in discussions of obscenity . . .), the Bible or Shakespeare might turn out to have these unfortunate consequences, in which case government would have a reason for banning these books that did not require a comparable hypothesis about them.

This possibility raises a slightly more subtle point. Suppose it were discovered that all forms of emotionally powerful literature (including Shakespeare, the Bible, and many forms of pornography) contributed significantly to crime. But the government responded to this discovery selectively, banning most examples of pornography and other literature it considered worthless, but allowing Shakespeare and the Bible nevertheless, on the ground that these were of such literary and cultural value that it was worth the crime they caused to preserve them. Nothing in this selection and discrimination (as so far stated) violates the right to moral independence. The judgment in question—that pornography does not in fact contribute enough of literary value, or that it is not sufficiently informative or imaginative about the different ways in which people might express themselves or find value in their lives, to justify accepting the damage of crime as the cost of its publication—is not the judgment that those who do enjoy pornography have worse character on that account. Any judgment of literary or cultural value will be a judgment about which honest and reasonable people will disagree. But this is true of many other kinds of judgments that government must nevertheless make. The present judgment is no doubt special because it may be used as a screen to hide a different judgment that would offend the right to independence, the judgment that pornography should be treated differently from the Bible because the people who prefer it are worse people. That danger might be sufficiently strong so that a society jealous of the right of moral independence will, for prophylactic reasons, forbid officials to make the literary judgment that would distinguish *Sex Kittens* from *Hamlet* if both were found to provoke crime. That does not touch the present point, that the literary judgment is different, and does not itself threaten the right of independence; and it is worth adding that very few of the people who do admit to enjoying pornography claim distinct literary merit for it. They claim at most the kind of merit that others, with more conventional ideas about amusement, claim for thrillers.

But this is, in any case, only academic speculation, because there is no reason to suppose a sufficiently direct connection between crime and either *Sex Kittens* or *Hamlet* to provide a ground for banning either one as private entertainment. But what about public display? Can we find a plausible justification for restricting the display of pornography that does not violate the right of moral independence? We can, obviously, construct a certain argument in that direction, as follows. "Many people do not like to encounter genital displays on the way to the grocer. This taste is not, nor does it necessarily reflect, any adverse view of the character of those who do not mind such encounters. Someone who would not like to find pornography in his ordinary paths may not even object to finding it elsewhere. He may simply have tastes and preferences that reject certain combinations in his experience, like someone who likes pink sunsets but not pink houses in Belgravia, who does not object to neon in Leicester Square but would hate it in the Cotswolds. Or he may have a more structured or more consequentialist scheme of preferences about his environment. He may find or believe, for example, that his own delight in other peoples' bodies is lessened or made less sharp and special if nakedness becomes either too familiar to him or less peculiar to those occasions in which it provides him special pleasure, which may be in museums or his own bedroom or both. Or that sex will come to be different and less valuable for him if he is too often or too forcefully reminded that it has different, more commercial or more sadistic, meaning for others. Or that his goal that his children develop certain similar tastes and opinions will be thwarted by the display or advertising that he opposes. None of these different opinions and complaints *must* be the product of some conviction that those with other opinions and tastes are people of bad character, any more than those who hope that state-supported theater will produce the classics exclusively must think that those who prefer experimental theater are less worthy people."

This picture of the motives people might have for not wanting to encounter pornography on the streets is a conceivable picture. But I suspect . . . that it is far too crude and one-dimensional as a picture of what these motives actually are. The discomfort many people find in encountering blatant nudity on the hoardings is rarely so independent of their moral convictions as these various descriptions suggest. It is at least part of the offense, for many people, that they detest themselves for taking the interest in the proceedings that they do. It is a major part of the offense, for others, that they are so forcefully reminded of what their neighbors are like and, more particularly, of what their neighbors are getting away with. People object to the display of naked men and women in erotic poses, that is, even when these displays occur (as for commercial reasons they inevitably do) in those parts of cities that would be in no sense beautiful or enlightening even without the pornography. Even if we took the descriptions of peoples' motives in the argument I set out at face value, moreover, we should be forced to recognize the substantial influence of moral convictions just in those motives, for someone's sense of what he wants his own attitudes toward sex to be, and certainly his sense of what attitudes he hopes to encourage in his children, are not only influenced by, but constitute, his moral opinions in the broad sense.

We therefore encounter, in peoples' motives for objecting to the advertising or display of pornography, at least a mix and interaction of attitudes, beliefs, and tastes that rule out any confident assertion that regulation justified by appeal to these motives would not violate the right to moral independence. We do not know whether, if we could disentangle the different strands of taste, ambition, and belief, so as to winnow out those that express moral condemnation or would not exist but for it, the remaining strands would justify any particular scheme of regulation of display. This is not just a failure of information that would be expensive to obtain. The problem is more conceptual than that: the vocabulary we use to identify and individuate motives—our own as well as those of others—cannot provide the discrimination we need.

A society anxious to defend the abstract right to moral independence in the face of this complexity has two options at least. It might decide that if popular attitudes toward a minority or a minority practice are mixed in this way, so that the impact of adverse moral convictions can be neither excluded nor measured, then these attitudes should all be deemed to be corrupted by such convictions, and no regulation is permissible. Or it might decide that the case of mixed attitudes is a special kind of case in the administration of the abstract right, so that more concrete statements of what people are entitled to have under the right must take the fact of mixed attitudes into account. It might do this, for example, by stipulating, at the more concrete level, that no one should suffer *serious* damage through legal restraint when this can only be justified by the fact that what he proposes to do will frustrate or defeat preferences of others that we have reason to believe are mixed with or are consequences of the conviction that people who act in that way are people of bad character. This second option, which defines a concrete right tailored to the problem of mixed preferences, is not a relaxation or compromise of the abstract right, but rather a (no doubt controversial) application of it to that special situation. Which of the two options (or which further option) provides the best response to the problem of mixed motives is part of the more general problem of justification that I postponed to the next section. The process of making an abstract right successively more concrete is not simply a process of deduction or interpretation of the abstract statement but a fresh step in political theory.

If society takes the second option just described in the case of pornography (as I think it should, for reasons I describe later), then its officials must undertake to decide what damage to those who wish to publish or read pornography is serious and what is trivial. Once again reasonable and honest officials will disagree about this, but we are trying to discover, not an algorithm for a law of obscenity, but rather whether a plausible concrete conception of a plausible abstract right will yield a sensible scheme of regulation. We should therefore consider the character of the damage that would be inflicted on consumers of pornography by, say, a scheme of zoning that requires that pornographic materials be sold and films shown only in particular areas, a scheme of advertising that prohibits in public places advertisements that would widely be regarded as indecent, and a scheme of labeling so that those entering cinemas or shops whose contents they might find indecent would be warned. There are three main heads of damage that such a regime might inflict on consumers: inconvenience, expense, and embarrassment. Whether the inconvenience is serious will depend on the details of, for example, the zoning. But it should not be considered serious if shoppers for pornography need travel on average only as far as, say, shoppers for stereo equipment or diamonds or secondhand books need travel to find the centers of such trade. How far this scheme of restriction would increase the price of pornography is harder to predict. Perhaps the constraint on advertising would decrease the volume of sales and therefore increase unit costs. But it seems unlikely that this effect would be very great, particularly if the legal ban runs to the character not to the extent of the advertising, and permits, as it should, not only stark "tombstone" notices, but the full range of the depressingly effective techniques through which manufacturers sell soap and video cassette recorders.

Embarrassment raises a more interesting and important question. Some states and countries have required people to identify themselves as belonging to a particular religion or holding certain political convictions just for the sake of that identification, and for the sake of the disadvantage it brings in its train. The Nazi's regime of yellow armbands for Jews, for example, or the registry of members of civil rights groups that some southern states established and the Supreme Court ruled unconstitutional in *NAACP v. Alabama ex rel Patterson*.[1] Since in cases like these identification is required just as a mark of public contempt, or just to provide the social and economic pressure that follows from that contempt, these laws are ruled out by even the abstract form of the right. But the situation is rather different if identification is a by-product rather than the purpose of a scheme of regulation, and is as voluntary as the distinct goals of regulation permit. It would violate the right of moral independence, plainly, if pornography houses were not allowed to use plain-brown-wrapper mail for customers who preferred anonymity, because embarrassment would be the point of that restriction, not a by-product. Also, I think, [the same would be true] if the law forbade pornography shops from selling anything but pornography, so that a shy pornographer could not walk out of the shop with a new umbrella as well as a bulge in his coat pocket. But the right of moral independence does not carry with it any government obligation to insure that people may exercise that right in public places without its being known by the public that they do. Perhaps the government would be obliged to take special measures to guard against embarrassment in a society in which people actually were likely to suffer serious economic harm if they were seen leaving a shop carrying the wrong sign. But that is unlikely to be true about shy pornographers in this country now, who might sensibly be required to bear the social burden of being known to be the kind of people they are.

I conclude that the right to moral independence, if it is a genuine right, requires a permissive legal attitude toward the consumption of pornography in private, but that a certain concrete conception of that right nevertheless permits a scheme of restriction rather like the scheme that the Williams Report recommends. It remains to consider whether that right and that conception can themselves be justified in political theory. . . .

Equality

A Trump over Utility

The rest of this essay considers the question of how the right to moral independence might be defended, both in its abstract form and in the more concrete conception we discussed in considering public display of pornography. This question is important beyond the relatively trivial problem of obscenity itself: the right has other and more important applications, and the question of what kinds of arguments support a claim of right is an urgent question in political theory.

Rights, I have argued elsewhere,[2] are best understood as trumps over some background justification for political decisions that states a goal for the community as a whole. If someone has a right to moral independence, this means that it is for some reason wrong for officials to act in violation of that right, even if they (correctly) believe that the community as a whole would be better off if they did. There are many different theories in the field about what makes a community better off on the whole; many different theories, that is, about what the goal of political action should be. One prominent theory (or rather group of theories) is utilitarianism in its familiar forms, which suppose that the community is better off if its members are on average happier or have more of their preferences satisfied. Another, and in certain ways different, theory is the theory . . . which argues that the community is better off if it provides the most desirable conditions for human development. There are of course many other theories about the true goal of politics, many of them much more different from either of these two theories than these are from each other. To some extent, the argument in favor of a particular right must depend on which of these theories about desirable goals has been accepted; it must depend, that is, on what general background justification for political decisions the right in question proposes to trump. In the following discussion I shall assume that the background justification with which we are concerned is some form of utilitarianism, which takes, as the goal of politics, the fulfillment of as many of peoples' goals for their own lives as possible. This remains, I think, the most influential background justification, at least in the informal way in which it presently figures in politics in the Western democracies.

Suppose we accept then that, at least in general, a political decision is justified if it promises to make citizens happier, or to fulfill more of their preferences, on average, than any other decision could. Suppose we assume that the decision to prohibit pornography altogether does meet that test, because the desires and preferences of publishers and consumers are outweighed by the desires and preferences of the majority, including their preferences about how others should lead their lives. How could any contrary decision, permitting even the private use of pornography, then be justified?

Two modes of argument might be thought capable of supplying such a justification. First, we might argue that, though the utilitarian goal states one important political ideal, it is not the only important ideal, and pornography must be permitted in order to protect some other ideal that is, in the circumstances, more important. Second, we might argue that further analysis of the grounds that we have for accepting utilitarianism as a background justification in the first place—further reflection of why we wish to pursue that goal—shows that utility must yield to some right of moral independence here. The first form of argument is pluralistic: it argues for a trump over utility on the ground that though utility is always important, it is not the only thing that matters, and other goals or ideals are sometimes more important. The second supposes that proper understanding of what utilitarianism is, and why it is important, will itself justify the right in question.

I do not believe that the first, or pluralistic, mode of argument has much prospect of success, at least as applied to the problem of pornography. But I shall not develop the arguments now that would be necessary to support that opinion. I want instead to offer an argument in the second mode, which is, in summary, this. Utilitarianism owes whatever appeal it has to what we might call its egalitarian cast. (Or, if that is too strong, would lose whatever appeal it has but for that cast.) Suppose some version of utilitarianism provided that the preferences of some people were to count for less than those of others in the calculation how best to fulfill most preferences overall either because these people were in themselves less worthy or less attractive or less well loved people, or because the preferences in question combined to form a contemptible way of life. This would strike us as flatly unacceptable, and in any case much less appealing than standard forms of utilitarianism. In any of its standard versions, utilitarianism can claim to provide a conception of how government treats people as equals, or, in any case, how government respects the fundamental requirement that it must treat people as equals. Utilitarianism claims that people are treated as equals when the preferences of each, weighted only for intensity, are balanced in the same scales, with no distinctions for persons or merit. The corrupt version of utilitarianism just described, which gives less weight to some persons than to others, or discounts some preferences because these are ignoble, forfeits that claim. But if utilitarianism in practice is not checked by something like the right of moral independence (and by other allied rights), it will disintegrate, for all practical purposes, into exactly that version.

Suppose a community of many people including Sarah. If the Constitution sets out a version of utilitarianism which provides in terms that Sarah's preferences are to count for twice as much as those of others, then this would be the unacceptable, nonegalitarian version of utilitarianism. But now suppose that the constitutional provision is the standard form of utilitarianism, that is, that it is neutral toward all people and preferences, but that a surprising number of people love Sarah very much, and therefore strongly prefer that her preferences count for twice as much in the day-to-day political decisions made in the utilitarian calculus. When Sarah does not receive what she would have if her preferences counted for twice as much as those of others, then these people are unhappy, because their special Sarah-loving preferences are unfulfilled. If these special preferences are themselves allowed to count, therefore, Sarah will receive much more in the distribution of goods and opportunities than she otherwise would. I argue that this defeats the egalitarian cast of the apparently neutral utilitarian Constitution as much as if the neutral provision were replaced by the rejected version. Indeed, the apparently neutral provision is then self-undermining because it gives a critical weight, in deciding which distribution best promotes utility, to the views of those who hold the profoundly un-neutral (some would say anti-utilitarian) theory that the preferences of some should count for more than those of others.

The reply that a utilitarian anxious to resist the right to moral independence would give to this argument is obvious: utilitarianism does not give weight to the truth of that theory, but just to the fact that many people (wrongly) hold that theory and so are disappointed when the distribution the government achieves is not the distribution they believe is right. It is the fact of their disappointment, not the truth of their views, that counts, and there is no inconsistency, logical or pragmatic, in that. But this reply is too quick. For there is a particularly deep kind of contradiction here. Utilitarianism must claim (as I said earlier, any political theory must claim) truth for itself, and therefore must claim the falsity of any theory that contradicts it. It must itself occupy, that is, all the logical space that its content requires. But neutral utilitarianism claims (or, in any case, presupposes) that no one is, in principle, any more entitled to have any of his preferences fulfilled than anyone else is. It argues that the only reason for denying the fulfillment of one person's desires, whatever these are, is that more or more intense desires must be satisfied instead. It insists that justice and political morality can supply no other reason. This is, we might say, the neutral utilitarian's *case* for trying to achieve a political structure in which the average fulfillment of preferences is as high as possible. The question is not whether a government can achieve that political structure if it counts political preferences like the preferences of the Sarah-lovers or whether the government will then have counted any particular preference twice and so contradicted utilitarianism in that direct way. It is rather whether the government can achieve all this without implicitly contradicting that case.

Suppose the community contains a Nazi, for example, whose set of preferences includes the preference that Aryans have more and Jews less of their preferences fulfilled just because of who they are. A neutral utilitarian cannot say that there is no reason in political morality for rejecting or dishonoring that preference, for not dismissing it as just wrong, for not striving to fulfill it with all the dedication that officials devote to fulfilling any other sort of preference. For utilitarianism itself supplies such a reason: its most fundamental tenet is that peoples' preferences should be weighed on an equal basis in the same scales, that the Nazi theory of justice is profoundly wrong, and that officials should oppose the Nazi theory and strive to defeat rather than fulfill it. A neutral utilitarian is barred, for reasons of consistency, from taking the same politically neutral attitude to the Nazi's political preference that he takes toward other sorts of preferences. But then he cannot make the case just described in favor of highest average utility computed taking that preference into account.

I do not mean that endorsing someone's right to have his preference satisfied automatically endorses his preference as good or noble. The good utilitarian, who says that the pinball player is equally entitled to satisfaction of that taste as the poet is entitled to the satisfaction of his, is not for that reason committed to the proposition that a life of pinball is as good as a life of poetry. Only vulgar critics of utilitarianism would insist on that inference. The utilitarian says only that nothing in the theory of justice provides any reason why the political and economic arrangements and decisions of society should be any closer to those the poet would prefer than those the pinball player would like. It is just a matter, from the standpoint of political justice, of how many people prefer the one to the other and how strongly. But he cannot say that about the conflict between the Nazi and the neutral utilitarian opponent of Nazism, because the correct political theory, his political theory, the very political theory to which he appeals in attending to the fact of the Nazi's claim, does speak to the conflict. It says that what the neutral utilitarian prefers is just and accurately describes what people are, as a matter of political morality, entitled to have, but that what the Nazi prefers is deeply unjust and describes what no one is entitled, as a matter of political morality, to have. But then it is contradictory to say, again as a matter of political morality, that the Nazi is as much entitled to the political system he prefers as is the utilitarian.

The point might be put this way. Political preferences, like the Nazi's preference, are on the same level—purport to occupy the same space—as the utilitarian theory itself. Therefore, though the utilitarian theory must be neutral between personal preferences like the preferences for pinball and poetry, as a matter of the theory of justice, it cannot, without contradiction, be neutral between itself and Nazism. It cannot accept at once a duty to defeat the false theory that some people's preferences should count for more than other people's and a duty to strive to fulfill the political preferences of those who passionately accept that false theory, as energetically as it strives for any other preferences. The distinction on which the reply to my argument rests, the distinction between the truth and the fact of the Nazi's political preferences, collapses, because if utilitarianism counts the fact of these preferences, it has denied what it cannot deny, which is that justice requires it to oppose them.

We could escape this point by distinguishing two different forms or levels of utilitarianism. The first would be presented simply as a thin theory about how a political constitution should be selected in a community whose members prefer different kinds of political theories. The second would be a candidate for the constitution to be so chosen; it might argue for a distribution that maximized aggregate satisfaction of personal preferences in the actual distribution of goods and opportunities, for example. In that case, the first theory would argue only that the preferences of the Nazi should be given equal weight with the preferences of the second sort of utilitarian in the choice of a constitution, because each is equally entitled to the constitution he prefers, and there would be no contradiction in that proposition. But of course the neutral utilitarian theory we are now considering is not a thin theory of that sort. It proposes a theory of justice as a full political constitution, not just a theory about how to choose one, and so it cannot escape contradiction through modesty.

Now the same argument holds (though perhaps less evidently) when the political preferences are not familiar and despicable, like the Nazi theory, but more informal and cheerful, like the preferences of the Sarah-lovers who think that her preferences should be counted twice. The latter might, indeed, be Sarahocrats who believe that she is entitled to the treatment they recommend by virtue of birth or other characteristics unique to her. But even if their preferences rise from special affection rather than from political theory, these preferences nevertheless invade the space claimed by neutral utilitarianism and so cannot be counted without defeating the case utilitarianism provides. My argument, therefore, comes to this. If utilitarianism is to figure as part of an attractive working political theory, it must be qualified so as to restrict the preferences that count by excluding political preferences of both the formal and informal sort. One very practical way to achieve this restriction is provided by the idea of rights as trumps over unrestricted utilitarianism. A society committed to utilitarianism as a general background justification which does not in terms disqualify any preferences might achieve that disqualification by adopting a right to political independence: the right that no one suffer disadvantage in the distribution of goods or opportunities on the ground that others think he should have less because of who he is or is not, or that others care less for him than they do for other people. The right of political independence would have the effect of insulating Jews from the preferences of Nazis, and those who are not Sarah from the preferences of those who adore her.

The right of moral independence can be defended in a parallel way. Neutral utilitarianism rejects the idea that some ambitions that people might have for their own lives should have less command over social resources and opportunities than others, except as this is the consequence of weighing all preferences on an equal basis in the same scales. It rejects the argument, for example, that some people's conception of what sexual experience should be like, and of what part fantasy should play in that experience, and of what the character of that fantasy should be, are inherently degrading or unwholesome.

But then it cannot (for the reasons just canvassed) count the moral preferences of those who do hold such opinions in the calculation whether individuals who form some sexual minority, including homosexuals and pornographers, should be prohibited from the sexual experiences they want to have. The right of moral independence is part of the same collection of rights as the right of political independence, and it is to be justified as a trump over an unrestricted utilitarian defense of prohibitory laws against pornography, in a community of those who find offense just in the idea that their neighbors are reading dirty books, in much the same way as the latter right is justified as a trump over a utilitarian justification of giving Jews less or Sarah more in a society of Nazis or Sarah-lovers.

It remains to consider whether the abstract right to moral independence, defended in this way, would nevertheless permit restriction of public display of pornography in a society whose preferences against that display were backed by the mixed motives we reviewed in the last part. This is a situation in which the egalitarian cast of utilitarianism is threatened from not one but two directions. To the extent to which the motives in question are moral preferences about how others should behave, and these motives are counted, then the neutrality of utilitarianism is compromised. But to the extent to which these are the rather different sort of motives we reviewed, which emphasize not how others should lead their lives, but rather the character of the sexual experience people want for themselves, and these motives are disregarded, the neutrality of utilitarianism is compromised in the other direction, for it becomes unnecessarily inhospitable to the special and important ambitions of those who then lose control of a crucial aspect of their own self-development. The situation is therefore not an appropriate case for a prophylactic refusal to count any motive whenever we cannot be sure that that motive is unmixed with moralism, because the danger of unfairness lies on both sides rather than only on one. The alternative I described in the preceding section is at least better than that. This argues that restriction may be justified even though we cannot be sure that the preferences people have for restriction are untinged by the kind of preferences we should exclude, provided that the damage done to those who are affected adversely is not serious damage, even in their own eyes. Allowing restrictions on public display is in one sense a compromise; but it is a compromise recommended by the right of moral independence, once the case for that right is set out, not a compromise of that right. . . .

NOTES

1. 357 U.S. 449 (1958).

2. Dworkin, *Taking Rights Seriously* (Cambridge, Mass.: Harvard University Press, 1977).

RAE LANGTON

Whose Right?
Ronald Dworkin, Women,
and Pornographers

*Rae Langton is a lecturer in philosophy at Monash University
(Melbourne, Australia). She works in moral and political
philosophy, metaphysics, and the history of philosophy. She is also
author of "Speech Acts and Unspeakable Acts," parts of which
appear in Part Four. She is writing her doctoral dissertation at
Princeton University on Kant.*

Amidst the heated and often acrimonious controversies about pornography
and government policy, the answer to one question at least has always
seemed obvious. Should liberal theorists be in favor of permitting pornography? As champions of our basic liberties, and as champions especially of free
speech, liberals have found it easy to answer this question with a simple
"yes." They are of course accustomed to viewing their opponents in this debate as conservatives, who want pornography prohibited because it is immoral; liberals view moralistic motives of this kind with deep (and doubtless
justified) suspicion. But there are other voices in the debate, too, voices

This article has benefited from the thoughtful comments and suggestions of many, includ-
ing Susan Brison, Gilbert Harman, Sally Haslanger, Richard Holton, Will Kymlicka, Mark van
Roojen, Michael Smith, Scott Sehon, Natalie Stoljar, and the Editors of *Philosophy & Public
Affairs.* I am grateful to all of them.

91

arguing that we have reason to be concerned about pornography, not because it is morally suspect, but because we care about equality and the rights of women. This aspect of the debate between liberals and their opponents can begin to look like an argument about liberty and equality—freedom of speech versus women's rights—and so, apparently, it has been regarded by the courts.[1]

Ronald Dworkin is one liberal theorist who has defended a right to pornography, addressing the topic in "Do We Have a Right to Pornography?"[2] He is, in addition, a liberal who thinks that there can be no real conflict between liberty and equality.[3] Given that the pornography issue can be seen as apparently posing just such a conflict, it is natural to wonder whether Dworkin is right. In this article I put to Dworkin the question raised at the outset: Should liberals, or should Dworkin, at any rate, be in favor of permitting pornography? In the light of Dworkin's general theoretical commitments, the answer is not as obvious as it might appear.

In commenting elsewhere on the topical relevance of the argument he presented in "Do We Have a Right to Pornography?" Dworkin remarks that the controversy it deals with is one that has been given "fresh shape and importance" by recent history. "Old wars over pornography and censorship have new armies," he writes, "in radical feminists and the Moral Majority."[4] The recent history here alluded to presumably includes the controversy over a feminist antipornography ordinance that was passed in 1984 by the Indianapolis City Council, was swiftly challenged, and was judged by the district court to be unconstitutional.[5]

One modest aim of this article is to show that, whatever success Dworkin's argument may have against the armies of the Moral Majority, it does not even begin to address the approach he labels "radical feminist." A second and more substantial aim is to show that the latter "feminist" argument is not only consistent with Dworkin's liberalism, but is, so far as I can tell, demanded by it. My strategy here will be to work entirely within the Dworkinian theoretical system, and to show how that system yields a conclusion about pornography that is radically at odds with Dworkin's own, as expressed in his article on this topic. I argue that Dworkin's principle of equal concern and respect requires a policy about pornography that conflicts with commonly held liberal views about the subject, and that coincides instead with the restrictive or prohibitive policy favored by his feminist foes. In the course of my argument I restrict my attention to pornography of a certain kind, and I make use of certain empirical claims that Dworkin does not consider. But, granted these not overly controversial claims, Dworkin's theoretical commitments appear to supply ample resources for the justification of a prohibitive strategy. Dworkin, of course, agrees that some empirical premises would be sufficient to support a prohibitive argument. If, for example, there were conclusive evidence linking pornography to violence, one could justify a prohibitive strategy on the basis of a simple harm principle. However, the

prohibitive arguments advanced in this article do not require empirical premises as strong as this, nor do they rely on a simple harm principle. They rely
instead on the notion of equality that forms the linchpin of Dworkinian liberal theory.

Section I of this article sets out Dworkin's theoretical framework as it appears in *Taking Rights Seriously*[6] and, in particular, as it appears in the essay
"What Rights Do We Have?"[7] . . . [Note: Section II has been omitted.] In
Section III I turn to the issue of pornography, considering Dworkin's own
treatment of the subject in "Do We Have a Right to Pornography?" Section
IV draws together the two issues of civil rights and pornography, presenting
a feminist case against pornography, largely as it was argued by those who
supported the above-mentioned ordinance—in particular, by Catharine
MacKinnon.[8] Armed with some insights from this latter perspective on the
pornography question, I return in Section V to the Dworkinian theoretical
framework, showing that the civil rights approach that Dworkin uses . . . is
an appropriate approach for pornography. . . .

I. Theoretical Framework

In "What Rights Do We Have?" Dworkin sets out some basic elements of his
political theory, and the role that rights have to play in that theory. Since I
need to draw on these views in some detail later on, I will take the opportunity to summarize some aspects that will become relevant.

Dworkin takes as his starting point certain "postulates of political morality" that are central, he says, to a liberal conception of equality.[9] They can
be summed up in the slogan "Government must treat those whom it gov-
erns with equal concern and respect." To treat citizens with concern is to
treat them as creatures capable of suffering and frustration; to treat citizens
with respect is to treat them as human beings capable of forming their own
intelligent views about how their lives should be lived, and of acting on
those views.[10]

This notion of equality, which Dworkin takes to be a straightforward ex-
plication of the common notion we all have, turns out, on closer inspection,
to be rather complex. First of all, the right of citizens to be treated with equal
concern by no means commits the state to the *equal treatment* of its citizens,
if by that is meant that each citizen is entitled to the same distribution of
goods and opportunities as everyone else. The right to equality is simply a
right to treatment *as an equal:* the right to have one's interests treated as
fully and as sympathetically as the interests of anyone else. Second, the
Dworkinian notion of equality appears to have a principle of *neutrality* at its
heart: to treat people with equal respect is to treat each citizen's view of the
good life with equal respect. While the principle of equal concern dictates
that the government "must not distribute goods or opportunities unequally

on the ground that some citizens are entitled to more because they are worthy of more concern," the principle of equal respect dictates that the government "must not constrain liberty on the ground that one citizen's
conception of the good life of one group is nobler or superior to
another's."[11] So Dworkin's principle of equality is double-pronged: a government subscribing to it will, first, treat its citizens as persons equally worthy of concern, and, second, treat them as persons whose conceptions of the
good life are equally worthy of respect.[12]

Dworkin goes on to distinguish two kinds of political argument: arguments of principle and arguments of policy. Arguments of principle invoke
the notion of a *right* that is central to Dworkin's theory. Arguments of policy,
on the other hand, do not involve rights: they are *goal*-based arguments,
which attempt to justify a particular course of action by showing that it will
achieve a state of affairs in which the community as a whole will be better off.
Arguments of policy come in two varieties, depending on the character of the
goal to be achieved. Utilitarian arguments of policy typically have as their end
the maximal satisfaction of citizens' preferences. Ideal arguments of policy
have a different end: they are not concerned with the preferences of citizens,
but attempt instead to arrange things so that the community will be "in some
way closer to an ideal community."[13]

Arguments of policy are vulnerable in a way that arguments of principle
are not. While arguments of principle are rights-based, and therefore embody
the conception of equality that Dworkin takes as foundational, arguments of
policy, by contrast, do not always yield conclusions that are consistent with
that conception; and where there is conflict, it is the "equal concern and respect" principle that must triumph. In other words, the conception of equality that Dworkin takes as his starting point is one that places constraints on
any argument of policy. Where the argument of policy is ideal in character,
urging us to constrain liberty in order to pursue a goal that many citizens do
not in fact want, the "neutrality" aspect of the notion of equality comes into
play: a government that is committed to treating its citizens with equal concern and respect is thereby committed to treating competing accounts of the
good life with equal respect; it cannot do this and claim that a particular form
of life is "inherently more valuable" than another.[14] Dworkin's example of an
argument of policy that might be defeated in this way is one supporting the
goal of achieving a culturally sophisticated community, in a situation in which
nobody in fact wants such sophistication.[15] If citizens value the pushpin way
of life, it might be wrong to force poetry on them.

Where the argument of policy is utilitarian in character, the notion of
equality places constraints upon it in a rather more sophisticated way. After
all, utilitarian arguments give every appearance of being thoroughly egalitarian; this was a feature evident in the original Benthamite idea that each man
is to count for one and no one for more than one. Dworkin notes that this
egalitarian appearance is what gives utilitarianism its appeal. But he goes on

to explain the way in which such an appearance is sometimes misleading: utilitarian arguments themselves may yield conclusions that conflict with principles of equal concern and respect. Consider, he says, the goal of utilitarian argument. The goal is simply the maximal satisfaction of citizens' preferences, taking into account both the number and the intensity of the preferences to be considered. Such a goal fails to take into account the status of citizens' preferences: it fails to attend to the important distinction between the preference of a citizen for his own enjoyment of goods and opportunities and the preference of a citizen for the assignment of goods and opportunities to others.[16]

This distinction between personal and external preferences is one that is crucial to the development of Dworkin's theory of rights. One simple way to see that theory (at least in the essays we are considering here) is as a response to the inadequacies of unrestricted utilitarianism when it is confronted with the demands of a liberal principle of equality.[17] In brief: Utilitarianism tells us to maximize the satisfaction of preferences; but if we do that without first disqualifying the preferences of any citizen for the assignment of goods and opportunities to citizens other than himself, the calculations may be distorted, a form of "double counting" may result, and the final outcome may be one that does not treat each citizen with equal concern and respect.[18] Rights are a useful theoretical means of preventing this unwelcome result; rights are a means of protecting individuals from the external preferences of other individuals.

What counts as an external preference? And how do such preferences disrupt the otherwise egalitarian character of utilitarian arguments? We can, says Dworkin, distinguish two ways in which the preferences of a citizen can be external, ways that correspond to the twin aspects of the equality principle. The citizen may, first, prefer that another citizen be assigned fewer goods and opportunities than others because he thinks that that *person* is simply worth less concern than others.[19] Consider, for example, a group of citizens who believe that blacks are simply worth less concern than whites, and whose preferences manifest this prejudice. They prefer, say, that the preferences of blacks be worth half those of whites in the utilitarian calculus. If such racist preferences are taken into account, says Dworkin, the utilitarian calculus will be distorted, and blacks will suffer unjustly as a result.

Alternatively, and here we have the second kind of preference, a citizen may prefer that another citizen be assigned fewer goods and opportunities than others because he believes the person's *conception of the good life* to be worthy of less respect than the conceptions of others. Dworkin gives as examples of this second variety the moralistic preferences of people who disapprove of various practices (such as homosexuality, pornography, Communist party adherence) and prefer that no one in society pursue such practices. If such preferences are taken into account, the individuals in question (homosexuals, pornographers, communists) will suffer, not simply because in the competing demands for scarce resources some preferences must lose out, and they happen to be the unlucky ones. They suffer [also] because their own views about how to live their lives are thought to be deserving of less respect.[20]

It is often difficult in practice, says Dworkin, to distinguish personal from external preferences. Democratic institutions usually do not have the resources to discriminate between them; and it is because of these pragmatic difficulties that the concept of a right comes into play. "The concept of an individual political right . . . is a response to the philosophical defects of a utilitarianism that counts external preferences and the practical impossibility of a utilitarianism that does not. It allows us to enjoy the institutions of political democracy, which enforce overall or unrefined utilitarianism and yet protect the fundamental right of citizens to equal concern and respect by prohibiting decisions that seem, antecedently, likely to have been reached by virtue of the external components of the preferences democracy reveals."[21] This characterization of rights provides a means of arguing for a further central Dworkinian thesis: namely, that rights to particular liberties—freedom of speech, religion, and so on—are derivable from the fundamental right to equality. A policy that constrains a particular liberty in the interests of utility may be shown to be probably based upon an argument utilizing external preferences; equality demands that such preferences be discounted; and in such cases the threatened citizen has a right to that liberty which will trump the opposing argument of utility. This approach contrasts sharply with a commonly held view that liberalism requires a right to liberty itself amongst its basic theoretical underpinnings. It is also an approach that attempts to answer the challenge that the right to liberty and the right to equality are often in conflict. Far from being antagonistic, says Dworkin, the one would not exist but for the other. . . .

III. Dworkin on Pornography

In "Do We Have a Right to Pornography?" Dworkin considers a question that has attracted attention from many political theorists, from liberals at one end of the spectrum to the redoubtable "new armies" of conservatives and feminists at the other. What might we expect Dworkin's approach to be? On the one hand, Dworkin is first and foremost a liberal theorist, and the freedom to produce and consume pornography has long been a liberal cause. But he is at the same time a writer famous for taking the principle of equality to be the starting point for sound political thinking; a writer whose sensitivity in dealing with the complex issues surrounding prejudice against an oppressed group we have already witnessed; and a writer who begins his discussion of the pornography question by drawing an analogy between laws concerning pornography and laws concerning racist speech. "Should we [*sic*] be free to incite racial hatred?" he asks his readers in the opening paragraph—an interesting question and one whose implications seem worth pursuing.

Given this hopeful start, and given also that the feminist "armies" had already begun to mass at the time of his writing,[22] we might reasonably expect that a rights-based argument *against* pornography would merit at least some brief mention in the essay. Such hopes, as it turns out, are disappointed, and Dworkin's question in the opening paragraph is not pursued in any detail. He considers, at various points throughout the essay, a vast number of ways in which pornography might more or less plausibly be construed as a harm. The sample that follows is by no means exhaustive, but I can assure my reader that there is one construal that is conspicuous by its absence, namely, that women as a group might be harmed by pornography.

Here is the quick sample. Since most people would prefer censorship, permitting pornography harms general utility by leaving the majority of preferences unsatisfied.[23] Pornography damages the cultural environment.[24] It upsets and disgusts people.[25] It limits people's ability to lead the kind of lives they would want for themselves and their children.[26] It makes sex seem less valuable.[27] People find discomfort in encountering blatant nudity because they detest themselves for taking an interest in the proceedings, and they are forcefully reminded of what their neighbors are like and of what their neighbors are getting away with.[28]

To be fair, Dworkin does indeed raise the issue of whether pornography ever presents a "special danger of personal harm narrowly conceived,"[29] and although he usually takes this to be a question about people's responses when directly confronted with pornography, he, along with the Williams Committee, "concedes . . . the relevance of the question whether an increase in the amount of pornography in circulation in the community is likely to produce more violence or more sexual crimes of any particular sort. . . ."[30] This is as close as Dworkin ever gets to considering whether or not it may be women who are, in the end, the ones hurt by the pornography industry. As a rule, when he raises the possibility of any link between pornography and harm to women of a concrete and familiar sort, he fails to take it seriously. Indeed, were it not for the evidence we already have of Dworkin's awareness of the subtle complexities surrounding questions of group oppression, the reader might be tempted to suppose that Dworkin's chief interest is to lampoon the idea. Imagining that pornography might lead to violence is like imagining that reading *Hamlet* might lead to violence.[31] Or, in another passage, he wonders whether pornography might be like "breakfast television": both might be found to encourage absenteeism from work, and thereby have (perish the thought!) "some special and deleterious effect on the general economy."[32] But as he continues with such comparisons, we begin to discover that he thinks that questions about concrete harm are mere "academic speculation";[33] the pornography issue is itself a "relatively trivial" problem.[34] By contrast, embarrassment—that is, embarrassment on the part of the "shy pornographer"—he describes as raising an "interesting and important question."[35] When it comes to the plight of the shy pornographer, Dworkin displays a touching concern; he suggests that legislators should make sure that the consumer can, should he so desire, buy an umbrella at his favorite adult bookstore, so as to disguise his secret and perhaps shameful habits.

Readers may have gathered by now that Dworkin and I do not share exactly the same view about what is and what is not an important question. Embarrassment is not, all things considered, a very important question; the well-being of women is. Leaving such sympathies aside, there are of course some relevant empirical questions to be addressed here. And on certain questions of this kind Dworkin accepts the findings of the Williams Committee, namely, that there is no persuasive evidence that pornography causes violent crime.[36] On other empirical questions—for example, questions about pornography's possible role in a society in which women happen to be widely oppressed—Dworkin is comfortably silent. . . . One does not always need conclusive evidence about crime to have cause for concern, nor is violence the only worry in situations in which there is widespread prejudice and discrimination against a particular group. In such situations, as Dworkin has already taught us, our investigation must take special care.

Readers of "Do We Have a Right to Pornography?" may be a little puzzled at this point. Why, we may be forgiven for asking, does Dworkin consider this "relatively trivial" issue to be worthy of serious attention, worthy in fact of a full forty-five pages of sophisticated political analysis? If we look again at the first of Dworkin's suggestions about the harm pornography brings about, we will find our answer. Most people, he says, would *prefer* censorship; if, in spite of this, we permit pornography, *general utility* will be harmed, since the majority preferences will be left unsatisfied.

This is enough to give us a fair idea of Dworkin's special interest in the question. We have the starting point for a familiar Dworkinian recipe for identifying rights, where one begins by noting that there is a good utilitarian argument for a certain policy, and that certain individuals will suffer as a result of this policy; investigates the preferences upon which the utilitarian argument is based; shows that they are external preferences; and finally concludes that the individuals concerned have rights that must defeat the policy in question. . . .

Dworkin proceeds to show how it is possible to mount an argument of principle against a prohibitive policy. Suppose, he says, that the policy of prohibiting pornography would satisfy the preferences of the majority,[37] and that the opportunities of the consumers of pornography would be curtailed as a result. Our next step, if we are interested in finding out whether pornographers might have rights against this policy, is to consider the character of the preferences upon which the policy relies, since the right to equality demands that certain preferences be disregarded. Does the prohibitive policy rely on any external preferences? Remember that external preferences can be of two broad types: one can prefer that another person receive fewer goods and opportunities because one thinks that that person is worth less concern, or, alternatively, because one thinks that that person's conception of the good life deserves less respect. . . . In the case of pornography I take it that Dworkin thinks they are of the latter. People want pornography to be prohibited chiefly because they think that it is ignoble or wrong, and that a conception of the good life that holds otherwise deserves less respect. "Moralistic" preferences of this kind must, says Dworkin, be defeated by a corresponding "right to moral independence," which he describes as "the right not to suffer disadvantage in the distribution of social goods and opportunities, including disadvantage in the liberties permitted to them by the criminal law, just on the ground that their officials or fellow citizens think that their opinions about the right way for them to lead their own lives are ignoble or wrong."[38] Insofar as the utilitarian argument hinges on moralistic preferences, the consumers of pornography have rights that trump the prohibitive policy, and our policy should be permissive.[39]

It is crucial to note that pornographers are said to have rights not because there is something special about speech per se, and pornography is speech; nor because there is something special about the private domain in which pornography is often consumed; but simply because they are vulnerable to the effects of the external preferences of others, and equality demands that such preferences be ignored. This essay provides a good illustration of Dworkin's strategy of deriving traditional liberties from the principle of equality alone. It is also worth pointing out that Dworkin claims that his own strategy, as illustrated here, does justice to deeply held liberal convictions about the value of free speech in a way that competing theoretical strategies cannot hope to do.[40]

IV. Pornography and Civil Rights: A Feminist Response

The purpose of this section is to review briefly a certain feminist civil rights argument about pornography, in the hope of showing how the question is transformed once it is placed in a civil rights context. Some, but by no means all, aspects of this argument will be relevant to the later argument in Section V of this paper, and at the beginning of that section I will outline the aspects that are. The reader should be aware that the argument reviewed in this section is one of a variety of feminist responses, many of which disagree with both the analysis and the course of action advocated by this one.[41]

In contrast to the argument discussed in Dworkin's paper on the topic, this feminist argument against pornography sets aside questions about "morality" and focuses instead on the civil status of women. The argument has been put very forcefully by Catharine MacKinnon,[42] who has written widely

on the subject, and who was involved in the drafting of the Indianapolis ordinance. In that ordinance pornography is defined as a civil rights violation:[43]
"We define pornography as the graphic sexually explicit subordination of
women through pictures or words that also includes women dehumanized as
sexual objects, things, or commodities; enjoying pain or humiliation or rape;
being tied up, cut up, mutilated, bruised, or physically hurt; in postures of
sexual submission or servility or display; reduced to body parts, penetrated by
objects or animals, or presented in scenarios of degradation, injury, torture;
shown as filthy or inferior; bleeding, bruised or hurt in a context which
makes these conditions sexual."[44] The ordinance distinguished pornography
from erotica, taking erotica to be sexually explicit material other than that
covered by the above definition. It should be emphasized that according to
this argument, and in contrast to "moralistic" arguments, there is nothing
wrong whatsoever with materials that are simply sexually arousing and explicit; the focus of concern lies elsewhere. Insofar as the ordinance is not concerned with explicit material per se, it departs of course from a more
traditional or popular conception that simply equates pornography with the
sexually explicit, a conception I take Dworkin to have been using. Pornography as defined above is a subset, though, of pornography as it is popularly
conceived, and Dworkin's remarks about the relevance of his own argument
to the "radical feminist" case indicate that he views pornographers as having
a right to this kind of pornography as well.

The distinctive feature of the MacKinnon argument is that it views pornography—as defined in the ordinance—as having implications for sexual
equality: pornography is seen as a practice that contributes to the subordinate
status of women, just as certain other practices (segregation among them)
contribute to the subordinate status of blacks. The argument seeks to establish at least two things: one is that women do not, as a matter of fact, currently have equal status; and the other is that pornography does, as a matter
of fact, contribute significantly to the continuing subordinate position of
women.

The first claim is, I think, not very controversial, and a cursory glance at
sociological facts about the distribution of income and power should be
enough to confirm it. One dimension to the inequality is the economic;
women earn substantially less than men, and a disproportionate number of
women live in poverty. A further dimension to the inequality is to be found
in the scale of the sexual abuse, including but not confined to rape, that
women suffer and that men, as a rule, do not.[45] The advent of feminism has
brought with it a new and more acute awareness of the conditions of women,
says MacKinnon. . . .

What is different about MacKinnon's approach to facts like these is that
she sees sexual violence not simply as "crime" (as Dworkin seemed apt to
do), but rather as a dimension to the inequality of the sexes, and one that
calls for an explanation. These things are done to women; they are not,
by and large done to men. To call such violence simply "crime," says

MacKinnon, without remarking upon the interesting fact that the perpetrators are nearly always members of one class of citizens, and the victims members of another, would be to disguise its systematically discriminatory nature.

Turning now to the second claim, the feminist argument can be seen as offering a hypothesis about the explanation for this pattern of sexual abuse: part of the explanation lies in the fact that certain kinds of pornography help to form) and propagate certain views about women and sexuality. Such pornography is said to work as a kind of propaganda, which both expresses a certain view about women and sexuality and perpetuates that view; it "sexualizes rape, battery, sexual harassment, prostitution, and child sexual abuse; it thereby celebrates, promotes, authorizes and legitimizes them."[46] To back up this claim, a substantial amount of empirical evidence was cited by those supporting the ordinance (in the form of both social science studies and testimony of people whose lives had been directly affected by pornography) which pointed to the conclusion that pornography influences behavior and attitudes, and does so in ways that undermine both the well-being of women and sexual equality.[47] In the light of evidence of this kind, the Indianapolis City Council issued the following findings:

> Pornography is a discriminatory practice based on sex which denies women equal opportunities in society. Pornography is central in creating and maintaining sex as a basis for discrimination. Pornography is a systematic practice of exploitation and subordination based on sex which differentially harms women. The bigotry and contempt it promotes, with the acts of aggression it fosters, harm women's opportunities for equality of rights in employment, education, access to and use of public accommodations, and acquisition of real property; promote rape, battery, child abuse, kidnapping and prostitution and inhibit just enforcement of laws against such acts; and contribute significantly to restricting women in particular from full exercise of citizenship and participation in public life.[48]

The case was viewed by the district court as presenting a conflict between First Amendment guarantees of free speech and the Fourteenth Amendment right to be free from sex-based discrimination.[49] The ordinance would survive constitutional scrutiny only if the state's interest in sex-based equality were "so compelling as to be fundamental," for "only then can it be deemed to outweigh interest of free speech."[50] And the court concluded, as a matter of law, that the state's interest in sex-based equality was not so compelling.[51]

It is worth noting that the empirical findings were not disputed; in fact, when the case went to the court of appeals, Judge Frank Easterbrook went so far as to say, "We accept the premises of this legislation. Depictions of subordination tend to perpetuate subordination. The subordinate status of women in turn leads to affront and lower pay at work, insult and injury at home, battery and rape on the streets." His conclusion, however, is that "this simply demonstrates the power of pornography as speech."[52]

V. A New Start

What I want to do now is take certain elements from the feminist case that was presented briefly in the preceding section and put them in the context of Dworkinian political theory. . . .

. . . I will be relying on a number of claims that Dworkin does not consider, which I draw largely from Section IV. Briefly, these are the claims: that women do not have equal status in this society; that widespread prejudice against women exists; that certain practices in this society express that prejudice and probably perpetuate that inequality, and thereby disadvantage women; and that the consumption of a certain kind of pornography is one such practice.

1. Prohibiting Pornography: An Argument of Principle

Let us begin by reminding ourselves of the general Dworkinian recipe for a good argument of principle . . . : (a) Begin with what looks like a good utilitarian argument for a particular policy; (b) look at the individuals who appear to suffer as a result of the policy, and ask whether the policy violates the rights of those individuals; (c) inspect the preferences upon which the utilitarian argument is based, and show that they are external preferences; (d) conclude that the individuals concerned do have rights that are trumps against the policy in question. This is precisely the recipe I now propose to follow. . . .

a. The Utilitarian Argument   . . . Could there be a utilitarian argument for *permitting* pornography? Such an idea sounds odd, since we are accustomed to casting the debate in the language of fundamental liberties, rather than utility. But I suggest that there might be at least a germ of a utilitarian argument in the background: people want pornography, so let them have it. If one were to take up this idea and add some other speculative premises, one might construct a simple utilitarian argument in favor of permitting pornography: most people would prefer that pornography be permitted, and so our policy should be to permit pornography.

To suppose this would be to question one of Dworkin's assumptions. In "Do We Have a Right to Pornography?" Dworkin assumed that unanalyzed preferences about pornography would come out in favor of prohibition. I am not so sure. The power of the pornography industry in sheer monetary terms[53] bears eloquent witness to the popularity of its product; and although it is difficult to gauge how much of this would count as pornography by MacKinnon's definition, it seems that pornography of the latter kind is a fairly widespread phenomenon, appearing in some guise on the shelves of most newsagents and video stores.[54] Given these facts, and given a general ignorance about or indifference to pornography's influence, can we be sure,

Women apparently suffer as a result of the policy of permitting violent and degrading pornography. We can now ask, Does that policy violate women's rights?

c. Preferences   At this point we must look more closely at the preferences upon which the utilitarian policy might be based. There are all kinds of reasons that people might have for wanting pornography to be permitted. Many people like pornography (including violent pornography), and want to be able to consume it without restriction; some people do not like it themselves, but are happy enough for others to enjoy it; some people are afraid of the "slippery slope," and worry that allowing the state to prohibit pornography would raise the likelihood of government abuse of power. It seems likely that the preferences upon which the argument hinges will be of the very first kind, namely, the preferences of the consumers of pornography for pornography itself.

What kind of preferences are these? On the face of it, they all seem to be personal. How could a preference for what one reads or watches behind closed doors fail to be anything other than personal? But we must not stop here, if we are to be true to the Dworkin of "Reverse Discrimination": there is more to the notion of an external preference than an explicit reference to the allocation of resources to another citizen. Dworkin has already endorsed a version of the view that the personal is sometimes political, or, more precisely, that apparently personal preferences can have implications for political questions about rights. . . . Is the situation we are considering one in which prejudice against the disadvantaged group is strong and pervasive in society? Surely that much at least is uncontroversial.

But if so, there are further questions to be asked. If the prejudice against women did not exist, would the preferences for this kind of pornography exist? This is a complicated hypothetical question, but at least one eminent liberal theorist has offered a fairly confident answer to it. This kind of violent pornography "does not appeal at all," says Feinberg, to a male who is "not in the grip of the macho cult. In fact these pictures, stories, and films have no other function but to express and reenforce the macho ideology. 'Get your sexual kicks,' they seem to say, 'but make sure you get them by humiliating the woman, and showing her who's boss.'"[63] Feinberg thinks that the possession of "macho" values is a necessary condition for the appeal of violent pornography; he also thinks that macho values embody a view about the worth of women.[64] If one were to accept his suggestion, one would be accepting that a preference for pornography of this kind depends upon a view about the worth of women, and hence that such preferences are, by Dworkinian standards, external preferences.

. . . To paraphrase Dworkin's words, an apparently personal preference for such pornography is really "parasitic upon external preferences . . . the consumer prefers pornography of this kind because he has macho social and political convictions, or because he has contempt for women as a group."

Feinberg's suggestion surely has some plausibility. One could, however, be somewhat more cautious. One could suppose that, while a great many such preferences depended on the possession of certain antecedent values, people were sometimes drawn to violent pornography through other motives, such as curiosity, or simple peer pressure. Such preferences might simply be personal. While there is some likelihood that many of the relevant preferences are affected by prejudice, it is possible that what one has here is a complicated situation of the kind Dworkin describes elsewhere, in which "personal and external preferences are so inextricably tied together, and so mutually dependent, that no practical test for measuring preferences will be able to discriminate the personal and external elements in any individual's overall preferences."[65] Suppose that this is the case. Suppose it is difficult to disentangle personal preferences about pornography of this kind from external preferences, difficult to answer the hypothetical question about the dependence of the desire on the prejudice. What should we conclude in such circumstances? We should still, if we are following the third of Dworkin's conditions[66] . . . , count the preferences in question as external.

In sum, if we are to be faithful to . . . Dworkin . . . , we ought, it seems, to conclude that the preferences of men for pornography of this kind are external preferences.

d. Conclusion   Women as a group have rights against the consumers of pornography, and thereby have rights that are trumps against the policy of permitting pornography. The permissive policy has a certain "objective feature," to use Dworkin's phrase; it relies on external preferences, that is, preferences that are dependent on views about the worth of other people. This is enough to establish that the permissive policy is in conflict with the principle of equal concern and respect, and that women accordingly have rights against it.[67]

It should be clear that this argument is rather different in kind to arguments against pornography that are based on a simple harm principle. Recall that Dworkin appeared to think that a successful antipornography argument would have to produce conclusive evidence of some grave harm, for example, evidence that pornography causes violent crime. This, I hope I have shown, is a mistake. The argument above does not need to claim that grave harm results from having a permissive policy, nor does it need to have conclusive evidence for the harm it cites. The argument focuses chiefly on the *preferences* underlying the permissive policy. To make this clear, let me sum up the argument once more, this time in the conditional mode. If there were a utilitarian argument for the policy of permitting violent and degrading pornography, women would have rights against it. Women are apparently disadvantaged by the permissive policy, and therefore have prima facie cause for complaint. Some women feel deeply distressed and insulted by it, and it is probable that the existence of such pornography reinforces and perpetuates attitudes and beliefs that undermine the well-being of women and undermine sexual equality; it probably contributes, for example, to an environment in which sexual abuse is more likely to occur. Given that women have cause to be concerned about the permissive policy, one can ask whether it violates their rights. Since it is likely that a utilitarian permissive policy would rely on the preferences of consumers for pornography of this kind, and since such preferences are external preferences, . . . women have rights against the permissive policy. . . .

NOTES

1. *American Booksellers, Inc. v. Hudnut*, 598 F. Supp. 1327 (S.D. Ind. 1984) (hereafter Hudnut).

2. Ronald Dworkin, "Do We Have a Right to Pornography?" *Oxford Journal of Legal Studies* 1 (1981): 177–212; repr. in *A Matter of Principle* (Cambridge, Mass.: Harvard University Press, 1985), pp. 335–72. Page references are to the reprint in *A Matter of Principle*.

3. Ronald Dworkin, "What Is Equality? Part 3: The Place of Liberty," *Iowa Law Review* 73 (1987): 9.

4. Dworkin, *A Matter of Principle*, p. 1.

5. See *Hudnut*; see also 771 F.2d 323 (7th Cir. 1985), affirmed 106 S.Ct. 1172 (1986).

6. Ronald Dworkin, *Taking Rights Seriously* (Cambridge, Mass.: Harvard University Press, 1977).

7. Ronald Dworkin, "What Rights Do We Have?" in *Taking Rights Seriously*, pp. 266–78.

8. Catharine MacKinnon, *Feminism Unmodified* (Cambridge, Mass.: Harvard University Press, 1987), esp. "Francis Biddle's Sister: Pornography, Civil Rights and Speech," pp. 163–97. Note that MacKinnon's argument is different [from] the "Dworkinian" argument in favor of prohibition which I advance, although the two arguments share some common premises and have similar conclusions. I take it that if my argument succeeds, it might offer support for MacKinnon's conclusion; but if my argument fails, it does not undermine hers.

9. Dworkin, "What Rights Do We Have?" p. 272.

10. Ibid., pp. 272–73. (The slogan slightly paraphrases Dworkin's description of the equality principle in this passage.)

11. Ibid., p. 273.

12. Ibid., pp. 273, 275.

13. Ibid., p. 274.

14. Ibid.

15. Ibid.

16. Ibid., p. 275.

17. My concern in this article is almost exclusively with Dworkin's theory as it appears in *Taking Rights Seriously* and *A Matter of Principle*. Since then Dworkin's views have undergone some changes (e.g., in "What Is Equality?"), but these are not, I think, changes that substantially affect the points I want to make here. . . .

18. For brevity's sake I am omitting further discussion of the "double counting" aspect of Dworkin's theory, a feature that has attracted a good deal of critical attention in its own right.

19. Again, for the sake of brevity I am omitting Dworkin's discussion of altruistic external preferences, which have their origins in views that another citizen is worth more (rather than less) concern than others.

20. Dworkin, "What Rights Do We Have?" p. 276.

21. Ibid., p. 277.

22. As demonstrated, for example, in the classic collection of essays *Take Back the Night: Women on Pornography* (New York: William Morrow, 1980), containing essays published earlier.

23. Dworkin, "Right to Pornography?" p. 335.

24. Ibid., pp. 337, 340.

25. Ibid., pp. 344–45.

26. Ibid., p. 349.

27. Ibid., p. 356.

28. Ibid.

29. Ibid., p. 340.

30. Ibid., p. 338.

31. Ibid., p. 355.

32. Ibid., p. 354.

33. Ibid., p. 355.

34. Ibid., p. 359.

35. Ibid., p. 358. Note that Dworkin uses the term *pornographer* to mean "consumer of pornography"; I follow his usage for the purposes of this article.

36. Ibid., p. 338. . . .

37. Dworkin, "Right to Pornography?" pp. 335, 360.

38. Ibid., p. 353.

39. Insofar as this permissive policy would in turn constrain the ability of other people to lead the lives of their choice, we have an argument for restriction of some form. So what Dworkin ends up with, balancing these conflicting considerations, is an endorsement of the compromise solution offered by the Williams Report, i.e., that most pornography should be permitted but restricted through measures such as zoning (ibid., p. 358).

40. Ibid., p. 352.

41. For a range of views other than MacKinnon's, see, e.g., Gail Chester and Julienne Dickey, eds., *Feminism and Censorship: The Current Debate* (Bridport, Eng.: Prism Press, 1988); Nan D. Hunter and Sylvia A. Law, "Brief Amici Curiae of Feminist Anti-Censorship Taskforce, *et al.*," in *American Booksellers, Inc. v. Hudnut,* 771 F.2d 323 (1985); Andrea Dworkin, *Pornography: Men Possessing Women* (London: The Women's Press, 1981); Varda Burstyn, ed., *Women Against Censorship* (Vancouver: Douglas and MacIntyre, 1985); and Edward Donnerstein, Daniel Linz, and Steven Penrod, *The Question of Pornography: Research Findings and Policy Implications* (New York: Free Press; London: Collier Macmillan, 1987), chaps. 7, 8.

42. See MacKinnon, *Feminism Unmodified,* esp. "Francis Biddle's Sister." There are many important aspects of MacKinnon's argument that I do not take time to consider in any detail here—for example, the claim that pornography constitutes a form of subordination (which has been considered by Melinda Vadas in "A First Look at the Pornography/Civil Rights Ordinance: Could Pornography Be the Subordination of Women?" *Journal of Philosophy* [1987], 487–511), and the claim (in answer to the champions of free speech) that pornography silences women, preventing women's exercise of free speech. The latter claim, if developed, might lead to an argument of a rather different kind, which saw the issue as presenting a conflict, not between liberty and equality, but between the liberty of men and the liberty of women.

43. It should be noted that the ordinance made pornography civilly actionable rather than a criminal offense. The definition used here is one that raises many difficult legal and philosophical questions in its own right, but I am afraid that such questions, while admittedly important, lie beyond the scope of this paper. . . .

44. MacKinnon, "Francis Biddle's Sister," p. 176.

45. This is not, of course, to say that it is only women who suffer sexual abuse, or to underrate the extent of the sexual violence suffered by children of both sexes, or by men in prisons. It is only to say that, as a pervasive phenomenon, sexual violence seems to be directed mainly against women.

46. MacKinnon, "Francis Biddle's Sister," pp. 171–72.

47. The question of what is involved in making a causal claim of this kind is an important one. No one is claiming, of course, that there is a simple link; one can agree with [Joel] Feinberg that "pornography does not cause normal decent chaps, through a single exposure, to metamorphose into rapists" (*Offense to Others,* [New York: Oxford University Press, 1985], p. 153). For an interesting discussion of the notions of causality that bear on questions of this kind, see Frederick Schauer, "Causation Theory and the Causes of Sexual Violence," *American Bar Foundation Research Journal* 1987, no. 4 (Fall 1987): 737–70.

48. *Hudnut* 1320.

49. *Hudnut* 1327.

50. *Hudnut* 1316. The case also raised constitutional problems in connection with the "due process" requirements of the Fifth and Fourteenth Amendments. The

ordinance was judged to be vague and to establish prior restraint of speech, and would therefore have been unconstitutional on those grounds alone.

51. *Hudnut* 1326.

52. 771 F.2d 329 (7th Cir. 1985).

53. According to Catherine Itzin, the pornography industry in the United States currently has a $10-billion-a-year turnover, although this total almost certainly includes material that would count as erotica by the ordinance definition ("Sex and Censorship: The Political Implications," in *Feminism and Censorship*. ed. Chester and Dickey, p. 45). See Gordon Hawkins and Franklin E. Zimring, *Pornography in a Free Society* (Cambridge and New York: Cambridge University Press, 1988) chap. 3, for a survey of attempts to estimate the size of the general pornography market.

54. Even if one leaves aside, for the sake of avoiding needless controversy, that clause of the definition which counts subordinating depictions of women in postures of "display" as pornography, it seems that some of the more straightforwardly "violent and degrading" material may have found a niche in magazines that have wide circulation (see Feinberg, *Offense to Others*, p. 151, for some *Penthouse* examples. . .). Accurate figures for pornography generally, let alone violent pornography, are hard to find. It seems that the pornography that concerns MacKinnon is prevalent, although it is almost certainly not "the *most* prevalent [form] of pornography," as is claimed in the *Report of the Attorney General's Commission on Pornography* ([Washington, D.C.: United States Government Printing Office, 1986], p. 323; italics mine), even if one does include "threatened violence" (p. 323). Certainly there has been a widespread perception that violent pornography is very much on the increase (Donnerstein et al., *The Question of Pornography*, p. 88). Donnerstein suggests that "we may be more aware of the sexually violent forms of pornography because all forms of pornography are more prevalent that they once were" (ibid., p. 91). Feinberg cites studies according to which some time ago (before 1980) the number of violent scenes in hard-core pornography was "as high as 20%," and in leading pornographic magazines such material constituted "as much as 10% of the total" number of cartoons and pictorials (*Offense to Others*, p. 149).

55. Dworkin, "Right to Pornography?" p. 345.

56. Dworkin, "Reverse Discrimination," in *Taking Rights Seriously*, p. 231.

57. Susan Brison has written convincingly on this subject in "Freedom of Expression and the Limits of Liberalism" (unpublished manuscript).

58. Feinberg, *Offense to Others*, pp. 150–151. Feinberg, it should be noted, does not think that violent pornography is like libel; he thinks that the macho ideology has done manifest harm to men as well; and although he thinks violent pornography "reenforces" that ideology, he does not think it is a major cause of it (p. 153).

59. Home Office, *Report of the Committee on Obscenity and Film Censorship*, Cmnd. 7772 (London: Her Majesty's Stationery Office, 1979), p. 59.

60. Ibid., p. 146.

61. Ibid., p. 145.

62. Ibid. I am indebted to the discussion in Hawkins and Zimring, *Pornography in a Free Society* (pp. 128–30) for drawing this aspect of the Williams Report to my attention.

63. Feinberg, *Offense to Others*, p. 151.

64. According to macho values, says Feinberg, men ought to be "utterly dominant" over women, treating them as little more than "trophies" (ibid., p. 150). In an earlier note I mentioned that while Feinberg thinks that violent pornography may "reenforce macho ideology," he thinks that it is not a major cause of either the macho ideology or the violence (the latter being an effect not of the pornography but of the macho cult). Feinberg seems to think that the considerations raised here—that having "macho values" is a prerequisite for the appeal of violent pornography—constitute evidence *against* the feminist claim that pornography is one of the causes of the pattern of sexual abuse suffered by women. Although his concessions (i.e., that pornography of this kind "reenforces" macho culture, which in turn manifests itself in abuse, and that it may in addition have some small but direct "spillover" effects into real-world violence) would be sufficient for my argument to go through, I think it would be a mistake to infer as Feinberg has done. Tracing causal connections of this kind is undoubtedly a difficult task, but it would surely be wrong to argue with respect to, for example, racist propaganda, that it made no difference, on the grounds that readers of such material would already be racist and hence that the material would be "merely" reinforcing existing attitudes. Such an argument would perhaps betray a rather simple view about how tastes and attitudes are formed. There is no contradiction involved in thinking that propaganda can sometimes appeal to people because they already have certain beliefs and values, or are disposed to have them; and that it can sometimes influence beliefs and values, reinforcing them in some cases, and pushing them in certain directions in others. I presume that it is precisely because expression does have this central role in forming beliefs and values that liberals think it so important. It is one thing to believe that pornography of this kind should be protected because it is expression, and expression must be protected at all costs; it is quite another to believe that it should be left alone because it is more or less causally inert, as Feinberg seems to be suggesting. Easterbrook recognized that expression is far from impotent when he concluded that the existence of pornography's pervasive effects was precisely what demonstrated "the power of pornography as speech" (771 F.2d 329 [7th Cir. 1985]).

    One could accept that not every case of apparently violent and degrading pornography embodies a view about the worth of others, while acknowledging that a significant number do have this feature (see, e.g., Feinberg, *Offense to Others*, pp. 144–46). It might be argued that some lesbian and homosexual pornography offers an example of apparently violent and degrading material that does not embody such a view.

65. Dworkin, "Reverse Discrimination," p. 236.

66. Editor's note: Langton is referring to Section II of her original paper, which has been omitted here. In that section she outlines three sufficient conditions for preferences to count as external according to Dworkin:

"(1) The preferences concern the allocation of resources to another citizen, *simpliciter.*

"(2) The following counterfactual holds: Were the prejudice not to exist, the preferences in question would not exist.

"(3) We find that the truth of the counterfactual in (2) is difficult to determine, and there is some likelihood that prejudice has affected the preferences."
(p. 322)

67. One possible response to this argument that I do not address here is that the argument, if correct, shows that pornography of this kind presents an apparent conflict of rights, the rights of pornographers against moralists and the rights of women against pornographers. How one goes about resolving such conflicts is not clear, but one way might be to think about what a fully reconstructed utilitarian argument might look like, that is, one that laundered out external preferences of both varieties. On this subject one must, perforce, be somewhat speculative; but if we were to talk of preferences at all, we might begin by considering the following three varieties: (i) preferences of some women that some pornography not be permitted because they view it as deeply insulting; preferences of women for an environment in which they can pursue their goals and life plans without the threat of the discrimination and sexual abuse that pornography of this kind arguably engenders; (ii) moralistic preferences of disapprovers, who want pornography prohibited because they view it as immoral; and (iii) preferences of pornographers that pornography be permitted. There may be others, but these would surely be among the most important. Dworkin considers chiefly the second and third varieties. By Dworkin's argument, the second set count as external; I accept this for the purposes of this article. I have argued that the preferences of the third variety are also external. This would leave the laundered utilitarian calculus with only the first to consider. I take it that preferences of the first variety are personal, and while pornographers may have rights against the second variety, they would have no rights against the first. So a fully reconstructed utilitarian argument would, it seems, yield a restrictive conclusion.

RONALD DWORKIN

Liberty and Pornography

When Isaiah Berlin delivered his famous inaugural lecture as Chichele Professor of Social and Political Theory at Oxford, in 1958, he felt it necessary
to acknowledge that politics did not attract the professional attention of most
serious philosophers in Britain and America. They thought philosophy had
no place in politics, and vice versa; that political philosophy could be nothing more than a parade of the theorist's own preferences and allegiances with
no supporting arguments of any rigor or respectability. That gloomy picture
is unrecognizable now. Political philosophy thrives as a mature industry; it
dominates many distinguished philosophy departments and attracts a large
share of the best graduate students almost everywhere.

Berlin's lecture, "Two Concepts of Liberty," played an important and
distinctive role in this renaissance. It provoked immediate, continuing,
heated, and mainly illuminating controversy. It became, almost at once, a
staple of graduate and undergraduate reading lists, as it still is. Its scope and
erudition, its historical sweep and evident contemporary force, its sheer interest, made political ideas suddenly seem exciting and fun. Its main polemical
message—that it is fatally dangerous for philosophers to ignore either the
complexity or the power of those ideas—was both compelling and overdue.
But chiefly, or so I think, its importance lay in the force of its central argument. For though Berlin began by conceding to the disdaining philosophers
that political philosophy could not match logic or the philosophy of language

Source: *The New York Review of Books*, October 21, 1993, pp. 12–15. Reprinted with permission from *The New York Review of Books*. Copyright © 1993 Nyrev, Inc.

as a theater for "radical discoveries," in which "talent for minute analyses is likely to be rewarded," he continued by analyzing subtle distinctions that, as it happens, are even more important now, in the Western democracies at least, than when he first called our attention to them.

I must try to describe two central features of his argument, though for reasons of space I shall have to leave out much that is important to them. The first is the celebrated distinction described in the lecture's title: between two (closely allied) senses of liberty. Negative liberty (as Berlin came later to restate it) means not being obstructed by others in doing what one might wish to do. We count some negative liberties—like the freedom to speak our minds without censorship—as very important and others—like driving at very fast speeds—as trivial. But they are both instances of negative freedom, and though a state may be justified in imposing speed limits, for example, on grounds of safety and convenience, that is nevertheless an instance of restricting negative liberty.

Positive liberty, on the other hand, is the power to control or participate in public decisions, including the decision how far to curtail negative liberty. In an ideal democracy—whatever that is—the people govern themselves. Each is master to the same degree, and positive liberty is secured for all.

In his inaugural lecture Berlin described the historical corruption of the idea of positive liberty, a corruption that began in the idea that someone's true liberty lies in control by his rational self rather than his empirical self, that is, in control that aims at securing goals other than those the person himself recognizes. Freedom, on that conception, is possible only when people are governed, ruthlessly if necessary, by rulers who know their true, metaphysical will. Only then are people truly free, albeit against their will. That deeply confused and dangerous, but nevertheless potent, chain of argument had in many parts of the world turned positive liberty into the most terrible tyranny. Of course, by calling attention to this corruption of positive liberty, Berlin did not mean that negative liberty was an unalloyed blessing, and should be protected in all its forms in all circumstances at all costs. He said later that on the contrary, the vices of excessive and indiscriminate negative liberty were so evident, particularly in the form of savage economic inequality, that he had not thought it necessary to describe them in much detail.

The second feature of Berlin's argument that I have in mind is a theme repeated throughout his writing on political topics. He insists on the complexity of political value, and the fallacy of supposing that all the political virtues that are attractive in themselves can be realized in a single political structure. The ancient Platonic ideal of some master accommodation of all attractive virtues and goals, combined in institutions satisfying each in the right proportion and sacrificing none, is in Berlin's view, for all its imaginative power and historical influence, only a seductive myth. He later summed this up:

> One freedom may abort another; one freedom may obstruct or fail to
> create conditions which make other freedoms, or a larger degree of free-

dom, or freedom for more persons, possible; positive and negative freedom may collide; the freedom of the individual or the group may not be fully compatible with a full degree of participation in a common life, with its demands for cooperation, solidarity, fraternity. But beyond all these there is an acuter issue: the paramount need to satisfy the claims of other, no less ultimate, values: justice, happiness, love, the realization of capacities to create new things and experiences and ideas, the discovery of the truth. Nothing is gained by identifying freedom proper, in either of its senses, with these values, or with the conditions of freedom, or by confounding types of freedom with one another.[1]

Berlin's warnings about conflating positive and negative liberty, and liberty itself, with other values seemed, to students of political philosophy in the great Western democracies in the 1950s, to provide important lessons about authoritarian regimes in other times and places. Though cherished liberties were very much under attack in both America and Britain in that decade, the attack was not grounded in or defended through either form of confusion. The enemies of negative liberty were powerful, but they were also crude and undisguised. Joseph McCarthy and his allies did not rely on any Kantian or Hegelian or Marxist concept of metaphysical selves to justify censorship or blacklists. They distinguished liberty not from itself, but from security; they claimed that too much free speech made us vulnerable to spies and intellectual saboteurs and ultimately to conquest.

In both Britain and America, in spite of limited reforms, the state still sought to enforce conventional sexual morality about pornography, contraception, prostitution, and homosexuality. Conservatives who defended these invasions of negative liberty appealed not to some higher or different sense of freedom, however, but to values that were plainly distinct from, and in conflict with, freedom: religion, true morality, and traditional and proper family values. The wars over liberty were fought, or so it seemed, by clearly divided armies. Liberals were for liberty, except, in some circumstances, for the negative liberty of economic entrepreneurs. Conservatives were for that liberty, but against other forms when these collided with security or their view of decency and morality.

But now the political maps have radically changed and some forms of negative liberty have acquired new opponents. Both in America and in Britain, though in different ways, conflicts over race and gender have transformed old alliances and divisions. Speech that expresses racial hatred, or a degrading attitude toward women, has come to seem intolerable to many people whose convictions are otherwise traditionally liberal. It is hardly surprising that they should try to reduce the conflict between their old liberal ideals and their new acceptance of censorship by adopting some new definition of what liberty, properly understood, really is. It is hardly surprising, but the result is dangerous confusion, and Berlin's warnings, framed with different problems in mind, are directly in point.

I shall try to illustrate that point with a single example: a lawsuit arising out of the attempt by certain feminist groups in America to outlaw what they consider a particularly objectionable form of pornography. I select this example not because pornography is more important or dangerous or objectionable than racist invective or other highly distasteful kinds of speech, but because the debate over pornography has been the subject of the fullest and most comprehensive scholarly discussion.

Through the efforts of Catharine MacKinnon, a professor of law at the University of Michigan, and other prominent feminists, Indianapolis, Indiana, enacted an antipornography ordinance. The ordinance defined pornography as "the graphic sexually explicit subordination of women, whether in pictures or words . . ." and it specified, as among pornographic materials falling within that definition, those that present women as enjoying pain or humiliation or rape, or as degraded or tortured or filthy, bruised or bleeding, or in postures of servility or submission or display. It included no exception for literary or artistic value, and opponents claimed that applied literally it would outlaw James Joyce's *Ulysses,* John Cleland's *Memoirs of a Woman of Pleasure,* various works of D. H. Lawrence, and even Yeats's "Leda and the Swan." But the groups who sponsored the ordinance were anxious to establish that their objection was not to obscenity or indecency as such, but to the consequences for women of a particular kind of pornography, and they presumably thought that an exception for artistic value would undermine that claim.[2]

The ordinance did not simply regulate the display of pornography so defined, or restrict its sale or distribution to particular areas, or guard against the exhibition of pornography to children. Regulation for those purposes does restrain negative liberty, but if reasonable it does so in a way compatible with free speech. Zoning and display regulations may make pornography more expensive or inconvenient to obtain, but they do not offend the principle that no one must be prevented from publishing or reading what he or she wishes on the ground that its content is immoral or offensive.[3] The Indianapolis ordinance, on the other hand, prohibited any "production, sale, exhibition, or distribution" whatever of the material it defined as pornographic.

Publishers and members of the public who claimed a desire to read the banned material arranged a prompt constitutional challenge. The federal district court held that the ordinance was unconstitutional because it violated the First Amendment to the United States Constitution, which guarantees the negative liberty of free speech.[4] The Circuit Court for the Seventh Circuit upheld the district court's decision,[5] and the Supreme Court of the United States declined to review that holding. The Circuit Court's decision, in an opinion by Judge Easterbrook, noticed that the ordinance did not outlaw obscene or indecent material generally but only material reflecting the opinion that women are submissive, or enjoy being dominated, or should be treated as if they did. Easterbrook said that the central point of the First

Amendment was exactly to protect speech from content-based regulation of that sort. Censorship may on some occasions be permitted if it aims to prohibit directly dangerous speech—crying fire in a crowded theater or inciting a crowd to violence, for example—or speech particularly and unnecessarily inconvenient—broadcasting from sound trucks patrolling residential streets at night, for instance. But nothing must be censored, Easterbrook wrote, because the message it seeks to deliver is a bad one, or because it expresses ideas that should not be heard at all.

It is by no means universally agreed that censorship should never be based on content. The British Race Relations Act, for example, forbids speech of racial hatred, not only when it is likely to lead to violence, but generally, on the grounds that members of minority races should be protected from racial insults. In America, however, it is a fixed principle of constitutional law that such regulation is unconstitutional unless some compelling necessity, not just official or majority disapproval of the message, requires it. Pornography is often grotesquely offensive; it is insulting, not only to women but to men as well. But we cannot consider that a sufficient reason for banning it without destroying the principle that the speech we hate is as much entitled to protection as any other. The essence of negative liberty is freedom to offend, and that applies to the tawdry as well as the heroic.

Lawyers who defend the Indianapolis ordinance argue that society does have a further justification for outlawing pornography: that it causes great harm as well as offense to women. But their arguments mix together claims about different types or kinds of harm, and it is necessary to distinguish these. They argue, first, that some forms of pornography significantly increase the danger that women will be raped or physically assaulted. If that were true, and the danger were clear and present, then it would indeed justify censorship of those forms, unless less stringent methods of control, such as restricting pornography's audience, would be feasible, appropriate, and effective. In fact, however, though there is some evidence that exposure to pornography weakens people's critical attitudes toward sexual violence, there is no persuasive evidence that it causes more actual incidents of assault. The Seventh Circuit cited a variety of studies (including that of the Williams Commission in Britain in 1979), all of which concluded, the court said, "that it is not possible to demonstrate a direct link between obscenity and rape. . . ."[6] A recent report based on a year's research in Britain said: "The evidence does not point to pornography as a cause of deviant sexual orientation in offenders. Rather, it seems to be used as part of that deviant sexual orientation."[7]

Some feminist groups argue, however, that pornography causes not just physical violence but a more general and endemic subordination of women. In that way, they say, pornography makes for inequality. But even if it could be shown, as a matter of causal connection, that pornography is in part responsible for the economic structure in which few women attain top jobs or equal pay for the same work, that would not justify censorship under the Constitution. It would plainly be unconstitutional to ban speech directly *advocating* that women occupy inferior roles, or none at all, in commerce and the professions, even if that speech fell on willing male ears and achieved its goals. So it cannot be a reason for banning pornography that it contributes to an unequal economic or social structure, even if we think that it does.

But the most imaginative feminist literature for censorship makes a further and different argument: that negative liberty for pornographers conflicts not just with equality but with positive liberty as well, because pornography leads to women's *political* as well as economic or social subordination. Of course pornography does not take the vote from women, or somehow make their votes count less. But it produces a climate, according to this argument, in which women cannot have genuine political power or authority because they are perceived and understood unauthentically—that is, they are made over by male fantasy into people very different from, and of much less consequence than, the people they really are. Consider, for example, these remarks from the work of the principal sponsor of the Indianapolis ordinance. "[Pornography] institutionalizes the sexuality of male supremacy, fusing the eroticization of dominance and submission with the social construction of male and female. . . . Men treat women as who they see women as being. Pornography constructs who that is. Men's power over women means that the way men see women defines who women can be."[8]

Pornography, on this view, denies the positive liberty of women; it denies them the right to be their own masters by recreating them, for politics and society, in the shapes of male fantasy. That is a powerful argument, even in constitutional terms, because it asserts a conflict not just between liberty and equality but within liberty itself, that is, a conflict that cannot be resolved simply on the ground that liberty must be sovereign. What shall we make of the argument understood that way? We must notice, first, that it remains a causal argument. It claims not that pornography is a consequence or symptom or symbol of how the identity of women has been reconstructed by men, but an important cause or vehicle of that reconstruction.

That seems strikingly implausible. Sadistic pornography is revolting, but it is not in general circulation, except for its milder, soft-porn manifestations. It seems unlikely that it has remotely the influence over how women's sexuality or character or talents are conceived by men, and indeed by women, that commercial advertising and soap operas have. Television and other parts of popular culture use sexual display and sexual innuendo to sell virtually everything, and they often show women as experts in domestic detail and unreasoned intuition and nothing else. The images they create are subtle and ubiquitous, and it would not be surprising to learn, through whatever research might establish this, that they indeed do great damage to the way women are understood and allowed to be influential in politics. Sadistic pornography, though much more offensive and disturbing, is greatly overshadowed by these dismal cultural influences as a causal force.

Judge Easterbrook's opinion for the Seventh Circuit assumed, for the sake of argument, however, that pornography did have the consequences the defenders of the ordinance claimed. He said that the argument nevertheless failed because the point of free speech is precisely to allow ideas to have whatever consequences follow from their dissemination, including undesirable consequences for positive liberty. "Under the First Amendment," he said, "the government must leave to the people the evaluation of ideas. Bald or subtle, an idea is as powerful as the audience allows it to be. . . . [The assumed result] simply demonstrates the power of pornography as speech. All of these unhappy effects depend on mental intermediation."

That is right as a matter of American constitutional law. The Ku Klux Klan and the American Nazi party are allowed to propagate their ideas in America, and the British Race Relations Act, so far as it forbids abstract speech of racial hatred, would be unconstitutional in the U.S. But does the American attitude represent the kind of Platonic absolutism Berlin warned against? No, because there is an important difference between the idea he thinks absurd, that all ideals attractive in themselves can be perfectly reconciled within a single utopian political order, and the different idea he thought essential, that we must, as individuals and nations, choose, among possible combinations of ideals, a coherent, even though inevitably and regrettably limited, set of these to define our own individual or national way of life. Freedom of speech, conceived and protected as a fundamental negative liberty, is the core of the choice modern democracies have made, a choice we must now honor in finding our own ways to combat the shaming inequalities women still suffer.

This reply depends, however, on seeing the alleged conflict within liberty as a conflict between the negative and positive senses of that virtue. We must consider yet another argument which, if successful, could not be met in the same way, because it claims that pornography presents a conflict within the negative liberty of speech itself. Berlin said that the character, at least, of negative liberty was reasonably clear, that although excessive claims of negative liberty were dangerous, they could at least always be seen for what they were. But the argument I have in mind, which has been offered by, among others, Frank Michelman of the Harvard Law School, expands the idea of negative liberty in an unanticipated way. He argues that some speech, including pornography, may be itself "silencing," so that its effect is to prevent other people from exercising their negative freedom to speak.

Of course it is fully recognized in First Amendment jurisprudence that some speech has the effect of silencing others. Government must indeed balance negative liberties when it prevents heckling or other demonstrative speech designed to stop others from speaking or being heard. But Michelman has something different in mind. He says that a woman's speech may be silenced not just by noise intended to drown her out but also by argument and images that change her audience's perceptions of her character, needs, desires, and standing, and also, perhaps, change her own sense of who she is and what she wants. Speech with that consequence silences her, Michelman supposes, by making it impossible for her effectively to contribute to the process Judge Easterbrook said the First Amendment protected, the process through which ideas battle for the public's favor. "[It] is a highly plausible claim," Michelman writes, "[that] pornography [is] a cause of women's subordination and silencing. . . . It is a fair and obvious question why our society's openness to challenge does not need protection against repressive private as well as public action."[9]

He argues that if our commitment to negative freedom of speech is consequentialist—if we want free speech in order to have a society in which no idea is barred from entry—then we must censor some ideas in order to make entry possible for other ones. He protests that the distinction that American constitutional law makes between the suppression of ideas by the effect of public criminal law and by the consequences of private speech is arbitrary, and that a sound concern for openness would be equally worried about both forms of control. But the distinction the law makes is not between public and private power as such, but between negative liberty and other virtues, including positive liberty. It would indeed be contradictory for a constitution to prohibit official censorship while protecting the right of private citizens physically to prevent other citizens from publishing or broadcasting specified ideas. That would allow private citizens to violate the negative liberty of other citizens by preventing them from saying what they wish.

But there is no contradiction in insisting that every idea must be allowed to be heard, even those whose consequence is that other ideas will be misunderstood, or given little consideration, or even not be spoken at all because those who might speak them are not in control of their own public identities and therefore cannot be understood as they wish to be. These are very bad consequences, and they must be resisted by whatever means our Constitution permits. But acts that have these consequences do not, for that reason, deprive others of their negative liberty to speak, and the distinction, as Berlin insisted, is very far from arbitrary or inconsequential.

It is of course understandable why Michelman and others should want to expand the idea of negative liberty in the way they try to do. Only by characterizing certain ideas as themselves "silencing" ideas—only by supposing that censoring pornography is the same thing as stopping people from drowning out other speakers—can they hope to justify censorship within the constitutional scheme that assigns a preeminent place to free speech. But the assimilation is nevertheless a confusion, exactly the kind of confusion Berlin warned against in his original lecture, because it obscures the true political choice that must be made. I return to Berlin's lecture, which put the point with that striking combination of clarity and sweep I have been celebrating:

> I should be guilt-stricken, and rightly so, if I were not, in some circumstances, ready to make [some] sacrifice [of freedom]. But a sacrifice is

not an increase in what is being sacrificed, namely freedom, however great the moral need or the compensation for it. Everything is what it is: liberty is liberty, not equality or fairness or justice or culture, or human happiness or a quiet conscience.

NOTES

1. Isaiah Berlin, *Four Essays on Liberty* (Oxford University Press, 1968), p. lvi.

2. MacKinnon explained that "if a woman is subjected, why should it matter that the work has other value?" See her article "Pornography, Civil Rights, and Speech," in *Harvard Civil Rights–Civil Liberties Law Review*, Vol. 28, p. 21.

3. See my article "Do We Have a Right to Pornography?" reprinted as Chapter 17 in my book *A Matter of Principle* (Harvard University Press, 1985).

4. *American Booksellers Association, Inc. et al. v. William H. Hudnut, III, Mayor, City of Indianapolis, et al.,* 598 F. Supp. 1316 (S.D. Ind. 1984).

5. 771 F. 2d 323 (US Court of Appeals, Seventh Circuit).

6. That court, in a confused passage, said that it nevertheless accepted "the premises of this legislation," which included the claims about a causal connection with sexual violence. But it seemed to mean that it was accepting the rather different causal claim considered in the next paragraph, about subordination. In any case, it said that it accepted those premises only for the sake of argument, since it thought it had no authority to reject decisions of Indianapolis based on its interpretation of empirical evidence.

7. See the *Daily Telegraph*, December 23, 1990. Of course further studies might contradict this assumption. But it seems very unlikely that pornography will be found to stimulate physical violence to the overall extent that nonpornographic depictions of violence, which are much more pervasive in our media and culture, do.

8. See MacKinnon's article cited in note 2.

9. Frank Michelman, "Conceptions of Democracy in American Constitutional Argument: The Case of Pornography Regulation." *Tennessee Law Review*, Vol. 56, No. 291 (1989), pp. 303–304.

STANLEY FISH

There's No Such Thing
as Free Speech, and
It's a Good Thing, Too

Stanley Fish is the author of, among other things, Doing What
Comes Naturally: Change, Rhetoric, and the Practice of
Theory in Literary and Legal Studies *(1989). He is professor of
English and professor of law at Duke University.*

> Nowadays the First Amendment is the First Refuge of Scoundrels.
>
> —S. Johnson and S. Fish

Lately, many on the liberal and progressive left have been disconcerted to
find that words, phrases, and concepts thought to be their property and gen-
erative of their politics have been appropriated by the forces of
neoconservatism. This is particularly true of the concept of free speech, for in
recent years First Amendment rhetoric has been used to justify policies and
actions the left finds problematical if not abhorrent: pornography, sexist language, campus hate speech. How has this happened? The answer I shall give
in this essay is that abstract concepts like free speech do not have any "natural" content but are filled with whatever content and direction one can manage to put into them. "Free speech" is just the name we give to verbal
behavior that serves the substantive agendas we wish to advance; and we give
our preferred verbal behaviors *that* name when we can, when we have the
power to do so, because in the rhetoric of American life, the label "free

---

speech" is the one you want your favorites to wear. Free speech, in short, is not an independent value but a political prize, and if that prize has been captured by a politics opposed to yours, it can no longer be invoked in ways that further your purposes, for it is now an obstacle to those purposes. This is something that the liberal left has yet to understand, and what follows is an attempt to pry its members loose from a vocabulary that may now be a disservice to them.

Not far from the end of his *Areopagitica,* and after having celebrated the virtues of toleration and unregulated publication in passages that find their way into every discussion of free speech and the First Amendment, John Milton catches himself up short and says, of course I didn't mean Catholics, them we exterminate:

> I mean not tolerated popery, and open superstition, which as it extirpates all religious and civil supremacies, so itself should be extirpated . . . that also which is impious or evil absolutely against faith or manners no law can possibly permit that intends not to unlaw itself.

Notice that Milton is not simply stipulating a single exception to a rule generally in place; the kinds of utterance that might be regulated and even prohibited on pain of trial and punishment constitute an open set; popery is named only as a particularly perspicuous instance of the advocacy that cannot be tolerated. No doubt there are other forms of speech and action that might be categorized as "open superstitions" or as subversive of piety, faith, and manners, and presumably these too would be candidates for "extirpation." Nor would Milton think himself culpable for having failed to provide a list of unprotected utterances. The list will fill itself out as utterances are put to the test implied by his formulation: would this form of speech or advocacy, if permitted to flourish, tend to undermine the very purposes for which our society is constituted? One cannot answer this question with respect to a particular utterance in advance of its emergence on the world's stage; rather, one must wait and ask the question in the full context of its production and (possible) dissemination. It might appear that the result would be ad hoc and unprincipled, but for Milton the principle inheres in the core values in whose name individuals of like mind came together in the first place. Those values, which include the search for truth and the promotion of virtue, are capacious enough to accommodate a diversity of views. But at some point—again impossible of advance specification—capaciousness will threaten to become shapelessness, and at that point fidelity to the original values will demand acts of extirpation.

I want to say that all affirmations of freedom of expression are like Milton's, dependent for their force on an exception that literally carves out the space in which expression can then emerge. I do not mean that expression (saying something) is a realm whose integrity is sometimes compromised by certain restrictions but that restriction, in the form of an underlying articulation of the world that necessarily (if silently) negates alternatively possible articulations, is constitutive of expression. Without restriction, without an inbuilt sense of what it would be meaningless to say or wrong to say, there could be no assertion and no reason for asserting it. The exception to unregulated expression is not a negative restriction but a positive hollowing out of value—we are for *this,* which means we are against *that*—in relation to which meaningful assertion can then occur. It is in reference to that value—constituted as all values are by an act of exclusion—that some forms of speech will be heard as (quite literally) intolerable. Speech, in short, is never a value in and of itself but is always produced within the precincts of some assumed conception of the good to which it must yield in the event of conflict. When the pinch comes (and sooner or later it will always come) and the institution (be it church, state, or university) is confronted by behavior subversive of its core rationale, it will respond by declaring "of course we mean not tolerated _____, that we extirpate," not because an exception to a general freedom has suddenly and contradictorily been announced, but because the freedom has never been general and has always been understood against the background of an originary exclusion that gives it meaning.

   This is a large thesis, but before tackling it directly I want to buttress my case with another example, taken not from the seventeenth century but from the charter and case law of Canada. Canadian thinking about freedom of expression departs from the line usually taken in the United States in ways that bring that country very close to the *Areopagitica* as I have expounded it. The differences are fully on display in a recent landmark case, *R. v. Keegstra.* James Keegstra was a high school teacher in Alberta who, it was established by evidence, "systematically denigrated Jews and Judaism in his classes." He described Jews as treacherous, subversive, sadistic, money loving, power hungry, and child killers. He declared them "responsible for depressions, anarchy, chaos, wars and revolution" and required his students "to regurgitate these notions in essays and examinations." Keegstra was indicted under Section 319(2) of the Criminal Code and convicted. The Court of Appeal reversed, and the Crown appealed to the Supreme Court, which reinstated the lower court's verdict.

   Section 319(2) reads in part, "Every one who, by communicating statements other than in private conversation, willfully promotes hatred against any identifiable group is guilty of . . . an indictable offense and is liable to imprisonment for a term not exceeding two years." In the United States, this provision of the code would almost certainly be struck down because, under the First Amendment, restrictions on speech are apparently prohibited without qualification. To be sure, the Canadian charter has its own version of the First Amendment, in Section 2(b): "Everyone has the following fundamental freedoms . . . (b) freedom of thought, belief, opinion, and expression, including freedom of the press and other media of communication." But Section 2(b), like every other section of the charter, is qualified by Section 1: "The

Canadian Charter of Rights and Freedoms guarantees the rights and freedoms set out in it subject only to such reasonable limits prescribed by law as can be demonstrably justified in a free and democratic society." Or in other words, every right and freedom herein granted can be trumped if its exercise is found to be in conflict with the principles that underwrite the society.

This is what happens in *Keegstra* as the majority finds that Section 319(2) of the Criminal Code does in fact violate the right of freedom of expression guaranteed by the charter but is nevertheless a *permissible* restriction because it accords with the principles proclaimed in Section 1. There is, of course, a dissent that reaches the conclusion that would have been reached by most, if not all, U.S. courts; but even in dissent the minority is faithful to Canadian ways of reasoning. "The question," it declares, "is always one of balance," and thus even when a particular infringement of the charter's Section 2(b) has been declared unconstitutional, as it would have been by the minority, the question remains open with respect to the next case. In the United States the question is presumed closed and can only be pried open by special tools. In our legal culture as it is now constituted, if one yells "free speech" in a crowded courtroom and makes it stick, the case is over.

Of course, it is not that simple. Despite the apparent absoluteness of the First Amendment, there are any number of ways of getting around it, ways that are known to every student of the law. In general, the preferred strategy is to manipulate the distinction, essential to First Amendment jurisprudence, between speech and action. The distinction is essential because no one would think to frame a First Amendment that began "Congress shall make no law abridging freedom of action," for that would amount to saying "Congress shall make no law," which would amount to saying "There shall be no law," only actions uninhibited and unregulated. If the First Amendment is to make any sense, have any bite, speech must be declared not to be a species of action, or to be a special form of action lacking the aspects of action that cause it to be the object of regulation. The latter strategy is the favored one and usually involves the separation of speech from consequences. This is what Archibald Cox does when he assigns to the First Amendment the job of protecting "expressions separable from conduct harmful to other individuals and the community." The difficulty of managing this segregation is well known: speech always seems to be crossing the line into action, where it becomes, at least potentially, consequential. In the face of this categorical instability, First Amendment theorists and jurists fashion a distinction within the speech/action distinction: some forms of speech are not really speech because their purpose is to incite violence or because they are, as the court declares in *Chaplinsky v. New Hampshire* (1942), "fighting words," words "likely to provoke the average person to retaliation, and thereby cause a breach of the peace."

The trouble with this definition is that it distinguishes not between fighting words and words that remain safely and merely expressive but between words that are provocative to one group (the group that falls under the rubric "average person") and words that might be provocative to other groups, groups of persons not now considered average. And if you ask what words are likely to be provocative to those nonaverage groups, what are likely to be *their* fighting words, the answer is anything and everything, for as Justice Holmes said long ago (in *Gitlow v. New York*), every idea is an incitement to somebody, and since ideas come packaged in sentences, in words, every sentence is potentially, in some situation that might occur tomorrow, a fighting word and therefore a candidate for regulation.

This insight cuts two ways. One could conclude from it that the fighting words exception is a bad idea because there is no way to prevent clever and unscrupulous advocates from shoveling so many forms of speech into the excepted category that the zone of constitutionally protected speech shrinks to nothing and is finally without inhabitants. Or, alternatively, one could conclude that there was never anything in the zone in the first place and that the difficulty of limiting the fighting words exception is merely a particular instance of the general difficulty of separating speech from action. And if one opts for this second conclusion, as I do, then a further conclusion is inescapable: insofar as the point of the First Amendment is to identify speech separable from conduct and from the consequences that come in conduct's wake, there is no such speech and therefore nothing for the First Amendment to protect. Or, to make the point from the other direction, when a court invalidates legislation because it infringes on protected speech, it is not because the speech in question is without consequences but because the consequences have been discounted in relation to a good that is judged to outweigh them. Despite what they say, courts are never in the business of protecting speech per se, "mere" speech (a nonexistent animal); rather, they are in the business of classifying speech (as protected or regulatable) in relation to a value—the health of the republic, the vigor of the economy, the maintenance of the status quo, the undoing of the status quo—that is the true, if unacknowledged, object of their protection.

But if this is the case, a First Amendment purist might reply, why not drop the charade along with the malleable distinctions that make it possible, and declare up front that total freedom of speech is our primary value and trumps anything else, no matter what? The answer is that freedom of expression would only be a primary value if it didn't matter what was said, didn't matter in the sense that no one gave a damn but just liked to hear talk. There are contexts like that, a Hyde Park corner or a call-in talk show where people get to sound off for the sheer fun of it. These, however, are special contexts, artificially bounded spaces designed to assure that talking is not taken seriously. In ordinary contexts, talk is produced with the goal of trying to move the world in one direction rather than another. In these contexts—the contexts of everyday life—you go to the trouble of asserting that X is Y only because you suspect that some people are wrongly asserting that X is Z or that

X doesn't exist. You assert, in short, because you give a damn, not about assertion—as if it were a value in and of itself— but about what your assertion is about. It may seem paradoxical, but free expression could only be a primary value if what you are valuing is the right to make noise; but if you are engaged in some purposive activity in the course of which speech happens to be produced, sooner or later you will come to a point when you decide that some forms of speech do not further but endanger that purpose.

Take the case of universities and colleges. Could it be the purpose of such places to encourage free expression? If the answer were "yes," it would be hard to say why there would be any need for classes, or examinations, or departments, or disciplines, or libraries, since freedom of expression requires nothing but a soapbox or an open telephone line. The very fact of the university's machinery—of the events, rituals, and procedures that fill its calendar—argues for some other, more substantive purpose. In relation to that purpose (which will be realized differently in different kinds of institutions), the flourishing of free expression will in almost all circumstances be an obvious good; but in some circumstances, freedom of expression may pose a threat to that purpose, and at that point it may be necessary to discipline or regulate speech, lest, to paraphrase Milton, the institution sacrifice itself to one of its *accidental* features.

Interestingly enough, the same conclusion is reached (inadvertently) by Congressman Henry Hyde, who is addressing these very issues in a recently offered amendment to Title VI of the Civil Rights Act. The first section of the amendment states its purpose, to protect "the free speech rights of college students" by prohibiting private as well as public educational institutions from "subjecting any student to disciplinary sanctions solely on the basis of conduct that is speech." The second section enumerates the remedies available to students whose speech rights may have been abridged, and the third, which is to my mind the nub of the matter, declares as an exception to the amendment's jurisdiction any "educational institution that is controlled by a religious organization," on the reasoning that the application of the amendment to such institutions "would not be consistent with the religious tenets of such organizations." In effect, what Congressman Hyde is saying is that at the heart of these colleges and universities is a set of beliefs, and it would be wrong to require them to tolerate behavior, including speech behavior, inimical to those beliefs. But insofar as this logic is persuasive, it applies across the board, for all educational institutions rest on some set of beliefs—no institution is "just there" independent of any purpose—and it is hard to see why the rights of an institution to protect and preserve its basic "tenets" should be restricted only to those that are religiously controlled. Read strongly, the third section of the amendment undoes sections one and two— the exception becomes, as it always was, the rule—and points us to a balancing test very much like that employed in Canadian law: given that any college or university is informed by a core rationale, an administrator faced with complaints about offensive speech should ask whether damage to the core would be greater if the speech were tolerated or regulated.

The objection to this line of reasoning is well known and has recently been reformulated by Benno Schmidt, former president of Yale University. According to Schmidt, speech codes on campuses constitute "well intentioned but misguided efforts to give values of community and harmony a higher place than freedom" (*Wall Street Journal,* May 6, 1991). "When the goals of harmony collide with freedom of expression," he continues, "freedom must be the paramount obligation of an academic community." The flaw in this logic is on display in the phrase "academic community," for the phrase recognizes what Schmidt would deny, that expression only occurs in communities—if not in an academic community, then in a shopping mall community or a dinner party community or an airplane ride community or an office community. In these communities and in any others that could be imagined (with the possible exception of a community of major league baseball fans), limitations on speech in relation to a defining and deeply assumed purpose are inseparable from community membership.

Indeed, "limitations" is the wrong word because it suggests that expression, as an activity and a value, has a pure form that is always in danger of being compromised by the urgings of special interest communities; but independently of a community context informed by interest (that is, purpose), expression would be at once inconceivable and unintelligible. Rather than being a value that is threatened by limitations and constraints, expression, in any form worth worrying about, is a *product* of limitations and constraints, of the already-in-place presuppositions that give assertions their very particular point. Indeed, the very act of thinking of something to say (whether or not it is subsequently regulated) is already constrained—rendered impure, and because impure, communicable—by the background context within which the thought takes its shape. (The analysis holds too for "freedom," which in Schmidt's vision is an entirely empty concept referring to an urge without direction. But like expression, freedom is a coherent notion only in relation to a goal or good that limits and, by limiting, shapes its exercise.)

Arguments like Schmidt's only get their purchase by first imagining speech as occurring in no context whatsoever, and then stripping particular speech acts of the properties conferred on them by contexts. The trick is nicely illustrated when Schmidt urges protection for speech "no matter how obnoxious in content." "Obnoxious" at once acknowledges the reality of speech-related harms and trivializes them by suggesting that they are *surface* injuries that any large-minded ("liberated and humane") person should be able to bear. The possibility that speech-related injuries may be grievous and *deeply* wounding is carefully kept out of sight, and because it is kept out of sight, the fiction of a world of weightless verbal exchange can be maintained, at least within the confines of Schmidt's carefully denatured discourse.

To this Schmidt would no doubt reply, as he does in his essay, that harmful speech should be answered not by regulation but by more speech; but that would make sense only if the effects of speech could be canceled out by additional speech, only if the pain and humiliation caused by racial or religious epithets could be ameliorated by saying something like "So's your old man." What Schmidt fails to realize at every level of his argument is that expression is more than a matter of proffering and receiving propositions, that words do work in the world of a kind that cannot be confined to a purely cognitive realm of "mere" ideas.

It could be said, however, that I myself mistake the nature of the work done by freely tolerated speech because I am too focused on short-run outcomes and fail to understand that the good effects of speech will be realized, not in the present, but in a future whose emergence regulation could only inhibit. This line of reasoning would also weaken one of my key points, that speech in and of itself cannot be a value and is only worth worrying about if it is in the service of something with which it cannot be identical. My mistake, one could argue, is to equate the something in whose service speech is with some locally espoused value (e.g., the end of racism, the empowerment of disadvantaged minorities), whereas in fact we should think of that something as a now-inchoate shape that will be given firm lines only by time's pencil. That is why the shape now receives such indeterminate characterizations (e.g., true self-fulfillment, a more perfect polity, a more capable citizenry, a less partial truth); we cannot now know it, and therefore we must not prematurely fix it in ways that will bind successive generations to error.

This forward-looking view of what the First Amendment protects has a great appeal, in part because it continues in a secular form the Puritan celebration of millenarian hopes, but it imposes a requirement so severe that one would expect more justification for it than is usually provided The requirement is that we endure whatever pain racist and hate speech inflicts for the sake of a future whose emergence we can only take on faith. In a specifically religious vision like Milton's, this makes perfect sense (it is indeed the whole of Christianity), but in the context of a politics that puts its trust in the world and not in the Holy Spirit, it raises more questions than it answers and could be seen as the second of two strategies designed to delegitimize the complaints of victimized groups. The first strategy, as I have noted, is to define speech in such a way as to render it inconsequential (on the model of "sticks and stones will break my bones, but . . ."); the second strategy is to acknowledge the (often grievous) consequences of speech but declare that we must suffer them in the name of something that cannot be named. The two strategies are denials from slightly different directions of the *present* effects of racist speech; one confines those effects to a closed and safe realm of pure mental activity; the other imagines the effects of speech spilling over into the world but only in an ever-receding future for whose sake we must forever defer taking action.

I find both strategies unpersuasive, but my own skepticism concerning them is less important than the fact that in general they seem to have worked; in the parlance of the marketplace (a parlance First Amendment commentators love), many in the society seemed to have bought them. Why? The answer, I think, is that people cling to First Amendment pieties because they do not wish to face what they correctly take to be the alternative. That alternative is *politics,* the realization (at which I have already hinted) that decisions about what is and is not protected in the realm of expression will rest not on principle or firm doctrine but on the ability of some persons to interpret— recharacterize or rewrite—principle and doctrine in ways that lead to the protection of speech they want heard and the regulation of speech they want heard and the regulation of speech they want silenced. (That is how George Bush can argue *for* flag-burning statutes and *against* campus hate-speech codes.) When the First Amendment is successfully invoked, the result is not a victory for free speech in the face of a challenge from politics but a *political victory* won by the party that has managed to wrap its agenda in the mantle of free speech.

It is from just such a conclusion—a conclusion that would put politics *inside* the First Amendment—that commentators recoil, saying things like "This could render the First Amendment a dead letter," or "This would leave us with no normative guidance in determining when and what speech to protect," or "This effaces the distinction between speech and action," or "This is incompatible with any viable notion of freedom of expression." To these statements (culled more or less at random from recent law review pieces) I would reply that the First Amendment has always been a dead letter if one understood its "liveness" to depend on the identification and protection of a realm of "mere" expression distinct from the realm of regulatable conduct; the distinction between speech and action has always been effaced in principle, although in practice it can take whatever form the prevailing political conditions mandate; we have never had any normative guidance for marking off protected from unprotected speech; rather, the guidance we have has been fashioned (and refashioned) in the very political struggles over which it then (for a time) presides. In short, the name of the game has always been politics, even when (indeed, especially when) it is played by stigmatizing politics as the area to be avoided.

In saying this, I would not be heard as arguing either for or against regulation and speech codes as a matter of general principle. Instead my argument turns away from general principle to the pragmatic (anti)principle of considering each situation as it emerges. The question of whether or not to regulate will always be a local one, and we can not rely on abstractions that are either empty of content or filled with the content of some partisan agenda to generate a "principled" answer. Instead we must consider in every case what is at stake and what are the risks and gains of alternative courses of action. In the course of this consideration many things will be of help, but among them will not be phrases like "freedom of speech" or "the right of individual expression," because, as they are used now, these phrases tend to obscure rather than clarify our dilemmas. Once they are deprived of their talismanic force, once it is no longer strategically effective simply to invoke them in the act of walking away from a problem, the conversation could continue in directions that are now blocked by a First Amendment absolutism that has only been honored in the breach anyway. To the student reporter who complains that in the wake of the promulgation of a speech code at the University of Wisconsin there is now something in the back of his mind as he writes, one could reply, "There was always something in the back of your mind, and perhaps it might be better to have this code in the back of your mind than whatever was in there before." And when someone warns about the slippery slope and predicts mournfully that if you restrict one form of speech, you never know what will be restricted next, one could reply, "Some form of speech is always being restricted, else there could be no meaningful assertion; we have always and already slid down the slippery slope; someone is always going to be restricted next, and it is your job to make sure that the someone is not you." And when someone observes, as someone surely will, that antiharassment codes chill speech, one could reply that since speech only becomes intelligible against the background of what isn't being said, the background of what has already been silenced, the only question is the political one of which speech is going to be chilled, and, all things considered, it seems a good thing to chill speech like "nigger," "cunt," "kike," and "faggot." And if someone then says, "But what happened to free-speech principles?" one could say what I have now said a dozen times, free-speech principles don't exist except as a component in a bad argument in which such principles are invoked to mask motives that would not withstand close scrutiny.

An example of a wolf wrapped in First Amendment clothing is an advertisement that ran recently in the Duke University student newspaper, the *Chronicle*. Signed by Bradley R. Smith, well known as a purveyor of anti-Semitic neo-Nazi propaganda, the ad is packaged as a scholarly treatise: four densely packed columns complete with "learned" references, undocumented statistics, and an array of so-called authorities. The message of the ad is that the Holocaust never occurred and that the German state never "had a policy to exterminate the Jewish people (or anyone else) by putting them to death in gas chambers." In a spectacular instance of the increasingly popular "blame the victim" strategy, the Holocaust "story" or "myth" is said to have been fabricated in order "to drum up world sympathy for Jewish causes." The "evidence" supporting these assertions is a slick blend of supposedly probative facts "not a single autopsied body has been shown to be gassed"—and sly insinuations of a kind familiar to readers of *Mein Kampf* and *The Protocols of the Elders of Zion*. The slickest thing of all, however, is the presentation of the argument as an exercise in free speech— the ad is subtitled "The Case for Open Debate"—that could be objected to only by "thought police" and censors. This strategy bore immediate fruit in the decision of the newspaper staff to accept the ad despite a long-standing (and historically honored) policy of refusing materials that contain ethnic and racial slurs or are otherwise offensive. The reasoning of the staff (explained by the editor in a special column) was that under the First Amendment advertisers have the "right" to be published. "American newspapers are built on the principles of free speech and free press, so how can a newspaper deny these rights to anyone?" The answer to this question is that an advertiser is not denied his rights simply because a single media organ declines his copy so long as other avenues of publication are available and there has been no state suppression of his views. This is not to say that there could not be a case for printing the ad, only that the case cannot rest on a supposed First Amendment obligation. One might argue, for example, that printing the ad would foster healthy debate, or that lies are more likely to be shown up for what they are if they are brought to the light of day, but these are precisely the arguments the editor *disclaims* in her eagerness to take a "principled" free-speech stand.

What I find most distressing about this incident is not that the ad was printed but that it was printed by persons who believed it to be a lie and a distortion. If the editor and her staff were in agreement with Smith's views or harbored serious doubts about the reality of the Holocaust, I would still have a quarrel with them, but it would be a different quarrel; it would be a quarrel about evidence, credibility, documentation. But since on these matters the editors and I are in agreement, my quarrel is with the reasoning that led them to act in opposition to what they believed to be true. That reasoning, as I understand it, goes as follows: although we ourselves are certain that the Holocaust was a fact, facts are notoriously interpretable and disputable; therefore nothing is ever really settled, and we have no right to reject something just because we regard it as pernicious and false. But the fact—if I can use that word—that settled truths can always be upset, at least theoretically, does not mean that we cannot affirm and rely on truths that according to our present lights seem indisputable; rather, it means exactly the opposite: in the absence of absolute certainty of the kind that can only be provided by revelation (something I do not rule out but have not yet experienced), we must act on the basis of the certainty we have so far achieved. Truth may, as Milton said, always be in the course of emerging, and we must always be on guard against being so beguiled by its present shape that we ignore contrary evidence; but, by the same token, when it happens that the present shape of truth is compelling beyond a reasonable doubt, it is our moral obligation to act on it and not defer action in the name of an interpretative future that may never arrive. By running the First Amendment up the nearest flagpole and rushing to salute it, the student editors defaulted on that obligation and gave over their responsibility to a so-called principle that was not even to the point.

Let me be clear. I am not saying that First Amendment principles are inherently bad (they are *inherently* nothing), only that they are not always the appropriate reference point for situations involving the production of speech, and that even when they are the appropriate reference point, they do not constitute a politics-free perspective because the shape in which they are invoked will always be political, will always, that is, be the result of having drawn the relevant line (between speech and action, or between high-value speech and low-value speech, or between words essential to the expression of ideas and fighting words) in a way that is favorable to some interests and indifferent or hostile to others. This having been said, the moral is not that First Amendment talk should be abandoned, for even if the standard First Amendment formulas do not and could not perform the function expected of them (the elimination of political considerations in decisions about speech), they still serve a function that is not at all negligible: they slow down outcomes in an area in which the fear of overhasty outcomes is justified by a long record of abuses of power. It is often said that history shows (itself a formula) that even a minimal restriction on the right of expression too easily leads to ever-larger restrictions; and to the extent that this is an empirical fact (and it is a question one could debate), there is some comfort and protection to be found in a procedure that requires you to jump through hoops—do a lot of argumentative work—before a speech regulation will be allowed to stand.

I would not be misunderstood as offering the notion of "jumping through hoops" as a new version of the First Amendment claim to neutrality. A hoop must have a shape—in this case the shape of whatever binary distinction is representing First Amendment "interests"—and the shape of the hoop one is asked to jump through will in part determine what kinds of jumps can be regularly made. Even if they are only mechanisms for slowing down outcomes, First Amendment formulas by virtue of their substantive content (and it is impossible that they be without content) will slow down some outcomes more easily than others, and that means that the form they happen to have at the present moment will favor some interests more than others. Therefore, even with a reduced sense of the effectivity of First Amendment rhetoric (it can not assure any particular result), the counsel with which I began remains relevant: so long as so-called free-speech principles have been fashioned by your enemy (so long as it is *his* hoops you have to jump through), contest their relevance to the issue at hand; but if you manage to refashion them in line with your purposes, urge them with a vengeance.

It is a counsel that follows from the thesis that there is no such thing as free speech, which is not, after all, a thesis as startling or corrosive as may first have seemed. It merely says that there is no class of utterances separable from the world of conduct and that therefore the identification of some utterances as members of that nonexistent class will always be evidence that a political line has been drawn rather than a line that denies politics entry into the forum of public discourse. It is the job of the First Amendment to mark out an area in which competing views can be considered without state interference; but if the very marking out of that area is itself an interference (as it always will be), First Amendment jurisprudence is inevitably self-defeating and subversive of its own aspirations. That's the bad news. The good news is that precisely *because* speech is never "free" in the two senses required—free of consequences and free from state pressure—speech always matters, is always doing work; because everything we say impinges on the world in ways indistinguishable from the effects of physical action, we must take responsibility for our verbal performances—*all* of them—and not assume that they are being taken care of by a clause in the Constitution. Of course, with responsibility comes risks, but they have always been our risks, and no doctrine of free speech has ever insulated us from them. They are the risks, respectively, of permitting speech that does obvious harm and of shutting off speech in ways that might deny us the benefit of Joyce's *Ulysses* or Lawrence's *Lady Chatterly's Lover* or Titian's paintings. Nothing, I repeat, can insulate us from those risks. (If there is no normative guidance in determining when and what speech to protect, there is no normative guidance in determining what is art—like free speech a category that includes everything and nothing—and what is obscenity.) Moreover, nothing can provide us with a principle for deciding which risk in the long run is the best to take. I am persuaded that at the present moment, right now, the risk of not attending to hate speech is greater than the risk that by regulating it we will deprive ourselves of valuable voices and insights or slide down the slippery slope toward tyranny. This is a judgment for which I can offer reasons but no guarantees. All I am saying is that the judgments of those who would come down on the other side carry no guarantees either. They urge us to put our faith in apolitical abstractions, but the abstractions they invoke—the marketplace of ideas, speech alone, speech itself—only come in political guises, and therefore in trusting to them we fall (unwittingly) under the sway of the very forces we wish to keep at bay. It is not that there are no choices to make or means of making them; it is just that the choices as well as the means are inextricable from the din and confusion of partisan struggle. There is no safe place. . . .

PART THREE

Pornography, Sexuality, and Politics

The papers in the first two parts of this book have been concerned mainly with heterosexual pornography. However, there is a rather large gay pornography industry and a growing lesbian market. Gay and lesbian pornography raise difficult and interesting questions, especially for the analyses of pornography offered by the writers in Part One. One of the reasons that feminists such as Catharine MacKinnon object to heterosexual ("straight") pornography is that its appeal depends on the subordination of women. As MacKinnon puts it, "[Pornography] makes dominance and submission into sex. Inequality is its central dynamic. . . ." And Steinem says, "The subject [of pornography] is not mutual love, or love at all, but domination and violence against women. (Though, of course, *homosexual pornography may imitate this violence by putting a man in the 'feminine' role of victim* [emphasis added].)" So, the question naturally arises, do certain feminist critiques of straight pornography apply with equal force to gay pornography? Lesbian pornography—in particular, lesbian sadomasochistic pornography—also poses a challenge for the type of feminist objections to pornography raised in Part One. Perhaps authentic lesbian pornography—as opposed to *Penthouse*'s pseudolesbian scenes—is a crucial part of women's own attempts to explore the parameters of female sexuality. If so, then some pornography might have a positive role to play in the liberation of women. Indeed, it might be argued that some straight pornography can play this role too, whether or not it is produced by women.

Thomas Waugh and John Stoltenberg tackle the uneasy relationship between feminism and gay pornography. As a gay man who grants the centrality of pornography in the experience and construction of gay male identity, Thomas Waugh asks, "How . . . am I to express my solidarity in words and actions with women's rightful denunciations of pornography as an instrument of anti-feminist backlash, . . . of the incitement to rape and violence against women?" As his "topographical comparison" of gay and straight (male) pornography shows, Waugh is mindful of the potentially problematic elements of gay male pornography. For example, in gay pornography, depictions of sexual violence and rape are not uncommon, and victimization is often eroticized. (This is a theme on which Stoltenberg expands in his essay.) Like its straight counterpart, gay male pornography is phallocentric—that is, focused on the penis. But gay pornography also differs in crucial respects from straight pornography. In gay male pornography the relationship of the spectator to the material is quite different; for example, in many films, characters play multiple roles—sometimes being penetrated, sometimes penetrating—and the viewer may find himself identifying alternately with each role. Furthermore, in gay male pornography, men are often invited to identify with the role of the victim; whereas in straight pornography, men are represented predominantly as victimizers, thus making possible only one same-gender identification. Finally, quite apart from its content, Waugh suggests that gay male pornography plays a social role very different from straight male pornography. For instance, the venues in which gay pornography is shown are often "liberated spaces"—that is, spaces in which gay men can safely express their sexuality to the point of participating in sexual encounters. So, arguably, gay male pornography is very much a part of gay sexual politics. Pornography and its consumption are not peripheral but perhaps central to gay men's struggles to lead free and open erotic lives.

This last point provides a possible basis for a case against state censorship of gay pornography. The argument would not be that the erotic lives of citizens are none of the state's business (though that *is* an argument that some people make in support of permissive policies on both gay and straight pornography). Rather, the claim would be that, in a homophobic society, a sphere of activity and expression that is accessible to heterosexual people is not accessible to homosexual men. By and large, heterosexual people are not prevented by either convention or law from leading erotic lives. However, in many U.S. states sodomy is illegal; and in Canada the depiction of anal intercourse is sufficient grounds for customs agents to stop material at the border.

Thus the "problem" of gay male pornography can be construed as a matter of equality.

Now we can see how the relation between anti-pornography feminists and gay men is especially complicated. As Waugh says, "Sexual liberation is still an essential component of political liberation. . . ." If this is right, then the elimination or restriction of pornography might hinder the political struggles of marginalized sexual minorities such as gays and lesbians. Thus, the political agenda of anti-pornography feminists might collide with that of these other groups. Waugh agrees that gay male pornography "is shaped by . . . [gay men's] conditioning as men in patriarchy," but he also insists that it has been shaped by gay men's experience of oppression. He does not deny that gay men need to investigate the content of their pornography critically. But he suggests that this critique not take place in abstraction from a broader political context. (This brings to mind Stanley Fish's contention that every decision about free speech is essentially a political decision.)

In his paper, "Gays and the Pro-Pornography Movement: Having the Hots for Sex Discrimination," John Stoltenberg elucidates the connections he sees between sexism, homophobia, and gay pornography. He contends that both sexism and homophobia are manifestations of misogyny (hatred of women); gay men are held in contempt because they are "smeared with female status." He also argues that much gay pornography serves to uphold the "sex-class system," which is "an eroticized power structure" of men over women.

Stoltenberg briefly discusses the content of gay male sex films and cites several examples of gay personal advertisements. In such media, domination and submission are sexualized. Echoing MacKinnon and Andrea Dworkin, Stoltenberg argues that in our current society all men are conditioned to find sexual pleasure in the possession of power over someone else. He writes, "We are *supposed* to respond orgasmically to power and powerlessness, to violence and violation; our sexuality is *supposed* to be inhabited by a reverence for supremacy, for unjust power over and against other human life." Under patriarchy, it is essentially the possession of power that distinguishes male from female, and thus sex itself becomes a manifestation of inequality.

Gay men are not immune to this conditioning, Stoltenberg claims. Indeed, he thinks that it explains why some gay men internalize homophobia. "When you're living in an erotic hierarchy, where to be demeaned in sex is to be feminized, and to have power over someone else is to be male . . . it leaves you eroticizing masculinity as power over other people." This makes the fact of being gay in our society problematic; if sex essentially involves a power asymmetry, who is to be the "man" in a gay sexual encounter? Stoltenberg suggests that gay men have a vested interest in the production and consumption of pornography that reiterates the sexual values of male supremacists. Such pornography provides a way of dealing with homophobia. If the sex depicted in gay pornography is sex that mirrors heterosexual patterns of domination and submission, then gay men can reassure themselves that they are still "really men." "There is a sexiness in subordination, and its sexiness for gay men in particular has a lot to do with the fact that subordination in sex helps resolve a misogynist struggle to cling to male supremacy."

Although there appear to be points of agreement between Waugh and Stoltenberg, they differ with respect to the question of whether the political interests of anti-pornography feminists and gay men converge. Waugh urges caution, suggesting that gay men might run the risk of losing something of value were pornography to be curtailed. Stoltenberg, in contrast, believes that both the oppression of gay men (through homophobia) and the oppression of women (through sexism) are cut from the same cloth, and that both gay and straight male pornography play a role in maintaining this oppression.

The topic of political alliances also arises within feminism. It is by now a commonplace that there is no monolithic theory (or practice or set of commitments) that defines feminism. So it is hardly surprising that not all people who identify themselves as feminists—or who "advocate feminism," to use Bell Hooks' phrase[1]—take the same view of pornography. As you will see from the bibliography, there is now an extensive literature that addresses, in one way or another, feminist critiques of pornography, and another anthology would be required to cover all aspects of this complicated debate. However, it is possible to identify four related disputes between those feminists who are sympathetic with the analysis of pornography presented in Part One and those feminists who are not. The papers by Ellen Willis and Mariana Valverde in Part Three serve to illustrate some of the complexity of these disputes.

A first site of disagreement between feminists concerning pornography has to do with how it is defined. This is an issue we have touched on before. In the introduction to Part One, we saw that it is crucial to distinguish between normative and descriptive characterizations of pornography. Normative definitions have their place, but they are rarely uncontroversial and often

---

[1]Bell Hooks, "Black Women and Feminism," in *Talking Back: Thinking Feminist, Thinking Black* (Toronto: Between the Lines, 1988).

make the identification of the material in question quite difficult. For example, one can simply stipulate that "pornography is . . . a form of forced sex,"[2] but then one will have to show that pornography so defined exists. Moreover, as Ellen Willis worries, some feminist analyses that use a normative characterization of pornography (like the one above) leave no room for distinguishing *types* of pornography. They take all pornography either to be or at least to represent violence against women. But perhaps not all pornography is problematic in this respect. Willis warns, "If feminists define pornography, per se, as the enemy, the result will be to make a lot of women ashamed of their sexual feelings and afraid to be honest about them. And the last thing women need is more sexual shame, guilt, and hypocrisy—this time served up as feminism."

A second site of feminist disagreement concerns a cluster of issues relating to freedom of expression. At least three concerns can be distinguished. First, some feminist critics fear that a campaign to censor pornography will foster equally repressive measures against things that women would not want restricted—for example, safe-sex information. Second, there is the objection that freedom of expression is crucial for political change, and hence for feminism. To the extent that feminists need to be able to rely on freedom of speech to achieve their political ends they cannot consistently recommend the censorship of someone else's views. Finally, there is the idea that the open discussion of sexuality and its complexity is central to understanding women's subordination. Women must be able both to investigate what kind of pornography is available and to explore their own desires, perhaps through producing pornography of their own. Advocating the censorship or restriction of sexually explicit material will frustrate this aim. As Willis writes, "The basic purpose of obscenity laws is and always has been to reinforce cultural taboos on sexuality and suppress feminism, homosexuality, and other forms of sexual dissidence." If this is right, then anti-pornography feminists who argue for censorship might unwittingly be contributing to a backlash against feminism.

In the third area of dispute, some feminists have worried about what appears to be a pernicious essentialism at work in the writings of MacKinnon and Andrea Dworkin. We have seen that these theorists, along with John Stoltenberg, contend that sex itself is constructed in a way injurious to

---

[2]Catharine A. MacKinnon, "Not a Moral Issue," in *Feminism Unmodified: Discourses on Life and Law* (Cambridge, Mass.: Harvard University Press, 1987), 148.

women. MacKinnon, Andrea Dworkin, and Stoltenberg argue that domination and submission are necessary to sex; so without inequality, sex would
not be sexy. They contend that pornography plays the central role in maintaining the so-called sex-class system of patriarchy. On this account, several
questions demand answers. For example, is it even possible for women to
have egalitarian sexual relations with men? If not, do heterosexual women
collaborate in their own oppression simply by having sex with men? What are
we to say to women who derive sexual pleasure from consuming some types
of pornography?

It is difficult to determine whether Andrea Dworkin and MacKinnon believe that women are essentially victims. Much depends on how one inter-
prets their central thesis that pornography is the subordination of women.
Are they asserting a causal connection between some types of pornography
and, let us say, the systematic mistreatment of women in our society? Or is
their thesis asserting an identity claim? According to this second interpretation, pornography does not simply contribute to the subordination of
women; it itself subordinates women. This is a claim that has kindled considerable debate. Some philosophers have suggested that the claim might even
be incoherent, for pornography does not seem to be the kind of thing that
can subordinate.[3] Moreover, if pornography determines who women are and
what sex is, as MacKinnon suggests, then while her analysis "intends to empower women . . . [it] portray[s] women as victims—of rape, of sexual harassment, of pornography"—or so Valverde concludes.

In contrast, feminists might embrace the weaker empirical reading of the
claim that pornography is the subordination of women. To be precise, this
would require recasting it as "pornography contributes to the subordination
of women," which may suggest that this is not what MacKinnon and Andrea
Dworkin intend. However, feminists might be happier to work with the revised suggestion, if only because it appears to leave room for the possibility
that women can simultaneously work against some types of pornography—
namely, those types that appear to be causally implicated in violence against
women—and use pornography to map the contours of their own sexual de-

---

[3]See W. A. Parent, "A Second Look at Pornography and the Subordination of Women," in
Journal of Philosophy 87 (1990): 202–211; but compare Melinda Vadas, "A First Look at the
Pornography/Civil Rights Ordinance: Could Pornography Be the Subordination of Women,"
in *Journal of Philosophy* 84 (1987): 487–511. This difficulty is addressed in Part Four in Rae
Langton's "Speech Acts and Unspeakable Acts."

sires. Of course, the latter would require that we think about how our desires are formed by our social milieu.

Feminists such as MacKinnon and Andrea Dworkin clearly see the fight against pornography at the very center of feminist struggles. And this "privileging" of the problem of pornography is a fourth matter on which feminists diverge. Most feminists agree that some forms of pornography are problematic; however, many argue that women's subordination is not the result of pornography alone, but rather is to be explained in terms of a multiplicity of factors. This distinction between so-called monocausal and multicausal theories of women's oppression is much discussed in contemporary feminist theory. Both Willis and Valverde are skeptical of the strategic wisdom of identifying pornography as the single root of women's problems. Willis claims, "If *Hustler* were to disappear from the shelves tomorrow, I doubt that rape or wife-beating statistics would decline," thereby suggesting that there are other causes of violence against women that feminists might usefully address. Valverde is also critical of MacKinnon for overemphasizing "the *sexual* component of women's oppression, to the detriment of economic and social factors. . . ." Finally, a persistent worry is that, in the face of scarce resources, it might be a practical error to invest the bulk of feminist energies in combating pornography. Perhaps the situation of women would be more effectively improved by a combination of strategies.

It would be a mistake to infer that feminists have theorized about sex and sexuality only in the context of thinking about pornography. As Valverde notes, questions about sex have been central in the history of feminism. But certainly the topic of pornography has given rise to much intense debate between feminists, breaking old alliances and forging new and sometimes surprising ones. Pornography, it seems, cannot be divorced from sex or politics.

T H O M A S   W A U G H

Men's Pornography: Gay vs. Straight

Thomas Waugh has taught film, as well as gay and
interdisciplinary studies, in the Cinema Department of the
Concordia University Faculty of Fine Arts, Montreal, since
1976. His publications include the anthology "Show Us Life":
Towards a History and Aesthetics of the Committed
Documentary *(1984), and* Hard to Imagine: Gay Male
Eroticism in Photography and Film from Their Beginnings to
Stonewall *(1995), as well as articles in many periodicals and*
anthologies.

Introduction: Labels and Red Herrings

Taking part in a debate about pornography, I am painfully aware of contradictions involved in my position as a person to whom a great many compromising labels may be applied (in alphabetical order: academic, anti-patriarchal, Canadian, cinephile, contributor-to-a-magazine-on-trial-for-obscenity, cyclist, gay, male, socialist, teacher, thirty-five, unattached, vanilla-sexual, wasp, etc.).

I belong to a cultural and political context—the urban gay male community/ies—in which dirty pictures have a hard-won centrality, both historically and at present. I am also an individual consumer: I couldn't begin to describe

Source: Tom Waugh, "Men's Pornography: Gay vs. Straight." *Jump Cut* 30 (Spring 1985):
30–36. Reprinted by permission.

the importance in my own political/personal growth of the erotic components in the work of Baldwin, Genet, Pasolini, Warhol/Morrissey,
Burroughs, Michelangelo, and even Gore Vidal (to begin with the most respectable list), not to mention *Tomorrow's Man* (the crypto-gay physique
magazine I discovered on the sports rack of the local newsstand as a trembling teenager in Presbyterian Ontario in the mid sixties), and *Straight to
Hell* (the underground folk-raunch magazine of readers' narratives I discovered as a trembling grad student in the early seventies, when I was wonder-
ing whether marching in Gay Pride could blow my comprehensives).

How then am I to express my solidarity in words and actions with
women's rightful denunciations of pornography as an instrument of anti-
feminist backlash, of the usurpation by industrial capitalism of the private
sexual sphere, of the merchandising and degradation of women's bodies, of
the incitement to rape and violence against women? Can I do so without ap-
ing the standard liberal male guilt-trip or its "we're oppressed and alienated
too" refrain? without echoing the occasional anti-feminist tirades in the gay
press by beleaguered men who think they see women lining up alongside the
cops? Can I do so while insisting that sexual liberation is still an essential
component of political liberation and that erotica has a rightful, even indispensable, place in the culture and politics of sexual liberation—gay, lesbian,
feminist, and yes, straight-male?

Is it enough for me to repeat that anti-woman pornography, a symptom,
can only be eradicated by a fundamental transformation of society along
feminist-socialist lines? And [is it enough] that, in the meantime, if I had
time, I could support various proposed liberal stopgap measures by the bourgeois state towards curbing pornography's worst social effects, that is, *measures short of obscenity provisions in criminal codes,* such as: the use of labor
and criminal codes to halt child exploitation, forced labor, non-consensual
sexual relations and the incitement of violence; the regulation of an above-
ground sex industry by means of unionization, taxation, labor codes, public
visibility restrictions, in short, the kind of state intervention that regulates
tobacco and alcohol (even though this kind of regulation has led in France to
a kind of de facto suppression of gay culture)[?] I also obviously support
non-state strategies of consumer resistance like boycotts and education, such
as those led around "non-pornographic" films such as *Cruising, Windows,*
and *Dressed To Kill* in which I have participated.

Censorship is both a red herring and a real issue, and often a means of
halting debate. . . . For me, a gay man struggling against continuing, in fact
escalated, censorship of gay newspapers and films, and in the Canadian context, resisting the most ferocious police suppression of our culture in any
Western society, censorship is a real issue. Even though many of the most visible anti-porn activists have repeatedly renounced legal sanctions against pornography and some have stressed the necessity of gay-lesbian rights
education as part of the anti-porn discourse, many mainstream spokespeople

are not so careful. As just one example, in 1978, the year that *The Body Politic,* the Canadian national gay-lesbian paper, began its still ongoing struggle to survive the obscenity courts, Canadian feminist spokespeople testified before a parliamentary committee and saw their proposals for revision of obscenity statutes (to provide for violence) manipulated and appropriated by homophobic liberals and the New Right alike.[1] The coincidence may or may not be only symbolic, but we don't have the time to wonder. In 1980, the National Organization of Women in the U.S. resolved that pornography is not a genuine lesbian-gay rights issue, nor are pedophilia, sadomasochism, and public sexuality (all of which overlap with the issues of pornography). All four of these issues have been central concerns within the gay community/ies since Stonewall, and favorite pretexts for our persecution. But some feminists, straight and lesbian alike, have tended to regard them as areas where we are struggling merely to exercise our full patriarchal privileges as men (a view that has sometimes been partly justified). Within the last few years, the lesbian-feminist community has learned not only that it will not be able to resolve these issues away but also that they are of utmost pertinence to feminism and lesbian liberation, and furthermore, that (who ever would have thought?) the interests of gay men and feminists on these issues are not necessarily reconcilable. The so-called choice between censorship and pornography, art and life, is falsely formulated: women's right to defend themselves against patriarchal violence and the right of women and sexual minorities to full cultural, sexual, and political expression, are allied rights, both threatened in the current conjuncture. To prioritize or rank them on our agenda greatly damages the anti-patriarchal movement (just as reproductive rights must not have less priority on the agenda than lesbian rights or vice versa).

The recent debate on sexuality within the feminist community, in the headlines of the alternative media since the *Heresies* sex issue, has already had some input from the gay men's movement. In all modesty, anti-patriarchal gay men still have an important contribution to make. It may be no accident that some of the first utterances of the new feminist sexual outlaws appeared in gay newspapers (with varying degrees of lesbian input, from a little (*The Advocate*), to some (*The Body Politic*), to tons (*Gay Community News*)). Gay men were struck from the beginning by how much the new discourse for women's pleasure echoed but went further than the discourse of early gay liberation (in the days when gay groups used to call themselves the Gay Liberation Front instead of the National Task Force), profiting directly from two decades of feminist debate. Of course the anti-porn right saw our satisfaction as patronizing and the use of our media as conspiratorial:

> The lesbian S & M [*sic*] movement is a growing and organized one, especially in San Francisco. One of the leaders, Pat Califia, who has a slave, wrote the article, "The New Puritans," which was published in

The Advocate. One of her arguments is that she doesn't want anyone taking her fist fucking magazines away from her. I think it is very interesting to note that most articles on this appear in primarily gay male publications. It seems to make a lot of sense since gay men tend to like porn, have a stake in it, and reinforce these attitudes to their advantage. This is again our colonization, women being taken over by gay men instead of straight men.[2]

. . . I would like to explore in this article our "stake" in porn, to sketch some of the contours of our contribution to the debate on sexuality and porn. Specifically, I would like to situate gay male pornography in relation to straight male pornography in terms of its uniquely contradictory mixture of progressive and reactionary characteristics in its relation of production, exhibition, consumption and representation. Far from wishing to offer an apologetics for gay porn against homophobic dismissals from within the women movements, both from the NOW center and the WAP right (I realize that my refutation of such dismissals is open to being misread as defensiveness, an unnecessary attitude I may not be wholly successful in avoiding), I feel that an objective analysis of gay pornography will clarify and expand many of the terms of the current debate.

The following "topographical" chart is largely contemporary in its focus, that is, post-sixties, though reference is made to the historical evolution of gay pornography particularly since the establishment of embryonic modern-day gay ghettos following World War II (I also refer here and there to classical stag movies). My main object is a relatively loose comparison of gay male pornography to straight male pornography, referring wherever relevant to its major product divisions: theatrical films; hardcore and softcore; rental or mail-order video; "arcade"/adult bookstore materials, mostly film loops and hardcore magazines; mail-order films and photographic sets (beefcake); glossy mass-distribution *Playboy*-imitation magazines like *Blueboy*; and finally, porn that may be called "artisanal," amateur or "folk," both written and visual, e.g., *Straight to Hell*. (Obviously these categories sometimes overlap, as with video versions of theatrical films, and some exclusions are arbitrary— "live" performances, written materials except for the artisanal STH, and ancillary branches of the industry like gadgets.)

The comparison is organized in terms of relations of production (making), exhibition (showing), consumption (looking), and representation (depiction). Obviously, this chart, with its illustrations and appendages, is a work-in-progress, and I welcome any corrections or additions; it may reflect also a certain unavoidable bias and a greater expertise in the left-hand column which readers are asked to tolerate. On the sidelines, I also offer a brief reflection trying to connect the feminist conception of patriarchal public space to the gay ghetto and its pornographic cultural form. . . .

Men's Pornography, Gay vs. Straight: A Topographical Comparison

RELATIONS OF PRODUCTION

Gay Male Pornography

—gay male producer employs gay male models

—small-scale industrial or artisanal production and distribution base for all commercial categories, reputedly some mafia presence in theatrical films

—producer control, non-union employees paid low flat rate, even for "stars", stigma usually prevents career crossover for performers

—theatrical industry stagnant since mid-seventies with only a few dozen showcases; mail-order business strong; growth only in video area; market seems saturated in present political situation

—small capital outlay and modest profits in theatres, with budgets never exceeding $80,000 for Joe Gage's features (*L.A. Tool and Die*), all in 16mm; according to Gage, theatrical market allows only one or two major films a year; reruns endemic

—highly developed star system (Richard Locke, Al Parker), and brand-name auteurs (Toby Ross, Joe Gage), especially in theatrical features; also brand-name mail-order houses (Colt, Falcon)

—overlapping of porno constituency with gay community at large, side-by-side existence within the ghetto: Artie Bressan has made political documentary, porn features, and a legit feature; porn ads appear alongside feminist women's ad in *Gay Community News*, "danglie"* moghul Pat Rocco sang in the Metropolitan Community Church choir; theatrical star Richard Locke currently campaigning for AIDS research

Straight Male Pornography

—straight male producer employs female models

—large-scale industrial apparatus for production and distribution with lots of small-scale competition; pervasive presence of mafia and other multinationals, links to other branches of sex industry

—producer control, mostly non-union employees with low flat-rate; some performers in "legit" areas receive high rewards and occasional career crossover, e.g. Sylvia Kristel, Pets of the Year, etc.

—still apparently a growth industry with 1000's of theatrical outlets and video boom, expansion continues into "legit" films (*Lady Chatterley's Lover*) and spinoff industries

—huge capital outlays relatively common, especially in pseudo-legit area, e.g. *Caligula*, where films can cross over out of the combat-zone market; huge profits

—wide range of star and auteur recognition in legit softcore films and in "prestige" hardcore features

—no straight equivalent; straight porn has no self-defined constituency or community base other than the straight male gender caste, extending across class, race and zoning divisions

—straight equivalent is marginal or industry adjunct, e.g. "Playboy Forum," advice columns, *Hustler* photos of readers' partners, swingers' newletters, cable TV . . .

—artistic avant-garde: less important historical role (e.g. *Geography of the Body*, Brakhage's late-fifties fuck films); current role negligible, though Michael Snow *has* been censored in Toronto

Straight Male Pornography

—same, straight equivalent even more pervasive, e.g. pay TV, cable

—no equivalent: theatrical exhibition space is zone of terror for unaccompanied female potential partners, except for sex industry workers

*danglie: a short-lived porno genre of the late sixties. after court decisions allowing nudity but before the hardcore explosion: hyper-kinetic but flaccid nude males facing camera and doing a lot of jumping up and down

—flourishing presence of non-industrial erotica (i.e. amateur, folk, artisanal), e.g. readers' narratives in *Straight to Hell*, classified ads culture, home movies, amateur beefcake, extension of pre-ghetto underground culture

—artistic avant-garde: historically an important role as producer of gay erotica in pre-liberation era (police harassed Kenneth Anger and beefcake studios equally); currently a much diminished but still visible role, e.g. Curt McDowell; Barbara Hammer as source of lesbian erotica

RELATIONS OF EXHIBITION

Gay Male Pornography

—commoditization of private/individual sexual space (bedside stroke mags, home video); telephone sex services a recent extension

—theatrical, arcade and bookstore space as social terrain, meeting place and setting for sex

(continued)

Men's Pornography, Gay vs. Straight: A Topographical Comparison (continued)

RELATIONS OF EXHIBITION (continued)

Gay Male Pornography

—exhibition space as liberated zone, extension of the gay ghetto, as gay refuge from heterosexist territory; favored space for anonymous contacts and for individuals who are dysfunctional in bars and saunas

—huge mail-order and rental video market is much more important than theatrical market; important glossy magazine industry. Strongest market away from gay ghettos.

—in isolated areas, straight theatres and adult bookstores service gay community; in New York and elsewhere, cheap straight theatres service poor and minority gays

—porno theatres restricted to ghettos and combat-zones; glossies are mass distributed but far less accessible than *Penthouse*

Straight Male Pornography

—no real equivalent in contemporary context: combat zone is extension of straight male domain. Remote equivalent to gay situation might be seen in straight male's escape from family, respectability, and suburbia. Some women have argued for similar function for women: Lisa Orlando (pornography as "first glimpse of freedom," aid in "adolescent search for validation and pleasure and sexual autonomy"); Ellen Willis (porn as "protest against the repression of nonmarital, nonprocreative sex . . . resistance to a culture that would allow women no sexual pleasure at all"); Deirdre English (porn district as "small zone of sexual freedom").[a]

—straight equivalent to mail-order market has all but disappeared except for specialty areas, e.g. fetish, SM; glossies are huge multi-national industry; video is eclipsing theatrical exhibition

—no equivalent

—pervasiveness and respectability of straight male theatres; shopping-center and neighborhood outlets in addition to combat zones; glossies omnipresent, iconography having long since seeped into popular culture and advertising

RELATIONS OF CONSUMPTION

Gay Male Pornography

—privatized, individual masturbation aid, in all categories, including theatrical and arcade

—accessory to sexual relations between strangers and between familiars; theatres and arcades are lively meeting and sex places, saunas often have film or video rooms

—the spectator's positions in relation to the representations are open and in flux. These include: non-viewing with the images functioning as background visual muzak; direct unmediated look at image-object, especially in solo-jerk films; look mediated by narrative—spectator's position fluctuates or is simultaneously multiple, among different characters and types, roles, etc. Spectator's identificatory entry into the narrative is not predetermined by gender divisions; mise-en-scene does not privilege individual roles, top or bottom, inserter or insertee, in any systematic way

Straight Male Pornography

—same

—only rarely a similar phenomenon (motel movies?); probable use as accessory to prostitution?

—spectator's position tends to be rigidly gender-determined; in all categories, straight male spectator looks at female image-object, *without* mediation of straight male narrative surrogates (*Penthouse* centerfolds) or *with* (narrative features). Mise-en-scene privileges women's roles and visibility, i.e. as insertee, whether active/top or passive/bottom. This is why closeup fellatio scenes (cock as prop) are far more common than male–female cunnilingus (a gynephobic taboo also operates here). Male figure has far less visual weight even in films headlining male stars such as Harry Reems. In hardcore, the privileging of women's roles is more emphatic than in classy/crossover softcore (e.g. *Private Lessons, Lady Chatterley's Lover*) because of strong narrative lines and appeal to women spectators (still such privileged male personae tend not to have cocks). (For further research: am I wrong in assuming that straight men's fantasies never flirt with forbidden corners of the text? Do they never project on/identify with the female roles? I'm afraid to ask any.)

(continued)

Men's Pornography, Gay vs. Straight: A Topographical Comparison (continued)

RELATIONS OF CONSUMPTION *(continued)*

Gay Male Pornography

—gay male spectator habitually invited to identify narratively with victimization and/or penetration of the Self, i.e. of gay male, often by straight male. Eroticization of victimization or submission is most common in noncommercial porn, e.g. of 110 randomly chosen *Straight to Hell* anecdotes, 30 eroticized active role on the part of the narrator, 33 were submissive or victimized, 43 were both or interchangeable

—gay porn functions as progressive, educative or ideological (consciousness-raising) force, as challenge to self-oppression, the closet and isolation (Oklahoma is reputedly the strongest mail-order market); gay porn often serves as isolated teenager's first link to community

—gay porn functions as potential regressive force, valorizing sexism, looks-ism, size-ism, racism, ageism and so on, as well as violent behaviors; reinforces the closet by providing anonymous, impersonal outlets? legitimizes straight-identified self-oppression (of 110 STH anecdotes, 43 valorized straight-defined men as erotic object)?

Straight Male Pornography

—straight male spectator habitually invited to identify narratively with victimizer, to eroticize victimization of the Other (woman-object), only rarely of the Self, as in the specialty dominatrix subgenre (*Ilsa, Tigress of Siberia*). (Distinction must be made between passive fantasy where narrative subject is in control (almost all fellatio scenes in het porn) and submissive fantasy where narrative object is controlled or victimized, extremely rare in mainstream het porn).

—no strict equivalent; historically stag movies had a loosely parallel function in sex-repressive society, as instruction and initiation for the dominant gender/sexual-orientation caste; in traditional Japanese society, pillowbooks had an important and respectable educative function

—straight porn can/does legitimize phallocentric, gynephobic, alienated, and violent attitudes and behavior; the "throwaway" woman

RELATIONS OF REPRESENTATION: DEPICTED SEXUAL PRACTICES

Gay Male Pornography

—gay men fuck and suck and are fucked and sucked, etc., in a wide range of combinations and roles not determined by gender; sometimes roles are defined by sexual practice, body type, age, class, race, or by the enunciation of sexual orientation (office employee short of cash for date with girl friend fucks gay boss for money), but just as often this is not so

—no equivalent to straight convention of lesbian sex, except perhaps relations among men narratively defined as "straight"

—in longer films, overall structure is as often purely episodic as climactic, e.g. J. Brian's *First Time Around* is a narrative daisy chain (A fucks with B fucks with C fucks with D fucks with A)

—within individual sequences, usually a climactic escalation of sexual practices, i.e. fucking after sucking, with staggered ejaculations of all participants as a drawn-out climax; rigid convention of external ejaculations of all participants as a drawn-out climax; rigid convention of external ejaculation often followed by ingestion of semen. Same for loops and short films.

—taboos: on male-female sex (Joe Gage's use of het coupling to establish straightness of a character is exception that proves the rule); on effeminacy, age, obesity, and drag (except in specialty materials or non-sexual roles, e.g. a drag queen in Wakefield Poole's *Bijou* leads butch construction worker down into labyrinthine sexual underworld)

Straight Male Pornography

—straight man (two or more men are less common because of rigid taboo on intermale sexuality) fucks and is sucked by one or more women in a more limited gender-defined range of roles and combinations, e.g. women frequently are active partners (i.e. aggressive fellators) as well as passive insertees, but the range of roles is quite rigidly prescribed. Would non-sexist hetero porn for men or women have the role-flexibility of much of gay porn?

—relations between women a routine formula, usually as prelude to entry of phallus

—features tend more often to be linear or climactic in narrative structure

—roughly the same with ejaculation coda more compressed because of scarcity of ejaculators (the gay taboo), and limited positions; straight men come outside too. Same for loops and shorts.

—taboos: on intermale sex; also on age, obesity, deviation from perceived ideals of femininity and beauty, etc.

(continued)

Men's Pornography, Gay vs. Straight: A Topographical Comparison (continued)

RELATIONS OF REPRESENTATION: DEPICTED SEXUAL PRACTICES *(continued)*

Gay Male Pornography

—in loops or short films, narrative is often solo performance, masturbation or just posing which can be either or both active (tense, upright) and/or passive (supine, exposed, languid, available). Same conventions in glossy centerfolds or photo-spreads. Solo performance materials establish eye contact with spectator.

—sexual practices stigmatized and often technically illegal are standard routine component in all categories: porn shows what legit media deny, suppress and stigmatize

—violence and rape, consensual and non-consensual, among gay men or perpetrated by characters defined as straight, is not uncommon

Straight Male Pornography

—same solo-stroke or posing conventions, except that poses are exclusively passive (supine, spread, seated, squatted, orifices offered, etc.). Same eye-contact conventions.

—illegal and stigmatized practices (other than violence) only in fringe subgenres such as kiddie-porn or scat, etc.; het porn shows what legit media imply, simulate, or present "tastefully"

—violence and rape is common, consensual and non-consensual, perpetrated on women by straight men, rarely vice versa except in dominatrix subgenre; in some respectable crypto-porn, violence is perpetrated by gay man or transsexual-transvestite, e.g. *Looking for Mr. Goodbar, Dressed to Kill*

RELATIONS OF REPRESENTATION: COMMON NARRATIVE FORMULAE

Gay Male Pornography

—5 common elements (Kathleen Barry's list quoted from Kronhausen can be applied):

—seduction (often of straight man)

—profanation (*Straight to Hell* is full of clerical motifs, but in post-clerical society the more common rendition is simple anti-authority—coach rims star athlete, sailor fucks officer)

Straight Male Pornography

—these 5 elements are still basic to much straight male narrative porn, though capitalist competition has tended to expand the repertory. Profanation is less important, nuns having all but disappeared. Insatiable nymphomaniac seems to be a new formula, whether comic (*Deep Throat*) or moralistic (*Devil and Miss Jones*).

—incest (*Straight to Hell* is full of father and older brother fantasies; less omnipresent in commercial porn but still very common)

—permissive-seductive parent (one film, title forgotten, depicts furtive father coming out at same time as teenage sons)

—defloration (in gay porn one version of this is initiation, another is the converse of the term—*being* deflowered)

—element unique to gay porn is "coming out," gay male assumption of gay identity and sexual practice; shedding of straight male identity or conversion of straight male can be part of this (Joe Gage's *Kansas City Trucking Company*)

—intra-narrative voyeur or photographer is common

—doctor or sex researcher as narrative mediator

—straight-identified institutional setting, e.g. ranch, hospital, school, military, construction site (of 110 STH anecdotes, 30 are situated in this way); military settings especially common

—sex-for-pay, especially straight hustlers and rough trade

—subversive humor (penile salute from Marines uniform in Jean-Claude von Italie's *American Cream*)

—back-to-nature, fucking in the forest or posing in the desert

—remote equivalent without the distinct ideological tenor might be woman's realization of her true desire (*Emmanuelle, Deep Throat*) or young male protagonist's assumption of his patriarchal sexual prerogatives (mostly in softcore such as *Private Lessons, Porky's* or *Spring Break*). Conversion formulae also present: lesbian is often converted by a good fuck; in *Roommates*, gay man is similarly converted.

—same

—same

—straight male interest in all-women institutions such as convents and brothels is related but has different ideological tenor and is now less common

—same, especially brothels, though now less common than in classical stag films; recent twist is suburban housewife who has sex to pay the bills

—humor not so evident, either prurient (guttural clitoris in *Deep Throat*) or flat (*Gone with the Wind*-style chorus-line rape production number in porno musical *Blond Ambition*)

—common in softcore (*Emmanuelle, Lady Chatterley*), less so in hardcore. Cheesecake, unlike beefcake, is usually interior.

(continued)

Men's Pornography, Gay vs. Straight: A Topographical Comparison (continued)

RELATIONS OF REPRESENTATION: COMMON NARRATIVE FORMULAE (continued)

Gay Male Pornography

—documentary gimmick, e.g. Peter de Rome's Super 8 sex on the subway, or location shooting and nonprofessional actors in Toby Ross's *Boys of the Slums* with acne and failed erections

—public sexuality a common element, e.g. glory holes of *Taxi Zum Klo* a frequent formula, 24 of 110 STH anecdotes take place in toilets and 38 in other public spaces such as parks, cars, and rest stops

—violence/rape as vengeance (at least one example, Joe Gage's *Heatstrokes*)

—rape of unconscious (Curt McDowell's *Nudes*) or of bound victim. Gang rape, passive fantasies of rape are common in STH, often with straight perpetrators

—rape victim comes to like it

—SM, fisting, gadgets, fetishes (boots most common, followed by jock straps: rapid escalation of these motifs in seventies hardcore has apparently leveled off; a recurring minor presence in mainstream glossies (*Blueboy*), dominant in other specialized mags (*Drum* the most common SM glossy)

Straight Male Pornography

—not common; exceptions include French feature on porn star *Exhibition*, or Vietnam brothel sequence of *Hearts and Minds*

—no straight equivalent since straight public sexuality is accepted social norm

—violence/rape as vengeance relatively common e.g. Russ Meyer's *Vixen*; an exception is *Those Naughty Victorians* where the rapist-protagonist is raped himself at the end by a (black) assailant hired by his earlier victims

—same (woman hitchhiker trapped by car window and raped from behind); gang rape relatively less common because of intermale taboo

—extremely common in legit media as softcore and hardcore films

—SM motifs more and more common in mainstream glossies (*Hustler*) as well as stable minority proportion of hardcore magazines, arcade materials and films; some osmosis of iconography into legit media, punk culture, high fashion, etc. Women usually bottom (e.g. *Swept Away . . .*, *The Night Porter*) but not always (*Maitresse*).

(continued)

—take-offs of legit media, especially with film titles, e.g. *Last Tango in Hollywood*

—racial difference as narrative angle: rare in hardcore features where nonwhite men often appear without racial enunciation. Subgenre of beefcake and hardcore mags specializing in racial difference presumably for white clientele (but question of race of producers and consumers is for future research), e.g. "Boys of Puerto Rico." 22 of 110 STH anecdotes had some kind of racial enunciation, frequently with black narrator.

—class enunciation relatively common, e.g. *Boys of the Slums*, blue-collar fantasies are omnipresent

—cock-size narrative gimmicks constructed around certain stars and in titles, e.g. *The Big Surprise*

—as a general rule, theatrical films have a more important narrative content than straight equivalents (Wakefield Poole's *Bijou* flopped because it was criticized for "too much story")

—same

—several racist subgenres of hardcore and softcore films and other categories where women and men are enunciated racially, e.g. "mixed combos," dozens of Thai *Emmanuelle*-spinoffs. Mainstream glossies are very white.

—probably less explicit, though no less prevalent through implicit and documentary codes, especially in cheaper mags and films. Maids are much less common than in classical and European films, often replaced now by secretary fantasies.

—same with breasts (e.g. Russ Meyer) and sometimes cocks

—narrative content relatively less important

Men's Pornography, Gay vs. Straight: A Topographical Comparison (continued)

RELATIONS OF REPRESENTATION: EXTRACTING SOME IDEOLOGICAL ESSENCES

Gay Male Pornography

—phallus obsession, the closeup a metaphor of corporal fragmentation and alienation, phallocentrism however not an explicit text in this fantasy universe where people not divided according to presence or absence of cock—everyone has one

—self-hatred, gay eroticization of victimization of self (some STH anecdotes eroticize abusive homophobic "dirty talk")

—racism: third world beefcake constructs spectator—object relation that is exact parallel of racist organization of society

—ideology of gay liberation: sex-positive attitudes, valorization of "coming out," acceptance of gay identity and community, challenge to masculinism; sex industry as economic base of autonomous, prosperous ghetto and therefore of political clout

—ideology of the closet: valorization of straight image reflect internalized homophobia, self-oppression

Straight Male Pornography

—phallocentrism: women as universally available caterers to pleasure of phallus

—women-hatred: women as deserving and willing victims, whose victimization is eroticized

—racism: nonwhite women as exaggeratedly sexual slaves, nonwhite men as instrument of patriarchal revenge

—ideology of sexual liberation? view of straight porn as therapeutic social safety valve, as vehicle of sex-positive values, espoused by straight male apologists and profiteers, by some social scientists, by some women pro-sex or libertarian feminists

—closest equivalent of self-oppression here is not a straight male pornography, which has no significant female audience, but women's romance pulp (Harlequins); men's lib line emphasizes straight male porn's oppression of men and well as of women

TOWARDS A SUMMARY: PORN AS INDEX/ECHO/PROP OF POLITICAL CONTEXT

Gay Male Pornography

PLUS—unlike straight male porn, gay porn does not directly and systematically replicate the heterosexist patriarchal order in its relations of production, exhibition, consumption, or representation. Kathleen Barry's assertion "Homosexual pornography acts out the same dominant and subordinate roles of heterosexual pornography,"[b] cannot be shown to be true of any of these terms. Produced by, depicting, and consumed exclusively by gay men, the fantasy universe of gay porn resembles the gay ghetto in its hermeticism as well as in its contradictory mix of progressive and regressive values, in its occupancy of a defensible enclave within heterosexist society. It subverts the patriarchal order by challenging masculinist values, providing a protected space for nonconformist non-reproductive and non-familial sexuality, encouraging many sex-positive values and declaring the dignity of gay people.

MINUS—at the same time, the ghetto is part of as well as separate from heterosexist society. The patriarchal privilege of male sexual expression and occupancy of public space is perpetuated. The patriarch is propped up equally by the reinforcement of the gay male spectator's self-oppression, by his ghettoization. Finally, capitalism's usurpation and commoditization of the private sphere is extended not threatened by gay commercial porn.

Straight Male Pornography

PLUS—porn as "liberated zone," social safety valve, as visualization of women's desire, as vehicle of the sexual revolution?

MINUS—gender-defined sexual roles and power imbalances, both within the narrative (woman as insertee, active or passive, woman as victim, woman as fetishized object of the camera) and outside of the narrative (woman as spectator), replicate the power relations of patriarchal capitalism and are thereby both its symptom and its reinforcement

---

[a] Lisa Orlando, "Bad Girls and 'Good' Politics," *Village Voice* (*Literary Supplement*), December 1982, p. 16; Ellen Willis, "Who Is a Feminist? A Letter to Robin Morgan," *ibid.* p. 17; Deirdre English, "Talking Sex: A Conversation on Sexuality and Feminism" (with Amber Hollibaugh and Gayle Rubin), *Socialist Review*, No. 58, July/Aug. 1981, p. 51.
[b] Kathleen Barry, *Female Sexual Slavery* (New York, 1979), p. 207.

A Note on Definitions

Much of the debate has been a war of definitions, of distinctions between sexist pornography and non-sexist erotica, between my art and your smut, and so on. All such definitions tend to be, for reasons of semantics, ideological rather than scientific. This is true whether explicitly so (as in any definition based on values, inherent artistic merit, or political or educational effectivity), or by implication, that is, expressed as formal/aesthetic, legalistic, physiological (Auden defined pornographic as anything that gave him an erection), historical, sociological or commercial (the definitions of pornographers themselves). I am not the first to insist that any advance in the debate must acknowledge all of the definitions currently in play since these definitions themselves are weapons in the ongoing struggle.

I will not add to the confusion by proposing a new definition (except insofar as the above caveat and a refusal to distinguish between erotica and pornography constitute a definition), since for gay people the definition imposed by police, censors and courts at any given point will always be the determining one.

However, since discussion of pornography is becoming increasingly acrimonious and difficult, and since misunderstandings are already being translated into social and legal practice, I will make a few prescriptions. Participants in the debate must situate themselves in relation to the definitions struggle and must specify exactly what images or texts they are referring to and exactly what social remedies they are proposing, if any.

This precision is indispensable in avoiding co-optation by the book-banners, the homophobes and the Moral Majority, who have gotten so far by blurred distinctions and misleading generalizations. Next, every exclusively single-issue intervention is a step backwards: connections must be established at every point between the porn debate and the other issues of the anti-patriarchal struggle, especially reproductive rights, sex education, and lesbian-gay rights. I would go even further to say that every comprehensive intervention on pornography must acknowledge the existence of gay male pornography. To pass over the stacks of *Blueboy* lined up beside *Penthouse* is either homophobic (as is the case of the National Film Board of Canada's *Not A Love Story*) or misguided liberalism, misguided even if the evasion arises out of solidarity with gay people. General propositions about pornography that do not apply to pornography are inadmissible (for example, does "All pornography degrades women"[3] apply to gay male pornography? if so, how? if not, why not?). Progressive gay men have nothing to fear from an open and non-homophobic confrontation with gay pornography, nor from our own self-critical confrontation with the abuses of pornography within our community.

Finally, the following distinctions are essential to any meaningful discussion: between pornography and violent pornography, between consent and coercion, between consensual power play (SM) and violence, between images and actions, between individual sexual practices and collective sexual politics. This latter distinction is crucial. The personal may be political, but there is no such thing as a politically correct individual sexuality. By this I mean that we must support the full rights of sexual outlaws to act out their individual (consensual) desires, whether sadomasochists or drag queens or Phyllis Schlafly. Andrea Dworkin's statement that all fucking is inherently sadistic discredits her other work, some of which is useful. Specific sexual practices as depicted in a given image do not necessarily coincide with relations of exploitation or domination nor with any other power relation. A man or a woman portrayed as getting fucked cannot automatically be seen as a victim; gay porn in particular, and of course gay sexuality in general, undermines the widespread assumption that penetration in itself is an act of political oppression. A sexual act or representation acquires ideological tenor only through its personal, social, narrative, iconographic, or larger political context.

The Ghetto: A Note on Space

One way of looking at the evolution of the gay movement since World War II is as the growth of our claims to space. Our first claim was to the inviolability of our private space (the state has no place in the bedrooms of the nation, said Trudeau, when he decriminalized consensual sodomy between two adults in 1969—a reform only a minority of American states have followed). Our next claim was for the inviolability of the ghetto, our gathering places and neighborhoods. Our final claim was full open access to all public space of our society, and in fact, many of us insisted, to alter the terms of that society. Our claim to our media and to our culture, including our pornography, is part of all three of these claims to space.

When we talk this over with our feminist allies, we often fail to strike a sympathetic chord. The space that we have been demanding is only the space we have been conditioned to expect as men in patriarchal society, space that had been only partly withheld because we suck cock. Women have not yet achieved access to that space, either literally in terms of public territory, or metaphorically in terms of media of cultural, sexual, and political expression. In short, gay pornography profits from and aspires to the institutionalized presence of patriarchal power built on the absence/silence of women, and is thus complicit in the oppression of women.

This is true and it hurts. But it's not all of the truth. Firstly, our claims to space, private, ghetto or public, have not been achieved except incompletely and provisionally, always subject to invasion and revocation. Ghettoized spaces, as women have always sensed in their kitchens and church basements and offices, are no substitute for autonomous political space; they are more like enclaves of self-defense and accommodation. Our pornography, in fact, reflects the recognition of this insufficiency: of the 110 STH anecdotes I mention elsewhere, only 8 take place in ghetto space (saunas, discos, backrooms, cinemas), whereas about 40 take place in our private homes and the rest all take place in non-ghetto public space. Our greatest visibility may be in the ghetto, but our fantasies and our everyday lives are elsewhere.

Pornography has become one of our privileged cultural forms, the expression of that quality for which we are stigmatized, queerbashed, fired, evicted, jailed, hospitalized, electroshocked, disinherited, raped in prison, refused at the U.S. border, silenced, and ghettoized—that quality being our sexuality. Our pornography is shaped both by the oppression told by my long chain of participles and by our conditioning as men in patriarchy. We must direct our claim to our pornographic culture, not towards occupying our share of patriarchal space, but towards shattering that space, transforming it.

On Getting Fucked

Richard Dyer's assertion . . . about the dominance of heterosexist modes of sexuality in gay porn narratives needs some qualification:

> . . . there seems to be no evidence that in the predominant form of how we represent our sexuality to ourselves (in gay porn) we in any way break from the norms of male sexuality . . . the narrative is never organized around the desire to be fucked, but around the desire to ejaculate (whether or not following from anal intercourse). Thus although at the level of public representation, gay men may be thought of as deviant and disruptive of masculine norms because we assert the pleasures of being fucked and the eroticism of the anus, in our pornography this takes a back seat.[4]

This may be true of many or even most theatrical films (though I think it requires further research—certainly lots of individual sequences I remember contradict this), however passive penetration fantasies are extremely common as narrative principles in many non-commercial films and anecdotes I have encountered (as are fellatio fantasies, active or passive, which do not seem to be organized around the narrator's ejaculation). Perhaps the non-commercial or artisanal origin of the examples that come to mind says more about the porn industry than our erotic culture as an audience, but that remains to be seen. What does a passive penetration fantasy look or sound like? This question is not only of academic interest. The active penetration fantasy is such a dominant one in the straight male porn industry and in patriarchal culture in general, that, in looking for alternatives, we should analyze the other side of the coin. I've talked about this with some women who, like many gay men and perhaps some straight men, are aware of and often disturbed by fantasies of passive penetration, of submission, even of rape. . . .

Gays and the Pro-Pornography Movement: Having the Hots for Sex Discrimination

John Stoltenberg is a speaker, writer, and activist. He is the author of Refusing to Be a Man: Essays on Sex and Justice *(1989) and* The End of Manhood: A Book for Men of Conscience *(1993).*

The World of Gay Male Sex Films

The typical gay male sex film is comprised of explicit sex scenes, frequently between strangers, often with a sound track consisting solely of music and dubbed-in groans. During these sex scenes there is almost always an erect penis filling the screen. If the camera cuts away from the penis, the camera will be back within seconds. Scenes are set up so that closeups of penises and what they are doing and what is happening to them show off to best advantage. Most of the closeups of penises are of penises fucking in and out of asses and mouths, being blown or being jacked off. A penis that is not erect, not being pumped up, not in action, just there feeling pretty good, is rarely to be seen: You wouldn't know it was feeling if it wasn't in action; and in the world of gay male sex films, penises do not otherwise feel anything.

Curiously, there is a great deal of repression of affect in gay male sex films—a studied impassivity that goes beyond amateur acting. The blankness of the faces in what is ostensibly the fever pitch of passion suggests an ners know when someone gets killed from something that looks a lot like extreme S/M; there are boys who have been molested, gay men who have been battered and raped in sexual relationships. Nevertheless, there is a sexiness in subordination, and its sexiness for gay men in particular has a lot to do with the fact that subordination in sex helps resolve a misogynist struggle to cling to male supremacy. For a gay man who wants to have that kind of identity—a femiphobic sexual connection with other men—subordinating someone helps reinforce during the time of sex his tenuous connection to an idea of manhood that only exists because it exists over and against women. It works—until it doesn't work. It tends to leave you rather addicted to forms of passion that exclude compassion, and it can lead very easily to forms of restraint and bondage, control-and-power head trips, and physical abuse that can leave someone in the relationship feeling very much unsafe, very unwhole, very unequal, and very ripped off.

Consider in this context the current political strategy to achieve social acceptability for queers loving queers. We cannot chip away at this thing called homophobia—through laws and litigation and luncheons and so on—without going to the root of the sex-class system, without dismantling the power structure of men over women, which is an *eroticized* power structure. So long as that structure stays in place, homophobia will stay put too, because homophobia is necessary to the maintenance of men's power over women. The system of male supremacy can't tolerate queerness; it will never tolerate queerness. It needs the hatred of women and of queerness in order to prevail, in order to keep men doing to women what men are supposed to do to women.

The system of gender polarity requires that people with penises treat people without as objects, as things, as empty gaping vessels waiting to be filled with turgid maleness, if necessary by force. Homophobia is, in part, how the system punishes those whose object choice is deviant. Homophobia keeps women the targets. Homophobia assures a level of safety, selfhood, self-respect, and social power to men who sexually objectify correctly. Those of us who are queer cannot fully appreciate our precarious situation without understanding precisely where we stand in male supremacy. And our situation will not change until the system of male supremacy ends. A political movement trying to erode homophobia while leaving male supremacy and misogyny in place won't work. Gay liberation without sexual justice can't possibly happen. Gay rights without women's rights is a male-supremacist reform.

The Eroticization of Sex Discrimination

Sex discrimination has been culturally eroticized—made sexy—and those of use who are stigmatized for being queer are not immune.

It may be difficult to realize how completely sex discrimination has constructed the homosexuality that many of us feel. Though some of us perhaps think we know something about how male supremacy constructs the heterosexuality we have observed, or participated in, we're probably less aware of how sex discrimination has affected the way our personal homoeroticism has taken shape in our lives. But try to imagine, if you can, the difference between making love with someone when gender is not important, when gender is totally irrelevant, and having some kind of sexual release with a partner when what is paramount is your urgency to feel your or your partner's sexedness. If I were to put into words something that would help jog your memory of these two different experiences (assuming you've had at least one of each), I would say it's the difference between, on the one hand, a kind of overwhelming blending or a deeply mutual and vigorous erotic melding, and on the other hand a kind of tactile combat or tension in which various hierarchy dramas have an erotic impact. The difference is the difference between eroticized empathy and eroticized power disparity—or between eroticized equality and eroticized subordination.

Being a male supremacist in relation to another body is a quite commonplace mode of sexual behaving. Sometimes, though not always, the urgency to "be the man there" gets expressed in ass-fucking—while one guy is fucking, for instance, he slaps the other guy's butt around and calls him contemptuous names, swats and insults that are sexually stimulating, which may progress to physically very brutal and estranging domination. Many gay men seem to think that there is no woman-hating in the sex that they have. Sexualized woman-hating, they believe, is the straight man's burden. So why do gay men sometimes find themselves all bent out of shape after a relationship between two lovers goes on the rocks—and it was a relationship in which one man was always objectified, or always pressured into sex, or forced, or battered, or perhaps always dominatingly ass-fucked, and in his growing unease over this arrangement of power and submission he found himself feeling "feminized" and resenting it, meanwhile his partner just kept fucking him over, both in and out of bed? No woman-hating in gay sex? Clap your hands if you believe. Sexualized woman-hating does not have a race or a class or a sexual orientation.[1] It does not even have gender, as lesbian devotees of sadomasochism have shown.[2] Gay men play at treating each other "like a woman" all the time. Sometimes in jest. Sometimes in grim earnest.

The personal classified ads in certain gay periodicals bear concise witness to the way in which the male-supremacist sex-class system has constructed many men's homoeroticism:

Hot blond model 30's hot buns & face loves to be degraded by sexy kinky guys . . .

Submissive WM [white male] 40 sks strict dad 35–50 for discipline sessions. Can be spanked with strap or whip. Can be tied up . . .

Wanted: Yng hot jocks to play pussy! Scene: I drop by your apt. U greet me in black lace panties, stockings, and bra. In my sweats is a 9" red hot tool. The fun begins . . .

Very dominant/aggressive master 29, 6'2", 170 lbs. hung 8" seeks slaves for verbal abuse, slapping, & handcuffing. You must be 6' in height, weigh over 180 lbs. and work out. Hairy chest and beard a plus . . .

White master & son need houseboy for lifetime ownership . . .

I am looking for slaves to fill an opening in my selective stable . . .

I'm seeking a dominant master in full leather who is willing to train a real novice. Age and looks are unimportant, but you must be a masculine, serious, demanding, health-conscious top . . .

[Gay white male] slave 35 6' 170 clnshvn broad shoulders big chest gdlking wishes to serve tall slim master 28–42. Training may include [verbal abuse, bondage, bootlicking, discipline] . . .

And finally, here's one headlined simply "Punishment":

Ass strapping, bend over paddling, abrasion, [deep fist-fucking, cock-and-ball torture, tit torture, bondage and discipline, humiliation] . . .[3]

The political reality of the gender hierarchy in male supremacy requires that we make it resonate through our nerves, flesh, and vascular system just as often as we can. We are *supposed* to respond orgasmically to power and powerlessness, to violence and violation; our sexuality is *supposed* to be inhabited by a reverence for supremacy, for unjust power over and against other human life. We are not supposed to experience any other erotic possibility; we are not supposed to glimpse eroticized justice. Our bodies are not supposed to abandon their sensory imprint of what male dominance and female subordination are supposed to be to each other—even if we are the same sex. Perhaps *especially* if we are the same sex. Because if you and your sex partners and not genitally different but you are emotionally and erotically attached to gender hierarchy, then you come to the point where you have to impose hierarchy on every sex act you attempt—otherwise it doesn't feel like sex.

Erotically and politically, those of us who are queer live inside a bizarre double bind. Sex discrimination and sex inequality require homophobia in order to continue. The homophobia that results is what stigmatizes our eroticism, makes us hateful for how we would love. Yet living inside this system of sex discrimination and sex inequality, we too have sexualized it, we have become sexually addicted to gender polarity, we have learned how hate and hostility can become sexual stimulants, we have learned sexualized antagonism toward the other in order to seem to be able to stand ourselves—and in order to get off. Sex discrimination has ritualized a homosexuality that dares not deviate from allegiance to gender polarity and gender hierarchy; sex discrimination has constructed a homosexuality that must stay erotically attached to the very male-supremacist social structures that produce homophobia. It's a little like having a crush on one's own worst enemy—and then moving in for life.

If indeed male supremacy simultaneously produces both a homophobia that is erotically committed to the hatred of homosexuality *and* a homosexuality that is erotically committed to sex discrimination, then it becomes easier to understand why the gay community, taken as a whole, has become almost hysterically hostile to radical-feminist antipornography activism. One might have thought that gay people—who are harassed, stigmatized, and jeopardized on account of prejudice against their preference for same-sex sex—would want to make common cause with any radical challenge to systematized sex discrimination. One might have thought that gay people, realizing that their self-interest lies in the obliteration of homophobia, would be among the first to endorse a political movement attempting to root out sex inequality. One might have thought that gay people would be among the first to recognize that so long as society tolerates and actually celebrates the "pornographizing" of women—so long as there is an enormous economic incentive to traffic in the sexualized subordination of women—then the same terrorism that enforces the sex-class system will surely continue to bludgeon faggots as well. One might have thought, for that matter, that gay men would not require the sexualized inequality of women in order to get a charge out of sex—or that a gay man walking through a porn store, perhaps on his way to a private booth in a back room, would stop and take a look at the racks and racks of pictures of women gagged and splayed and trussed up and ask himself exactly why this particular context of woman-hate is so damned important to his blow job. . . .

Why Pornography Matters

The political function of pornography is analogous to the centrality of segregation in creating and maintaining race discrimination. Segregation was speech in the sense that it expressed the idea that blacks are different and inferior. But it was speech embodied in action—wherever there was segregation, there was something done to a class of victims: There was discrimination created, perpetuated, and institutionalized; there was damage to hearts and minds. Similarly, pornography contains and expresses many ideas about the "natural" servility and sluttishness of women, about how much women want to be ravished and abused, but in the real world, pornography functions as speech embodied in a practice—a thing actually done to an individual victim, the woman in it, and a thing actually done to women as a class.

Mere sexual explicitness does not create sex discrimination. And no damage to anyone's civil rights is done by so-called erotica, which may be defined as sexually explicit materials premised on equality, mutuality, reciprocity, and so forth. Pornography is something else. Pornography, which creates and maintains sex discrimination, is that sexually explicit material which actively *subordinates* people on account of their sexual anatomy; it puts them down, makes them inferior. Subordination is something that is done *to* someone; and it is often invisible, because the values in pornography link it to what many people think of as sex: a social hierarchy between men and women; objectification, which robs a person of his or her human status; submission, as if it's a person's "nature" to be a slave, to be servile; and violence, viewed as "normal" when it comes to sex. Pornography is what does that; pornography is that which produces sex discrimination by making subordination sexy. . . .

NOTES

1. For a discussion of woman-hating in gay male pornography, see Andrea Dworkin, *Pornography: Men Possessing Women* (New York: Dutton, 1989), pp. 36–45.

2. See Robin Ruth Linden et al., eds. *Against Sadomasochism: A Radical Feminist Analysis* (East Palo Alto, Calif.: Frog in the Well, 1983).

3. Typical personal-ad excerpts culled from the *New York Native*, 24 February 1986, pp. 55–56. Portions in brackets spell out coded abbreviations in the original.

ELLEN WILLIS

Feminism, Moralism, and Pornography

Ellen Willis is author of Beginning to See the Light: Sex,
Hope, and Rock-and-Roll *(1992). She is a former senior editor
at the* Village Voice, *and is now associate professor of journalism
at New York University.*

For women, life is an ongoing good cop–bad cop routine. The good cops
are marriage, motherhood, and that courtly old gentleman, chivalry. Just co-
operate, they say (crossing their fingers), and we'll go easy on you. You'll
never have to earn a living or open a door. We'll even get you some romantic
love. But you'd better not get stubborn, or you'll have to deal with our
friend rape, and he's a real terror; we just can't control him.

Pornography often functions as a bad cop. If rape warns that without the
protection of one man we are fair game for all, the hard-core pornographic
image suggests that the alternative to being a wife is being a whore. As
women become more "criminal," the cops call for nastier reinforcements; the
proliferation of lurid, violent porn (symbolic rape) is a form of backlash. But
one can be a solid citizen and still be shocked (naively or hypocritically) by
police brutality. However widely condoned, rape is illegal. However loudly
people proclaim that porn is as wholesome as granola, the essence of its appeal is that emotionally it remains taboo. It is from their very contempt for

the rules that bad cops derive their power to terrorize (and the covert approbation of solid citizens who would love to break the rules themselves). The line between bad cop and outlaw is tenuous. Both rape and pornography reflect a male outlaw mentality that rejects the conventions of romance and insists, bluntly, that women are cunts. The crucial difference between the conservative's moral indignation at rape, or at *Hustler*, and the feminist's political outrage is the latter's understanding that the problem is not bad cops or outlaws but cops and the law.

Unfortunately, the current women's campaign against pornography seems determined to blur this difference. Feminist criticism of sexist and misogynist pornography is nothing new; porn is an obvious target insofar as it contributes to larger patterns of oppression—the reduction of the female body to a commodity (the paradigm being prostitution), the sexual intimidation that makes women regard the public streets as enemy territory (the paradigm being rape), sexist images and propaganda in general. But what is happening now is different. By playing games with the English language, antiporn activists are managing to rationalize as feminism a single-issue movement divorced from any larger political context and rooted in conservative moral assumptions that are all the more dangerous for being unacknowledged.

When I first heard there was a group called Women Against Pornography, I twitched. Could I define myself as Against Pornography? Not really. In itself, pornography—which, my dictionary and I agree, means any image or description intended or used to arouse sexual desire—does not strike me as the proper object of a political crusade. As the most cursory observation suggests, there are many varieties of porn, some pernicious, some more or less benign. About the only generalization one can make is that pornography is the return of the repressed, of feelings and fantasies driven underground by a culture that atomizes sexuality, defining love as a noble affair of the heart and mind, lust as a base animal urge centered in unmentionable organs. Prurience—the state of mind I associate with pornography—implies a sense of sex as forbidden, secretive pleasure, isolated from any emotional or social context. I imagine that in utopia, porn would wither away along with the state, heroin, and Coca-Cola. At present, however, the sexual impulses that pornography appeals to are part of virtually everyone's psychology. For obvious political and cultural reasons nearly all porn is sexist in that it is the product of a male imagination and aimed at a male market; women are less likely to be consciously interested in pornography, or to indulge that interest, or to find porn that turns them on. But anyone who thinks women are simply indifferent to pornography has never watched a bunch of adolescent girls pass around a trashy novel. Over the years I've enjoyed various pieces of pornography—some of them of the sleazy Forty-second Street paperback sort—and so have most women I know. Fantasy, after all, is more flexible than reality, and women have learned, as a matter of survival, to be adept at shaping male fantasies to their own purposes. If feminists define pornography, per se, as the enemy, the result will be to make a lot of women ashamed of their sexual feelings and afraid to be honest about them. And the last thing women need is more sexual shame, guilt, and hypocrisy—this time served up as feminism.

So why ignore qualitative distinctions and in effect condemn all pornography as equally bad? WAP organizers answer—or finesse—this question by redefining pornography. They maintain that pornography is not really about sex but about violence against women. Or, in a more colorful formulation, "Pornography is the theory, rape is the practice." Part of the argument is that pornography causes violence; much is made of the fact that Charles Manson and David Berkowitz had porn collections. This is the sort of inverted logic that presumes marijuana to be dangerous because most heroin addicts started with it. It is men's hostility toward women—combined with their power to express that hostility and for the most part get away with it—that causes sexual violence. Pornography that gives sadistic fantasies concrete shape—and, in today's atmosphere, social legitimacy—may well encourage suggestible men to act them out. But if *Hustler* were to vanish from the shelves tomorrow, I doubt that rape or wife-beating statistics would decline.

Even more problematic is the idea that pornography depicts violence rather than sex. Since porn is by definition overtly sexual, while most of it is not overtly violent, this equation requires some fancy explaining. The conference WAP held in September was in part devoted to this task. Robin Morgan and Gloria Steinem addressed it by attempting to distinguish pornography from erotica. According to this argument, erotica (whose etymological root is "eros," or sexual love) expresses an integrated sexuality based on mutual affection and desire between equals; pornography (which comes from another Greek root—"porne," meaning prostitute) reflects a dehumanized sexuality based on male domination and exploitation of women. The distinction sounds promising, but it doesn't hold up. The accepted meaning of erotica is literature or pictures with sexual themes; it may or may not serve the essentially utilitarian function of pornography. Because it is less specific, less suggestive of actual sexual activity, "erotica" is regularly used as a euphemism for "classy porn." Pornography expressed in literary language or expensive photography and consumed by the upper middle class is "erotica"; the cheap stuff, which can't pretend to any purpose but getting people off, is smut. The erotica-versus-porn approach evades the (embarrassing?) question of how porn is *used*. It endorses the portrayal of sex as we might like it to be and condemns the portrayal of sex as it too often is, whether in action or only in fantasy. But if pornography is to arouse, it must appeal to the feelings we have, not those that by some utopian standard we ought to have. Sex in this culture has been so deeply politicized that it is impossible to make clear-cut distinctions between "authentic" sexual impulses and those conditioned by patriarchy. Between, say, *Ulysses* at one end and *Snuff* at the other, erotica/

pornography conveys all sorts of mixed messages that elicit complicated and private responses. In practice, attempts to sort out good erotica from bad porn inevitably come down to "What turns me on is erotic; what turns you on is pornographic."

It would be clearer and more logical simply to acknowledge that some sexual images are offensive and some are not. But logic and clarity are irrelevant—or rather, inimical—to the underlying aim of the antiporners, which is to vent the emotions traditionally associated with the word "pornography." As I've suggested, there is a social and psychic link between pornography and rape. In terms of patriarchal morality both are expressions of male lust, which is presumed to be innately vicious, and offenses to the putative sexual innocence of "good" women. But feminists supposedly begin with different assumptions—that men's confusion of sexual desire with predatory aggression reflects a sexist system, not male biology; that there are no good (chaste) or bad (lustful) women, just women who are, like men, sexual beings. From this standpoint, to lump pornography with rape is dangerously simplistic. Rape is a violent physical assault. Pornography can be a psychic assault, both in its content and in its public intrusions on our attention, but for women as for men it can also be a source of erotic pleasure. A woman who is raped is a victim; a woman who enjoys pornography (even if that means enjoying a rape fantasy) is in a sense a rebel, insisting on an aspect of her sexuality that has been defined as a male preserve. Insofar as pornography glorifies male supremacy and sexual alienation, it is deeply reactionary. But in rejecting sexual repression and hypocrisy—which have inflicted even more damage on women than on men—it expresses a radical impulse.

That this impulse still needs defending, even among feminists, is evident from the sexual attitudes that have surfaced in the antiporn movement. In the movement's rhetoric pornography is a code word for vicious male lust. To the objection that some women get off on porn, the standard reply is that this only shows how thoroughly women have been brainwashed by male values—though a WAP leaflet goes so far as to suggest that women who claim to like pornography are lying to avoid male opprobrium. (Note the good-girl-versus-bad-girl theme, reappearing as healthy-versus-sick, or honest-versus-devious; for "brainwashed" read "seduced.") And the view of sex that most often emerges from talk about "erotica" is as sentimental and euphemistic as the word itself: lovemaking should be beautiful, romantic, soft, nice, and devoid of messiness, vulgarity, impulses to power, or indeed aggression of any sort. Above all, the emphasis should be on *relationships*, not (yuck) *organs*. This goody-goody concept of eroticism is not feminist but feminine. It is precisely sex as an aggressive, unladylike activity, an expression of violent and unpretty emotion, an exercise of erotic power, and a specifically genital experience that has been taboo for women. Nor are we supposed to admit that we, too, have sadistic impulses, that our sexual fantasies may reflect forbidden urges to turn the tables and get revenge on men. (When a woman is aroused by a rape fantasy, is she perhaps identifying with the rapist as well as the victim?)

At the WAP conference lesbian separatists argued that pornography reflects patriarchal sexual relations; patriarchal sexual relations are based on male power backed by force; ergo, pornography is violent. This dubious syllogism, which could as easily be applied to romantic novels, reduces the whole issue to hopeless mush. If all manifestations of patriarchal sexuality are violent, then opposition to violence cannot explain why pornography (rather than romantic novels) should be singled out as a target. Besides, such reductionism allows women no basis for distinguishing between consensual heterosexuality and rape. But this is precisely its point; as a number of women at the conference put it, "In a patriarchy, all sex with men is pornographic." Of course, to attack pornography, and at the same time equate it with heterosexual sex, is implicitly to condemn not only women who like pornography, but women who sleep with men. This is familiar ground. The argument that straight women collaborate with the enemy has often been, among other things, a relatively polite way of saying that they consort with the beast. At the conference I couldn't help feeling that proponents of the separatist line were talking like the modern equivalents of women who, in an era when straightforward prudery was socially acceptable, joined convents to escape men's rude sexual demands. It seemed to me that their revulsion against heterosexuality was serving as the thinnest of covers for disgust with sex itself. In any case, sanitized feminine sexuality, whether straight or gay, is as limited as the predatory masculine kind and as central to women's oppression; a major function of misogynist pornography is to scare us into embracing it. As a further incentive, the good cops stand ready to assure us that we are indeed morally superior to men, that in our sweetness and nonviolence (read passivity and powerlessness) is our strength.

Women are understandably tempted to believe this comforting myth. Self-righteousness has always been a feminine weapon, a permissible way to make men feel bad. Ironically, it is socially acceptable for women to display fierce aggression in their crusades against male vice, which serve as an outlet for female anger without threatening male power. The temperance movement, which made alcohol the symbol of male violence, did not improve the position of women; substituting porn for demon rum won't work either. One reason it won't is that it bolsters the good girl–bad girl split. Overtly or by implication it isolates women who like porn or "pornographic" sex or who work in the sex industry. WAP has refused to take a position on prostitution, yet its activities—particularly its support for cleaning up Times Square—will affect prostitutes' lives. Prostitution raises its own set of complicated questions. But it is clearly not in women's interest to pit "good" feminists against "bad" whores (or topless dancers, or models for skin magazines).

So far, the issue that has dominated public debate on the antiporn campaign is its potential threat to free speech. Here too the movement's arguments have been full of contradictions. Susan Brownmiller and other WAP organizers claim not to advocate censorship and dismiss the civil liberties issue as a red herring dragged in by men who don't want to face the fact that pornography oppresses women. Yet at the same time, WAP endorses the Supreme Court's contention that obscenity is not protected speech, a doctrine I—and most civil libertarians—regard as a clear infringement of First Amendment rights. Brownmiller insists that the First Amendment was designed to protect political dissent, not expressions of woman-hating violence. But to make such a distinction is to defeat the amendment's purpose, since it implicitly cedes to the government the right to define "political." (Has there ever been a government willing to admit that its opponents are anything more than antisocial troublemakers?) Anyway, it makes no sense to oppose pornography on the grounds that it's sexist propaganda, then turn around and argue that it's not political. Nor will libertarians be reassured by WAP's statement that "we want to change the definition of obscenity so that it focuses on violence, not sex." Whatever their focus, obscenity laws deny the right of free expression to those who transgress official standards of propriety—and personally, I don't find WAP's standards significantly less oppressive than Warren Burger's. Not that it matters, since WAP's fantasies about influencing the definition of obscenity are appallingly naive. The basic purpose of obscenity laws is and always has been to reinforce cultural taboos on sexuality and suppress feminism, homosexuality, and other forms of sexual dissidence. No pornographer has ever been punished for being a woman hater, but not too long ago information about female sexuality, contraception, and abortion was assumed to be obscene. In a male supremacist society the only obscenity law that will not be used against women is no law at all.

As an alternative to an outright ban on pornography, Brownmiller and others have advocated restricting its display. There is a plausible case to be made for the idea that antiwoman images displayed so prominently that they are impossible to avoid are coercive, a form of active harassment that oversteps the bounds of free speech. But aside from the evasion involved in simply equating pornography with misogyny or sexual sadism, there are no legal or logical grounds for treating sexist material any differently from (for example) racist or anti-Semitic propaganda; an equitable law would have to prohibit any kind of public defamation. And the very thought of such a sweeping law has to make anyone with an imagination nervous. Could Catholics claim they were being harassed by nasty depictions of the pope? Could Russian refugees argue that the display of Communist literature was a form of psychological torture? Would proabortion material be taken off the shelves on the grounds that it defamed the unborn? I'd rather not find out.

At the moment the First Amendment issue remains hypothetical; the movement has concentrated on raising the issue of pornography through demonstrations and other public actions. This is certainly a legitimate strategy. Still, I find myself more and more disturbed by the tenor of antipornography actions and the sort of consciousness they promote; increasingly their focus has shifted from rational feminist criticism of specific targets to generalized, demagogic moral outrage. Picketing an antiwoman movie, defacing an exploitative billboard, or boycotting a record company to protest its misogynist album covers conveys one kind of message, mass marches Against Pornography quite another. Similarly, there is a difference between telling the neighborhood news dealer why it pisses us off to have *Penthouse* shoved in our faces and choosing as a prime target every right-thinking politician's symbol of big-city sin, Times Square.

In contrast to the abortion rights movement, which is struggling against a tidal wave of energy from the other direction, the antiporn campaign is respectable. It gets approving press and cooperation from the city, which has its own stake (promoting tourism, making . . . area[s] safe for gentrification) in cleaning up Times Square. It has begun to attract women whose perspective on other matters is in no way feminist ("I'm anti-abortion," a participant in WAP's march on Times Square told a reporter, "but this is something I can get into"). Despite the insistence of WAP organizers that they support sexual freedom, their line appeals to the antisexual emotions that feed the backlash. Whether they know it or not, they are doing the good cops' dirty work.

MARIANA VALVERDE

Beyond Gender Dangers and Private Pleasures: Theory and Ethics in the Sex Debates

Mariana Valverde is the author of Sex, Power, and Pleasure
(1985, 1987) and The Age of Light, Soap and Water: Moral
Reform in English Canada 1885–1925 *(1991), as well as*
journal articles on social theory and historical sociology. She is
currently working on a historical sociology of urban "vices" and
their regulation by philanthropic state agencies. She is at the
Centre of Criminology, University of Toronto.

If the so-called sex debates have been generating so much heat in feminist gatherings during the last few years, this is not only because sex is a taboo and therefore hot topic. It is also because the debates on pornography, censorship, feminist erotica, sexual ethics, sadomasochism, and related topics involve some of the basic questions of women's liberation. These include the following: What is the place of sexuality in both our oppression and our project for liberation? To what extent do patriarchal relations determine our sexual fantasies and practices, and to what extent can we as individuals develop a "free" sexuality? Who is responsible for the sexual oppression of women—men, patriarchy, capitalism, the state? What ethical principles do we want to develop as a replacement for old moralities? Is sexuality really important to us, or is it only a Freudianized and commercialized society that tells us it is?

Source: This article is reprinted from *Feminist Studies,* Volume 15, number 2 (Summer 1989)
237–254, by permission of the publisher, *Feminist Studies,* Inc., c/o Women's Studies Program, University of Maryland, College Park, MD 20742.

177

This list of questions is obviously not exhaustive, and yet it covers many of the most important concerns of feminism as a historical movement; they have been with us for at least a century and are unlikely to be resolved in our lifetime. This article attempts not grand solutions but rather a clarification of some of the theoretical differences between two major camps in the current debates, recognizing that in these debates political commitments often precede and determine theoretical positions. This is certainly the case in the pleasure/danger controversy, in which feminists who emphasize sexual danger, and thus seek to control male abuse and protect and/or empower women, are opposed to those who emphasize the need for taking risks in the pursuit of both the theory and practice of women's sexual pleasure. There is no logical reason why one should have to choose between emphasizing one or the other aspect of women's sexual experience; but in the feminist political atmosphere of today, in North America at least, certain camps have been formed. A feminist theorist cannot leap over this political division, among other reasons because the theoretical positions developed by both sides are grounded in practical commitments which are all part of the feminist project but which often appear to be—and to some extent are—conflicting priorities. Having outlined some of the political and theoretical assumptions underlying the pleasure/danger debate, I will conclude with some brief remarks on a possible new concept of "sexual freedom."

Let us begin with an examination of the theory of Catharine MacKinnon, who is one of the key players in the sex debates. Her practical and strategic suggestions (such as the Minneapolis antipornography ordinance) have received much attention and criticism, but, surprisingly, her more theoretical writings have not.[1]

In two widely read articles published in *Signs* in 1982–83, MacKinnon argued that gender is crucially constituted in and by sexuality, while sexuality is in turn largely if not totally determined by gender. She asserts that "male and female are created through the erotization of dominance and submission" and that "sexual objectification" is "the central process within this dynamic."[2] In her recent book, *Feminism Unmodified: Discourses on Life and Law,* this is reiterated: "In my view—you will notice that I equate 'in my view' with 'feminism'—this argument is that the molding, direction, and expression of sexuality organize society into two sexes, women and men."[3] The centrality of sexual subordination in women's oppression is further explicated by stating quite boldly that "I use sex and gender relatively interchangeably" even though "much has been made of the distinction between sex and gender."[4]

MacKinnon's argument could be broken down into two parts. First, the long-standing feminist distinction between the sexes as biological categories and the genders as social constructions is being challenged. In a remarkable opinion, buried in a footnote, she states that "the intractability of maleness as a form of dominance suggests that social constructs, although they flow from human agency, can be less plastic than nature has proven to be. If experience trying to do so is any guide, it may be easier to change biology than society."⁵ This statement is reflected, at the level of strategy, in her skepticism about the ability of humanity to change its social relations as history unfolds. Unlike radical feminists with an optimist/heroic perspective, MacKinnon spends virtually no time recounting the victories of women against patriarchy, believing women's subordination to be virtually transhistorical: "Our status as a group relative to men has almost never, if ever, been much changed from what it is."⁶ The deliberate use of the word "male" to mean "masculine" thus serves to reinforce a philosophical pessimism of Schopenhauerian proportions. This pessimistic evaluation of the ontological status of patriarchy raises the question of whether women's patterns of submission can ever be changed. The "social constructs" which MacKinnon believes are "less plastic than nature" presumably include femininity as well as masculinity. As a feminist, MacKinnon must believe that it is possible for women to organize to defeat or at least transform patriarchy; but the theoretical framework she sets up has very little room for proactive strategies.⁷

The second part of her argument concerns the centrality of sexual processes and, notably, what she calls "sexual objectification" in the construction and subsequent reproduction of gender. What is meant by "sexual objectification"? Although this question is not explicitly answered, it would appear that MacKinnon wants to avoid philosophical idealism; it is not only men's ideas about sex that oppress women, she argues against Mary Daly.⁸ Sexual objectification is a set of practices, not an ideology; rape, sexual harassment, and the production and consumption of pornography are its key aspects.

MacKinnon thus distances herself from the philosophical idealism that plagues so much U.S. feminist theory, both radical and liberal. She is especially acerbic about the liberal notion that "gender roles" are the cause of women's oppression. In her attempt to undermine both the optimism of liberal role theory and the mysticism of Daly's radical feminism, however, she is led to state rather mysteriously that pornography is *not* a set of images and texts which influences people. She simply states that pornography is "a practice," without specifying whether she is using the word "practice" in the Marxian sense of a praxis determined by the mode of labor, in the poststructuralist sense of a signifying practice, or in some other sense. For her, pornography is *not* a cultural genre for whose analysis the tools of cultural studies might be mobilized; she bluntly states that "pornography, in the feminist view, is a form of forced sex."⁹ This denial of any significant difference between actual sex or violence, and representations of sex or violence, brings her, ironically, into the arms of the liberal state, whose concept of obscenity (which she rejects) is based precisely on a denial of the relative autonomy of representations. In obscenity law, certain pictures are obscene not because of their signification as pictures but simply because the *acts* depicted are illegal under other sections of the criminal code.

Leaving aside the problem of undialectical rejection not only of idealism but of any notion of culture (a rejection disguised by MacKinnon's use of the term "practice," which in the current intellectual atmosphere has semiotic connotations), queries can also be raised about her selection of the practices that are most crucial in the constitution of women as an oppressed gender. In all her writings, rape, sexual harassment, and pornography have pride of place. Now, these are undoubtedly constitutive of women's oppression and of masculine dominance, but the selection of these and omission of other phenomena, first, focuses attention primarily on extrafamilial sexual dangers; second, overemphasizes the *sexual* component of women's oppression, to the detriment of economic and social factors; and, third, concentrates on nega-tive male practices to the exclusion of women's practices of resistance.

Regarding the first point: rape goes on in marriage as well as outside of it, and MacKinnon would be the first to point this out. MacKinnon, how-ever, puts very little emphasis on the nuclear family as a site or a cause of women's oppression. One wonders if this is a tactical choice motivated by her (and Andrea Dworkin's) explicit attempt to court right-wing women or whether it is a principled stand. She makes no distinction between sex be-tween women and men, on the one hand, and sex between women and men in the context of a society in which the nuclear patriarchal family is norma-tive. As countless feminists have pointed out, in our society women are con-stantly pressured to limit their sexual activity to married monogamy, and part of the pressure involves constructing all other forms of sex as *per se* danger-ous. The dangers of extramarital rape and sexual harassment are often exag-gerated by right-wing forces wanting to show that "promiscuity" has its own punishment and that women ought not to walk down city streets alone or be in the labor force. One way of distinguishing the feminist critique of sexual danger from that of the right wing is precisely to emphasize the dangers of being in the "haven" of the family. These dangers include not only wife abuse, incest, and tyrannical sexual demands but also constraints on women's sexual freedom and plain sexual boredom (which is not the least of our sexual dangers).

This crucial failure to situate sexuality in its actual context (i.e., a society that privileges married sex as "safe" and confines everything else to the realm of risk) then mars the argument about the construction of gender through sexuality, as indicated in the second and third points above. MacKinnon as-sumes that the process of gender differentiation always has a sexual content: "Each element of the female *gender* stereotype is revealed as, in fact, *sexual*"; "what defines woman as such is what turns men on."[10] This is sexual reduc-tionism. It ignores the social and economic roots of women's oppression, and it presents a far too homogeneous picture of sexuality. Even within het-erosexuality there is a great deal of variation in the social meaning of sex. Ca-sual sex between an independent woman and a male friend, the rape of a girl by an older man, the rape of a black woman by a white man, and the rape of a black woman by a black man cannot be lumped together as though they had a unitary meaning. Perhaps more significantly, the only desire theorized by MacKinnon is the desire of men to objectify and conquer women. Female desires (or any male desire, such as homosexuality, which is not linked to the domination of women) are conspicuous by their absence in MacKinnon's discourse. During the lecture entitled "Desire and Power," a member of the audience asked: "What about female power?" MacKinnon replied: "That is a contradiction in terms" and explained that "in the society we currently live in, the content I want to claim for sexuality is the gaze that constructs women as objects for male pleasure."[11] This once more illustrates the undialectical character of MacKinnon's critique of patriarchy. Because the "male gaze" is largely constitutive of sexual relations in our society, she assumes that this objectifying gaze is the *only* possible meaning of the term "sexuality," thus denying women any position, however precarious, from which to reclaim or invent nonpatriarchal sexual desires.[12]

A consequence of this is that nonheterosexual sex remains untheorized. In *Feminism Unmodified,* MacKinnon appears to be saying that lesbian sex is implicated in the dynamic of domination which for her is the sole meaning of sexuality: "Women sexually choosing women can challenge the position of women as the sexually acted-upon. . . . But so long as gender is a system of power, and it is women who have less power, like any other benefit of abstract equality, it can merely extend this choice to women who can get the power to enforce it."[13] This is a puzzling statement. Lesbian feminists, and, for that matter, ordinary lesbians conducting their sexual lives, do not envisage lesbianism as an abstract right to share male access to women. Without glorifying lesbianism or exaggerating its political content, one can certainly see it, as most feminists do, as a *potentially* antipatriarchal practice that empowers women at large. Of course, it is true that exploitative power dynamics *can* take place among lesbians, but one wonders why a feminist writer would highlight this while remaining silent about the positive, joyful, and egalitarian aspects of lesbian community life.

The eventual result is a construction of sexuality as uniformly oppressive, a picture of relentless male violence drawn with the twin brushes of feminist functionalism (all phenomena are explained as serving a purpose for "patriarchy" in general) and philosophical pessimism. Resistance, subversion, and pleasure are written out of the account. MacKinnon's concept of sexuality parallels Schelling's concept of the Absolute Spirit as described by Hegel, that is, "the night in which all cows are black."

Having established the sexual reductionist framework, MacKinnon then goes on to argue quite consistently that contraception and abortion are really sexual, not reproductive, issues (in her sense of "sexual") and that rape is also a sexual question and not, as Susan Brownmiller and others have argued, primarily a question of violence. The implications of MacKinnon's viewpoint are developed in her discussions of rape, in which she appears to argue that there is virtually no difference between consenting and nonconsenting (heterosexual) sex. Her critique of liberal-democratic assumptions behind the notion of "consent" exposes the substantive and collective inequalities that lurk under the apparently egalitarian surface of "equal rights" discourse. The critique of individualistic notions of consent, however, is carried to the extreme of denying the possibility that individual women might genuinely consent to specific sexual acts with particular men. One can criticize Anglo-American jurisprudence for its disregard for the substantial inequalities between the genders that make consent arguments somewhat problematic. But it does not logically follow that heterosexual sex is always only a site for the constitution of gender oppression, and, therefore, what an individual woman feels or desires is of no consequence. MacKinnon argues this not by directly saying "women cannot consent" but rather by rhetorical questions along the lines of, "Is there really any difference between rape and non-rape?"—a rhetorical technique that allows her to disclaim responsibility for having said that women are not capable of giving consent. Another rhetorical technique with the same effect is visible in her either/or dichotomy to the effect that *either* heterosexuality is structurally oppressive *or* it is not,[14] a device which constructs anyone who disagrees with her as holding the view that heterosexuality is not oppressive, erasing any possible middle ground.

Consent is both conditioned and limited by social and historical factors, but it is rather absolutist to believe that the existence of patriarchy completely negates the possibility of consensual sex between women and men. Any theory of sexuality must take into account that even as we suffer patriarchal oppression, we continue to have genuine active desires, and these include, among others, some women's desire to have intercourse. The silence on female desire does not only result in a pessimistic worldview . . . more importantly, it denies even the theoretical possibility of individual or collective resistance through sexuality.

MacKinnon herself summarizes her argument by stating that "sex as gender and sex as sexuality are thus defined in terms of each other, but it is sexuality that determines gender, not the other way around."[15] Her definition of sexuality, however, is wholly derived from a certain view of sex/gender differences, as explicated, for instance, in her discussions of rape as the paradigmatic form of sexuality. One could thus say without injustice that although she sees sexuality as the main site for the constitution of gender, what she chooses to highlight in her discussion of sexuality is in turn determined by a preconceived view of gender; she consistently uses examples from the sphere of sexual danger, never from the sphere of sexual pleasure, and she furthermore takes sexuality out of its sociohistorical context by ignoring the constitution of the bourgeois patriarchal family and other gendered institutions within which sexuality is shaped.

MacKinnon begins by a rejection of Anglo-American liberal political and legal thought, whose patriarchal bias is in her view exemplified in the hypocritical practice of dividing legal from illegal sex by simply asking, "Did she consent?" She wants to emphasize that sexuality is not a private contract but is rather a relation between two sharply differentiated and unequal genders and is the main constitutive factor in the maintenance of gender difference and oppression. Given gender inequality, women and men do not face one another as liberal, "free" individuals engaging in a fair contract; hence, to speak of consent is to mystify and obscure patriarchal relations. Her critique of liberalism could be useful (as will be discussed below) in the formulation of a feminist framework for sexual ethics. She is so single-minded in her critique, however, that she forgets that women are not merely instances of an ideal gender and that women's bodies are not simply sites for the reproduction of patriarchy via sexual objectification. MacKinnon's view of gender is formally very similar to the vulgar Marxist view of class, which sees workers are mere instances of an Idea of class whose content is in turn given by impersonal forces and relations of production. Her famous analogy "sexuality is to feminism what work is to Marxism"[16] would suggest that "unmodified feminism" is formally equivalent to orthodox Marxism, with the important difference that, while Marxism envisages the possibility of meaningful work or nonalienated labor, there is no space in MacKinnon's theory for beginning to imagine a nonalienated sexuality.

MacKinnon's approach intends to empower women; however, its actual effect is to portray women as victims—of rape, of sexual harassment, of pornography. This results, at the level of political practice, in choosing strategies (such as the Minneapolis ordinance) that emphasize the *protection* of women against sexual danger to the detriment of all other strategies for our social and sexual liberation. It furthermore tends to abolish all differences among women (and among men), by not seriously examining individual variability in desire, fantasy, and consent and—perhaps more significantly—by a total disregard of factors such as race and class, which are also constitutive of sexual and gender experience. Although MacKinnon's critique of liberal individualism's failure to account for sexual danger leads only to a gender-sex reductionism, her opponents in the sex debate have experienced analogous difficulties in theorizing sexual pleasure from a nonindividualist, postliberal perspective. Let us begin by examining the work of one of MacKinnon's best-known opponents, Gayle Rubin.

In what was, in my view, the most interesting theoretical innovation contained in the 1984 anthology, *Pleasure and Danger: Exploring Female Sexuality,* Rubin criticizes her own much-acclaimed 1975 article, "The Traffic in Women," for conflating the "sex system" and the "gender system." She writes: "In contrast to my perspective in 'The Traffic in Women,' I am now arguing that it is essential to separate gender and sexuality analytically to more accurately reflect their separate social existence. This goes against the grain of much contemporary feminist thought, which treats sexuality as a derivation of gender." Rubin mentions that it is MacKinnon who has made the most thorough attempt to "subsume sexuality under feminist thought" and in particular under her own gender-reductionist thought. Rubin reacts to this by exploring precisely the distance between "the gender system" (which is loosely what many others call "patriarchy") and the "sex system." Sexual minorities have been and are oppressed not only because they include women or they threaten patriarchal domination; Rubin argues, along the lines first established by Freud and Reich, that a profound "sex negativity" characterizes Western culture, and that this negativity crosses the gender boundary.[17]

This is an interesting thought, for, ever since Kate Millett, feminists have tended to believe that the scope of "sexual politics" is solely determined by gender.[18] Rubin, who has been influenced by both sexology and gay liberation thought, has seen the fallacy of gender reductionism and pointed it out. (Her comment on this is echoed by Carole Vance in her introductory essay in *Pleasure and Danger*.) Indeed, anyone who is familiar with recent work in the history of sexuality would have to conclude that even if gender is the most important factor in sexual politics it is by no means the only one, and other aspects of sexuality cannot always be seen as derivative of gender oppression. (For instance, Michel Foucault's work on Greek and Roman sexual ethics shows that there were fundamental differences between the older systems of sexual ethics and the Christian view, differences which are intertwined with the history of gender relations but which are not reducible to derivations of gender.[19])

The precise meaning of the term "sex system" remains nevertheless somewhat elusive. Terms such as "sex negativism" and "benign sexual variation" are taken from the "science of sexuality," which has since its inception in the late nineteenth century been shaped, on the one hand, by post-Darwinian biology and, on the other, by the regulatory features of liberal states. For instance, Magnus Hirschfeld, founder of the German gay liberation movement and of an important sexological institute destroyed by the Nazis, explained the notion of benign sexual variation in his highly political keynote address to the 1929 meeting of the World League for Sex Reform: "Between the normal and the pathological type there is a range of border line cases which must be regarded as biological [i.e. benign] variations. . . . I believe we should extend our idea of the range of biological variations and limit the conception of pathological cases."[20] Rubin echoes this idea when she states that "it is difficult to develop a pluralistic sexual ethics without a concept of benign sexual variation. Variation is a fundamental property of life, from the simplest biological organisms to the most complex human social framework."[21]

Variation, the key concept in Kinsey's work, is certainly an improvement over the norm/pathology dichotomy, if only because the pathology approach has reactionary political implications, while the "variation thesis" legitimates liberal approaches to sexual regulation. Nevertheless, both frameworks arbitrarily privilege biological models as tools in social inquiry. The physiology of desire is the precondition of sexual relationships, but that does not mean the analytical tools useful to study the former are applicable to the realm of language and social life. The variations in body type and bodily experience that occur among human beings do not have any intrinsic, necessary social meaning.

Rubin's use of the term "variation" is especially problematic because, unlike Kinsey, she is explicitly engaged in a political debate about feminist sexual *ethics*. Her scientific references thus serve to enlist the authority of natural science in the service of a particular philosophical position on sexual conduct. The connection between the realm of bodily, extradiscursive experience and that of human communication has to be theorized and researched. It cannot be assumed that it is an easy matter to slide from "the simplest biological organism" to "the most complex human social framework." It may be true that sexual behavior can usefully be conceived as a range of "variations," although even this limited claim already assumes that one can reason by analogy and extend biological models to sexual-social experience. However, even if the analogy is justified, one certainly cannot leap up yet another level to the realm of ethics and assert that the more variations, the better.

Furthermore, I do not see how, after Foucault, any one can uncritically speak of "sex negativism"—as though bourgeois society were not responsible for what Foucault called "the deployment of sexuality," the obsession with speaking about sex and constituting sexual identities through expert discourse, supposedly in order to find "the truth" about human identity. Rubin, who is not a simplistic libertarian, avoids relying on the repression hypothesis to explain sexual history; but the passages inspired by Foucault clash with her praise of sexology's scientific objectivity.[22] Social construction and empiricism are juxtaposed without their conflicts being resolved, and both are counterposed to "the first principles of feminism." In the end, we are left without knowing exactly what the "sex system" consists of, much less how it interacts with the gender system.

Rubin's theoretical problems can, in my view, be traced to the contradiction between practical political needs (such as presenting "solid" lesbian and gay identities for public, political purposes) and the theoretical realization that gender and sexual orientation are far less fixed than our politics would imply. As someone speaking from a gay perspective said during the 1985 Sex and the State conference in Toronto, it's all very well to deconstruct homosexuality in theory, but "*we'll* deconstruct when *they* deconstruct." Practical realities have tended to discourage any critique of liberal sexology and its naturalist notion of "benign sexual variation."

Political exigencies may have thus led Rubin and others (e.g., Jeffrey Weeks)[23] to embrace sexology more warmly than their intellectual commitment to Foucault and deconstruction might have indicated. When faced with gender reductionism and feminist moralism (not to mention the Moral Majority), many of us feel obliged to defend the diversity of human sexual desire, especially female desire, even if this means employing a Kinsey-style taxonomic, amoral framework. Weeks's concept of "radical pluralism" may be the necessary starting point for a nonabsolutist sexual ethics, and it may give us a defense against the rising tide of conservatism that one can detect in the AIDS panic. However, it has to be admitted (at least among feminists) that the notion of "pluralism" cannot provide any content for a feminist sexual ethic. This is why women who are more interested in ethical values than in the vindication of abstract choice have often gravitated to feminist moralistic systems that fill the ethical void with arbitrary but spiritually satisfying content. The debate on sexual theory, therefore, cannot revolve only around the logic or lack of logic of various theories of sexuality. It has to address the ethical questions that, for most people, are far more pressing than the theoretical questions. Let us thus pursue our discussion of gender, sex, and community, incorporating into it the debate on sexual ethics that closely parallels the theoretical debate.

Lynne Segal has published a critique of Dale Spender, Mary Daly, and Andrea Dworkin which rejects, from a socialist and prosex perspective, their gender reductionism and their implicit or explicit belief in the moral superiority of women.[24] She argues that what I am here calling gender reductionism is the dominant philosophy of popular feminism in Britain, and she presents some cogent theoretical arguments against both the theoretical and ethical assumptions behind this position. (If she does not include MacKinnon in her critique, it may be because MacKinnon cannot be accused of making claims about the moral superiority of women, since she does not present women as subject, moral or otherwise—she addresses women's experience as victims.) But the feminists criticized by Segal agree with MacKinnon in suggesting that feminist sexual ethics is basically a matter of women saying "No" to men. Some, like Mary Daly, would elaborate on this "No" with many metaphysical and rhetorical flourishes; others, like MacKinnon, leave no room for any positive feminist discourse—for her, "No" is the *only* word in a feminist discourse on sexual ethics. But for all the radical feminists mentioned, there are no real ethical dilemmas among women. One is either for patriarchy or one is against it, and everything else is unimportant. (Men, on their part, are apparently exempt from any ethical responsibility, or at least they are not challenged to reflect on their actions.)

For those of us challenging both right-wing and feminist moralisms, sexual ethics is clearly not a question of individual women adhering to a monolithic "Race" of purified women.[25] The emphasis is not on general and absolute rules but, rather, on the elaboration of a framework within which concrete discussions of particular ethical dilemmas can take place. Insofar as there are any substantial, as opposed to merely formal, values, they generally revolve around mutual recognition and empowerment. Decisions about the presence or absence of mutuality and consent are not to be made from the point of view of a formalistic liberal individualism, however, but rather through an examination of how individual desire and individual consent are shaped and even constructed by both the larger oppressive social forces (gender, race, class) and the bonds one has to local communities of resistance.

Rubin, for instance, tempers her commitment to individual autonomy in sexual decision making with discussions of sexual desire as embodied in *communities* (e.g., the gay male leather community, the lesbian sadomasochistic community, etc.). However, in the discussion of the lesbian sadomasochistic communities by people such as Gayle Rubin, Pat Califia, and the Samois group[26] one gets the impression that all ethical conflicts occur on the boundaries separating communities (for instance, Women against Pornography has ethical values which clash with those of the Samois sadomasochistic group). Although intercommunity conflicts are obviously more visible and more heated, there must be some room to allow members of self-defined communities to dissent or to challenge the values of that subculture. And perhaps more fundamentally, it is not clear to me—even though I have resorted to the useful term "sexual communities" in public discussions—how one can define the boundaries of such communities. Califia and other advocates of lesbian sadomasochism, for instance, claim an ethical autonomy for the lesbian sadomasochistic community which would be denied by those who see all lesbians as a single community.

The notion of "sexual minorities" or "sexual communities" is thus quite problematic, partly because of its uneasy origins in sexology and partly because of the arbitrariness with which the boundaries of the community are drawn. However, it is a relatively new concept and perhaps it ought to be allowed some chance to be used in practice before the theoretical scalpel is used to dissect it. A community is a more concrete collectivity than the abstract and monolithic gender favored by Daly and MacKinnon. Therefore the concept, however difficult to define in practice, could be useful in navigating between gender reductionism and liberal individualism.

The concept of community can help in the elaboration of one of the thorniest elements of a new feminist discourse on sexual ethics, namely, a nonindividualistic notion of "consent" that does not disguise substantive power differentials through the ideology of liberal equality—a concept of "consent" that subverts liberalism instead of legitimating it.[27] Insofar as we see ourselves as members of (if not accountable to) a particular local community, we deprivatize the process of establishing consent in our otherwise fairly private sexual relationships. Whether one wants to have sex with a given individual or not, how or when or where one has sex, what rules one observes in a sexual relationship—these questions are never decided completely privately but, rather, are answered in the context of a certain community which gives us our reference point even when we dissent from its values. At the merely linguistic level, discourses of any type are always socially produced (as Wittgenstein said, the concept of a private language is a contradiction in terms). Hence, even if we want to stress the individuality of a particular statement, we cannot forget that the discourse within which that statement exists, and upon which it must rely for its meaning, is not in the least individual. This linguistic fact is reinforced at the nonlinguistic level by the feminist belief in collective empowerment. When feminists speak about gaining autonomy and self-determination for our sexual choices, what is usually meant is autonomy from male authority, tradition, and similar constraints; what is not meant is absolute autonomy, even if such a thing were possible. We seek to be free not as self-sufficient egos wandering in a void (an intrinsically bourgeois image of utopia) but as active participants in communities that are establishing a counterdiscourse on sexual ethics. I believe that many feminists share this general aim, even as they differ as to how to define a relevant "community." MacKinnon's notion of "sex," the notion of "sexual minorities," combinations of race and class analyses of sexuality—all these are in a sense attempts to move beyond both liberal individualism and essentialism, beyond the undialectical opposition of private pleasures and gender dangers.

Of course, there are limits to one's connection to or accountability toward any community, however enlightened. Thus, most writers on the question have emphasized the need to retain a sense of *individual* autonomy. Rosalind Petchesky makes this very clear in her brilliant discussion of the ethics of decision making around abortion. Although she rejects the liberal notion of abstract "choice" in favor of a socially and historically grounded concept of reproductive freedom, she is sharply critical of those who maintain that a woman's right to choose would be taken away "after the revolution," when the objective conditions constraining women now are absent and the community is willing to provide childcare and other support services.[28] Petchesky points out that no matter what the social conditions might be, there is still a basic fact: the pregnancy is taking place in the body of a particular woman. Even in a world where we do not experience our bodies as quite so private, pregnancy (like sexual pleasure, or like pain) will be a bodily as well as a social experience.

As well as allowing for individual moral judgments based on bodily autonomy, Petchesky avoids the simplistic reliance on one arbitrarily designated collectivity (be it gender or "sexual minority") in order to explain sexual identity and ground sexual discourse and values. This is one of her valuable contributions. She shows it is possible to reject liberalism without thereby resorting to reductionisms based on essentialist notions of class, gender, or sexual preference.

It may be that by pursuing the abortion movement's notion of "reproductive freedom" in the sexual realm, the discussion of sexual ethics can overcome the current impasse on the question of individual consent versus community values. The concept of "sexual freedom" has been tarnished by its association with the Playboy mentality, but it might be useful to try to reclaim it (as Carole Vance, Varda Burstyn, and others are doing). In the elaboration of a discourse on sexual ethics that is both postliberal and postmoralistic, the term "sexual freedom" would not signify individual hedonism undeterred by community ethics and motivated by false notions of individual sexual autonomy. Rather, "sexual freedom" would involve fighting for substantive sexual rights, beginning with women's economic, social, and emotional independence, which is the primary condition for the sexual empowerment of women.

In this context, it might be useful to experiment with the concept of sexual needs rather than sexual rights (taking our cue from Petchesky's discussion of abortion as a need, not a right.)[29] Sexual and emotional fulfillment, if seen as a basic human need, does not necessarily pit individuals either against one another or against the community. Just as the need for food and shelter only results in competition, exploitation, and poverty under certain social structures such as class divisions and imperialism, so too the human need for love and sex only results in competition, misery, and misogyny under certain structural conditions. The task before us is perhaps best envisaged as the effort to discern and bring about the conditions for a nonalienated sexuality, rather than as an attempt to maximize the sexual rights of individuals or groups.

Sexual freedom would also involve a recognition of class and race as well as gender differences in sexual identity and sexual experience. The new sexual "communities," if they exist at all, would not be based on sexological categories divorced from class, race, and gender realities. "Sexual freedom" would be both the collective freedom of communities that are countering the current sexual hegemony and claiming substantive sexual and reproductive rights, on the basis of bodily and psychic need (not abstract legal right), and the idiosyncratic participation of individuals in this project.

The sexual discourse within which "sexual freedom" would exist as a term would not seek to abolish the tension between desire and duty, individual pleasure and social goal. But it would also not automatically construct desire and duty, individual and collectivity, as necessarily opposed (a construction which underlies not only conservative but also liberal sexual ethics). It would also be resolutely antiessentialist, refusing all monocausal explanations of our complex and multifaceted oppression. Neither sexual objectification nor sexual negativism can be construed as the main enemy, as that which, in "the last instance," determines sexual oppression. Rather, these, as well as other concepts, such as my proposed notion of substantive sexual freedom, can only be regarded as elements in the elaboration of a new discourse on sexual theory and sexual ethics.

NOTES

1. See, for example, Varda Burstyn, ed., *Women against Censorship* (Toronto and Vancouver: Douglas & McIntyre, 1985).

2. Catharine MacKinnon, "Feminism, Marxism, Method, and the State: An Agenda for Theory," *Signs* 7 (Spring 1982): 515–44, and "Feminism, Marxism,

Method, and the State: Toward Feminist Jurisprudence," *Signs* 8 (Summer 1983): 635–58, 635–36.

3. Catharine MacKinnon, *Feminism Unmodified: Discourses on Life and Law* (Cambridge: Harvard University Press, 1987), 49.

4. MacKinnon, "Feminism, Marxism, Method, and the State: Toward Feminist Jurisprudence," 635 n. 1.

5. Ibid., 636 n. 3.

6. MacKinnon, *Feminism Unmodified,* 167.

7. MacKinnon's concentration, at the strategic level, on stopping sexual harassment, pornography, and rape (as opposed to achieving reproductive and economic freedom, for instance) is thus consistent with her theoretical framework.

8. MacKinnon, "Feminism, Marxism, Method, and the State: Toward Feminist Jurisprudence," 639 n. 8. MacKinnon remarks here that even though Mary Daly is "extreme" she is not a true radical feminist because her method is "idealist" and is therefore "formally liberal no matter how extreme or insightful."

9. MacKinnon, *Feminism Unmodified,* 148.

10. MacKinnon, "Feminism, Marxism, Method, and the State: An Agenda for Theory," 530, 531.

11. MacKinnon, *Feminism Unmodified,* 53.

12. Feminist semioticians and film theorists are certainly not agreed on whether the male gaze is as all-pervasive as MacKinnon believes. Laura Mulvey's "Visual Pleasure and Narrative Cinema," *Screen* 16 (Autumn 1975) has given rise to an extensive debate on this question. For one interpretation, see Teresa De Lauretis, *Alice Doesn't: Feminism, Semiotics, Cinema* (Bloomington: Indiana University Press, 1984).

13. MacKinnon, *Feminism Unmodified,* 14.

14. Ibid., 60–61.

15. MacKinnon, "Feminism, Marxism, Method, and the State: An Agenda for Theory," 531.

16. Ibid., 515. This is the opening sentence of the article.

17. Gayle Rubin, "Thinking Sex," in *Pleasure and Danger: Exploring Female Sexuality,* ed. Carole Vance (London and Boston: Routledge & Kegan Paul, 1984), 308, 278.

18. I owe this thought to Lorna Weir, "Sexual Rule, Sexual Politics: Studies in the Medicalization of Sexual Danger" (Ph.D. diss., York University, Toronto, 1986).

19. Michel Foucault, *Histoire de la sexualité,* vols. 2 and 3 (Paris: Gallimard, 1984).

20. Magnus Hirschfeld, "Presidential Address," *Proceedings of the Third Congress of the World League for Sexual Reform* (London: Kegan Paul, 1930), xiii.

21. Rubin, 283.

22. After praising Havelock Ellis's work without mentioning his profound sexism, Rubin writes: "Neither sexology nor sex research has been immune to the pre-

vailing sexual value system. . . . But sexology and sex research provide abundant detail, a welcome posture of calm. . . . These fields can provide an empirical grounding for a radical theory of sexuality more useful than the combination of psychoanalysis and feminist first principles to which so many texts resort" (p. 284).

23. Jeffrey Weeks, *Sexuality* (London: Tavistock and Ellis Horwood, 1986). In this book, which is more popular in style and content than his earlier *Sexuality and Its Discontents* (London: Routledge & Kegan Paul, 1984), one can clearly see the tension between the deconstruction of sexual science, on the one hand, and the use of sexological categories such as "sexual minorities," on the other. Weeks, however, is somewhat more critical of sexology than Rubin, possibly because he is more concerned to develop a framework for ethical decision making.

24. Lynne Segal, *Is the Future Female? Reflections on Contemporary Feminism* (London: Virago, 1986).

25. The term "Race" is applied to women by Mary Daly, *Pure Lust: Elemental Feminist Philosophy* (Boston: Beacon, 1984).

26. See Samois, *Coming to Power: Writings and Graphics on Lesbian S/M* (Boston: Alyson, 1982); Samois, *What Color Is Your Handkerchief?* (Berkeley: Samois, 1979); and Pat Califia's article in the *Advocate* in the early eighties.

27. Jeffrey Weeks makes a similar argument in his discussion of sexual ethics. See *Sexuality*, 81–86. His comments there parallel my discussion of sadomasochism in Mariana Valverde, *Sex, Power, and Pleasure* (Toronto: Women's Press, 1985, and Philadelphia, New Society, 1987), 170–76. Both Weeks's discussion and mine, however, remain sketchy and do not sufficiently theorize what is meant by "power" in a sexual context.

28. Rosalind Petchesky, *Abortion and Woman's Choice: The State, Sexuality, and Reproductive Freedom* (Boston: Northeastern, 1984), 13.

29. Ibid., 378.

PART FOUR

Pornography and Speech Acts

Two of the most influential and at the same time most controversial claims in the current debate about pornography are: (i) pornography *is* the (sexually explicit) subordination of women, and (ii) pornography *silences* women.[1] Many people who advocate a restrictive or prohibitive policy on pornography follow Catharine MacKinnon and Andrea Dworkin in endorsing these two claims. But, as we have already seen, objections to (i) and (ii) may be leveled from a liberal perspective (see Ronald Dworkin's paper "Liberty and Pornography" in Part Two), and from a feminist perspective (see Ellen Willis' paper in Part Three). Moreover, as I mention in the Introduction, (i) and (ii) give rise to several distinctly philosophical worries; indeed, it has been said that the idea that pornography subordinates women is "philosophically indefensible."[2] If only agents (that is, people) can subordinate other people, how can *pornography* subordinate women? Also, how, precisely, is pornography able to silence women? It is time to face those questions squarely.

In their model anti-pornography civil rights ordinance, MacKinnon and Andrea Dworkin say, "Pornography is the sexually explicit subordination of

---

[1]These claims are, to some extent, mutually supporting. One way of explaining how pornography subordinates women would be to explain how it silences women. And if it can be established that pornography silences women—on some plausible understanding of what it is to silence—then the claim that pornography subordinates women gains credence.

[2]W. A. Parent, "A Second Look at Pornography and the Subordination of Women," *Journal of Philosophy* 87 (1990): 205–211, 211.

women. . . ." Now, why might this claim be philosophically indefensible? Consider the following two sentences:

(a) Earth is the third planet from the sun.

(b) Joan's dog is loyal.

Sentence (a) says that Earth is the very same thing as the thing that is the third planet from the sun. Sentence (b), however, does not say that Joan's dog is the same thing as loyal, or that loyal is the same thing as Joan's dog. Indeed, it is hard to make any sense of this at all. Rather *is* in sentence (b) is used to say that Joan's dog has a particular property—namely, the property of being loyal. Thus, philosophers distinguish between what is called the "is" of identity and the "is" of predication; sentence (a) employs the former, and sentence (b) employs the latter.

Let us return to the idea that pornography *is* the subordination of women. On the basis of their essays in Part One, we can infer that MacKinnon and Andrea Dworkin intend the *is* in their definition to be read as the "is" of identity. No doubt they do believe that pornography both depicts and contributes to the subordination of women, but the point of their definition is different. Their point is that pornography really *is* the subordination of women; or, in other words, pornography *subordinates* women. But is pornography the kind of thing that can subordinate?

Let us take *subordinate* to mean "to place [a] person or group of persons socially in the class of those whose intrinsic or inherent moral worth or standing is not of the first rank, and whose rights are thereby of lesser scope, importance, or weight than the rights of others."[3] Then we must ask whether films, magazines, or books themselves can do this. It might be argued that to answer in the affirmative is to make what the philosopher Gilbert Ryle called a "category mistake."[4] We make a category mistake when we flout the "logic" of a concept. For example, were someone to say "The number five has a headache," or "My dream weighed 5 pounds," they would commit a category mistake, for numbers and dreams are not the appropriate kinds of things to have headaches and weights, respectively. Now, the verb *to subordinate* takes an agent as subject. Thus we might say that the "logic" of subordination implies that it is only human beings who can subordinate. Trees,

---

[3]Melinda Vadas, "A First Look at the Pornography/Civil Rights Ordinance: Could Pornography Be the Subordination of Women?" *Journal of Philosophy* 84 (1987): 487–511, 506.
[4]Gilbert Ryle, *The Concept of Mind* (London: Hutchinson University Library, 1949).

planets, racecourses—and, specifically, books, videos, and magazines—are simply unable to do this.

Notice as well that the verb *to silence* usually takes an agent, or person, as subject. Of course, expressions such as "The speaker was silenced by the passing garbage truck" are meaningful. Here, what is being asserted is that something (the garbage truck) made so much noise that someone (the speaker) could not be heard. Is that what some feminist critics of pornography have in mind about pornography? That is, do they think that pornography makes a loud noise, loud enough to drown out the speech of women differentially? It is not obvious that this is what they mean. At the very least, this sort of claim is little more than metaphorical, and anti-pornography feminists are concerned about demonstrating the *real* detrimental effects of some pornography. So the claim that pornography silences women—just like the claim that pornography is the subordination of women—must be read literally. For similar reasons we must ask after the coherence of this claim, does it make any sense?

MacKinnon is aware of the way in which her claims are interpreted; she writes, "To say that pornography is an *act* against women is seen as metaphorical or magical, rhetorical or unreal, a literary hyperbole or propaganda device [emphasis added]."[5] However, she does intend the assertion to be taken literally. In Part Four, Rae Langton and Jennifer Hornsby explain how no "metaphysical sleight-of-hand"[6] is involved in such an interpretation. In "Speech Acts and Unspeakable Acts," Langton argues that the claim that pornography subordinates is intelligible, and in "Speech Acts and Pornography," Hornsby shows how pornography might be able to silence. As the titles of their essays suggest, both philosophers make use of a particular theory in the philosophy of language known as speech act theory.

Speech act theory receives its earliest exposition in the work of British philosopher J. L. Austin.[7] The central theme of speech act theory is captured in Austin's own words: "To say something is to *do* something."[8] Speech act theorists contend that a satisfactory understanding of the way language

---

[5]Catharine A. MacKinnon, *Only Words* (Cambridge, Mass.: Harvard University Press, 1993), 11.

[6]Ronald Dworkin, "Women and Pornography," *New York Review of Books*, 21 October 1993, 38.

[7]J. L.Austin, *How to Do Things with Words* (London: Oxford University Press, 1962); see also John Searle, *Speech Acts* (Cambridge: Cambridge University Press, 1970).

[8]Austin, *How to Do Things with Words,* 12.

works requires that we pay attention not only (i) to what our utterances mean, but also (ii) to the effects our utterances have and especially (iii) to what we do in saying what we say. There is some terminology here that is important. When Sarah makes a meaningful utterance—for example, "It's raining outside"—she is performing what is called a "locutionary act"; she is reporting on some state of affairs in the world, and what she says is either true or false. Suppose, alternatively, that Sarah says to Bill, "Go on, apply for the job!"—and Bill does apply. We might say that Sarah has persuaded Bill to apply; the effect of her saying what she said to Bill, in a particular context, was to get him to send in his application form, say. To do something *by* saying something is to perform a "perlocutionary act." Finally, imagine that Bill says "I do" to Sarah in the presence of a minister and in the context of a marriage ceremony. In this instance, Bill does something *in* saying "I do"; namely, he marries Sarah. He performs what Austin calls an "illocutionary act." Other examples of illocutionary acts include ordering, reprimanding, congratulating, and promising. Philosophers do disagree about how exactly to draw the distinction between perlocutionary and illocutionary acts. For instance, is humiliation a perlocutionary or an illocutionary act? Perhaps the best way to think about the difference is this: When we speak of perlocutionary acts—that is, the doing of something *by* saying something—what is of interest is some (future) causal effect of the relevant utterance. When we speak of illocutionary acts—that is, the doing of something *in* saying something—what is of interest is the act constituted by the utterance.

Now, one very important point about illocutionary acts is this: in order to count as a particular illocutionary act, an utterance must satisfy certain "felicity conditions." As Langton explains, "Whether in saying 'I do' the speaker is marrying depends on the felicity conditions of marriage, which require that the speaker intends to marry, and that the utterance takes place in the course of a particular conventional procedure, with appropriate participants (adult heterosexual couple, unmarried, plus priest or registrar). The speaker will also need to secure 'uptake': that is to say, the hearer must recognize that an illocution of a certain kind is being performed." Hence, Bill does not succeed in marrying Sarah if he merely utters the words "I do" to a photograph of her on his desk.

How might this theory help us in understanding the claim that pornography subordinates and silences women? I shall begin with the matter of subordination. We have noted that MacKinnon intends the claim to be read literally. She is not only asserting that pornography conveys a message about women's inferior status (a locutionary act), nor is she simply pointing to the fact that pornography sometimes has the effect of encouraging its consumers to treat women as if they were inferior (a perlocutionary act). In addition, MacKinnon wants to say that pornography may be used to perform an illocutionary act—namely, the act of subordinating women. The problem, however, is to understand whether this could be true; does the claim make any sense? A separate issue is whether the claim *is* true.

In order to figure out whether it could be true that pornography subordinates, we need to determine whether *any* words (or expressions) could, in principle, subordinate. Consider Langton's two examples: "Blacks are not permitted to vote," uttered by a legislator in Pretoria, South Africa, and "Whites only." She writes of the former: "It is a locutionary act: by 'blacks' it refers to blacks. It is a perlocutionary act: it will have the effect, among others, that blacks stay away from polling booths. But it is, first and foremost, an illocutionary act: it makes it the case that blacks are not permitted to vote."[9] Similarly, Langton contends, uttering "Whites only" is an illocutionary act. "It orders blacks away, welcomes whites, permits whites to act in a discriminatory way towards blacks." At the outset, I suggested that *to subordinate* means (at least) "to place [a] person or group of persons socially in the class of those whose intrinsic or inherent moral worth or standing is not of the first rank, and whose rights are thereby of lesser scope, importance, or weight than the rights of others." More precisely, Langton argues that in order for an illocutionary act to be an act of subordination it must possess the following three features: it must (i) "*unfairly* rank" a person or group of people "as having inferior worth," (ii) "legitimate *discriminatory* behavior" on the part of some people towards that person or group of people, and (iii) "*unjustly* deprive" that person or group of people of some important powers. Arguably, "Blacks are not permitted to vote," and "Whites only" uttered in South Africa, *by a person who occupies a position of authority in the relevant domain,* have just these features and so constitute acts of subordination. That the utterances be made by a person in authority is crucial. Those same utterances performed by a black actor in a Johannesburg theater would not constitute subordinating speech acts. Put another

---

[9]Happily, due to recent events in South Africa, this example has lost some of its force. In April 1994, after hundreds of years of white domination, South Africa held its first open election. People of every race were permitted to vote and did so. Nelson Mandela of the African National Congress became President of South Africa.

way, that the speaker "occupy a position of authority in a relevant domain" is among the felicity conditions for an illocutionary act of subordination. As MacKinnon sums it up:

> Authoritatively *saying* someone is inferior is largely how structures of status and differential treatment are demarcated and actualized. Words and images are how people are placed in hierarchies, how social stratification is made to seem inevitable and right, how feelings of social inferiority and superiority are engendered, and how indifference to violence against those on the bottom is rationalized and normalized.[10]

On the basis of the foregoing analysis it is certainly intelligible to claim that pornography could subordinate women. Our question now is whether that claim is true. As the writers in Part One argue, some pornography does rank women as having inferior worth: MacKinnon, for example, says, "Pornography defines women by how . . . [they] look according to how . . . [they] can be sexually used." And Longino's characterization of pornography as "verbal or pictorial material which represents or describes sexual behavior that is degrading or abusive to one or more of the participants *in such a way as to endorse the degradation*" suggests that some pornography legitimates discriminatory behavior towards women. Finally, if some pornography operates in a such a way as to deprive women unjustly of certain important powers (for example, the right to participate equally in the political process), then, at the very least, *some* pornography does possess the features necessary for making it capable of subordinating.

However, we must move slowly here. In the first place, we need to investigate further the idea that pornography unjustly deprives women of important powers. So, for example, if it could be established that some pornography also silences women, then we could agree that some pornography possesses the third feature necessary to give it the illocutionary force of subordinating. In the second place, recall that subordinating speech must also be authoritative speech. That is, among the felicity conditions for an illocutionary act of subordination is that the speech act in question be performed by a person who occupies a position of authority in the relevant domain. Hence, we must determine whether pornography's speakers have the relevant authority. Before addressing the question of authority, however, let us see what can be said in support of the claim that pornography silences.

---

[10]MacKinnon, *Only Words,* 31.

Jennifer Hornsby contends that "communication is a relation between people, and . . . requires understanding on an audience's part attuned not only to the significance of the sounds the speaker produces [that is, the meaning of her words], but also to her intended performances." This idea should remind you of the notion of felicity conditions. Recall in the marriage example above that one important felicity condition of performing the illocutionary act of marrying (in saying "I do") is that the speaker "secure uptake." In other words, Bill will not succeed in marrying Sarah if she and others do not recognize that Bill has performed the relevant illocutionary act. For all his sincere efforts—he genuinely intends to marry Sarah, believes that saying "I do" is a (the) way to do this, and so on—Bill can fail to perform successfully the act of marrying if his audience does not understand him to have performed that act. Similarly, and more generally, for any illocutionary act (of a particular type) A, if a speaker is not understood by her audience to have performed A, she will not have (successfully) performed A. We might imagine that all communication involves performing some illocutionary act or other and so conclude that all successful communication depends upon a certain match between (i) a speaker's intention to perform a particular illocutionary act and (ii) her audience's recognition that she has performed that act.

Hornsby suggests that we call this match *reciprocity*. She says, reciprocity "obtains when people are such as to recognize one another's speech as it is meant to be taken, and thus to ensure the success of attempts to perform speech acts." Some examples will be helpful here. Suppose I say "I promise to return your book tomorrow," sincerely intending (in so saying) to be making a promise to you vis-à-vis your book. In saying what I say, I not only assume that you will understand the meaning of the words I utter; I also rely on your being willing and able to recognize that in saying what I say I have made you a promise. That is, I assume that reciprocity obtains. If it does—if you do indeed recognize that I have made you a promise—then I will have successfully performed the speech act I intended to perform. Alternatively, consider a woman who says no to a man in response to his sexual advances, intending to refuse them. Imagine also that for whatever reason her audience (the man in question) is not willing or able to recognize her speech act as the speech act she intended—namely, one of refusal. In such a situation reciprocity does not obtain, and it is impossible for the woman to perform the illocutionary act she intends. As Hornsby says, "To perform the illocutionary act of refusal successfully, an utterance of the word 'no' is not enough: to refuse successfully a woman must be understood as attempting to refuse. But a woman may mean to refuse, but be unable successfully to refuse, because a condition of her having successfully refused—that she be recognized as attempting to refuse—is not satisfied." The central point here is that circumstances can sometimes be such as to make it impossible for a person to perform the illocutionary acts she intends to perform—that is, to do the things with her words she intends to do. According to Hornsby, this is how we are to understand silencing. "The silenced person does not have it in her power to do with language what she might want to do"; she has been "deprived of illocutionary potential." As we have seen in the example above, a person is so deprived when reciprocity does not obtain: a refusal is not a refusal unless it is so taken to be.

Reciprocity can fail to obtain for any number of reasons. For example, I might have made promises to you in the past that I have never kept. If so, you may refuse to recognize that I have a made a promise to you now when I say "I promise to return your book." Similarly, we all know people who are systematically unreliable in reporting information, and as a result we do not take their pronouncements to be assertions of the truth, no matter how sincerely they are uttered. These are cases of what we might call "local" failures of reciprocity: reciprocity fails to obtain on the basis of some shared history of the speaker and the hearer in question. But reciprocity might be absent on a more global scale, and it might depend on things having little to do with any prior interaction between a particular speaker and a particular hearer. For example, as Hornsby points out, suppose that "embedded within the social practices in which our speech actions happen is a code of behavior . . . a code according to which men have uncontrollable sexual urges; women who do not behave and dress with great circumspection are ready and willing to gratify those urges, but will feign unwillingness, whether through decency, or through deceitfulness, or through a desire to excite." If this code underpins men's beliefs about themselves and women, and consequently gives rise to expectations about women's behavior in the face of sexual overtures, we might imagine that few women will be recognized to have refused a sexual advance when they say no. In other words, ideas about "proper" sexual etiquette could mitigate against the existence of reciprocity in certain sexual situations between men and women. Recall, on this account, an absence of reciprocity makes it impossible to perform certain illocutionary acts. If we agree that this is what it is to silence and, further, if it is plausible to claim that pornography is responsible for the sorts of beliefs and expectations that ensure an absence of reciprocity, then we can say that pornography is indeed able to silence. As Hornsby concludes, "My claim is that the promulgation of a demeaning view of women can have the effect of rendering women relatively powerless parties in communicative exchanges because it affects the reciprocity that is a precondition of illocution. For women as for men, the illocutionary acts that they are able to perform are only those they may be taken to be performing. But men more than women have determined when reciprocity obtains."

If Hornsby is right, then it is at least plausible to think that some pornography has the ability to silence women and thus that some pornography unjustly deprives women of the important power of free speech. Recall that this—namely, the unjust deprivation of some important power—was the third feature of Langton's characterization of subordinating speech. Thus, Hornsby's account of silencing lends further support to the intelligibility of the claim that pornography subordinates. There is, however, one last point to be considered, and that is whether pornography is authoritative speech.

In broad agreement with MacKinnon, Langton argues that it is at least worth asking, Is pornography *in the domain of sex* authoritative speech? She concedes that an answer here is not likely to be forthcoming "from the philosopher's armchair." Rather, we must investigate whether pornography is understood by its consumers as an authoritative source on sex, appropriate sexual behavior, and women's sexual desires. It is at least plausible that pornography represents, for many young men, the only detailed information about these matters. In the absence of alternative views, such people would have no reason to doubt the "truth" of pornography's pronouncements.

Langton appears, then, to have established a *prima facie* case for the intelligibility of the claim that pornography subordinates; she has shown that the idea is philosophically defensible. It is a separate question whether it is true that pornography either subordinates or silences, and thus we are driven back to the need for empirical research. But the empirical questions which face us now, under this new analysis, are different from the difficult-to-answer question: Does pornography lead to rape? Our new questions are: Is pornography authoritative speech in the domain of sex? What expectations do men have of women in sexual situations? and so on.

The appropriation of speech act theory into the debate about pornography also has implications for the assessment of liberal arguments against the restriction or prohibition of pornography. Recall that liberal philosopher Ronald Dworkin takes free speech to be a negative liberty, "something . . .

[one has] unless someone interferes with you." On this view, a person's free speech is threatened only if there are actual obstacles to her speaking—for example, when a speaker is drowned out by a heckling mob. As Hornsby notes, this liberal account assumes that "communication using speech is . . . a matter merely of getting out some audible sentences. . . ." However, as she shows, a person can get out all the audible sentences she wants, but if reciprocity fails to obtain, she will not be able to perform the illocutionary acts she intends. In short, sometimes circumstances can make it impossible for a person to communicate. If the right to free speech is a right to communicate, not simply to make noise, then the liberal has too narrow a view of what does and does not pose a threat to free speech. In particular, if Hornsby's account is on the right track, the strongest feminist anti-pornography argument against the liberal—that is, the argument that takes pornography to pose a conflict between the free speech of pornographers and that of women—looks more compelling.

Finally, the use of speech act theory to support the claim that pornography *can* subordinate enables an argument to the effect that pornography ought to be construed legally as a form of discrimination on a par with sexual harassment and racial segregation. In the Introduction, I discuss why this is a powerful argument in the hands of anti-pornography advocates. They can concede that pornography is a form of speech, but argue that it is also a practice—in particular, that it is sexual discrimination. What is problematic about pornography is not so much what it says as what it does. From this perspective, restrictive or prohibitive policies on pornography need not be understood as calls for *content-based* restriction—something which is eschewed by both the U.S. and Canadian courts. The speech act approach, if plausible, sets the stage for a new round of philosophical and legal arguments.

RAE LANGTON

Speech Acts and Unspeakable Acts

Pornography is speech. So the courts declared in judging it protected by the First Amendment. Pornography is a kind of act. So Catharine MacKinnon declared in arguing for laws against it.[1] Put these together and we have: pornography is a kind of speech act. In what follows I take this suggestion seriously.

If pornography is speech, what does it say? If pornography is a kind of act, what does it do? Judge Frank Easterbrook, accepting the premises of antipornography legislation, gave an answer. Pornography is speech that depicts subordination. In the words of the feminist ordinance passed in Indianapolis, pornography depicts women

> dehumanized as sexual objects, things or commodities; enjoying pain or humiliation or rape; being tied up, cut up, mutilated, bruised, or physically hurt; in postures of sexual submission or servility or display; reduced to body parts, penetrated by objects or animals, or presented in scenarios of degradation, injury, torture; shown as filthy or inferior; bleeding, bruised or hurt in a context which makes these conditions sexual.[2]

Source: Rae Langton, "Speech Acts and Unspeakable Acts," *Philosophy and Public Affairs* 22(4): 293–330. Copyright 1993 by Princeton University Press. Reprinted by permission of Princeton University Press.

Special thanks for comments on earlier drafts and ancestors of this paper are due to Susan Brison, Mark Hannam, Sally Haslanger, Richard Holton, Jennifer Hornsby, Lloyd Humberstone, Philip Petit, Sarah Richmond, Frederick Schauer, Michael Smith, Natalie Stoljar, and three anonymous referees of *Philosophy & Public Affairs*.

Pornography is a kind of act that has certain effects. Depictions of subordination, said Easterbrook, "tend to perpetuate subordination. The subordinate status of women in turn leads to affront and lower pay at work, insult and injury at home, battery and rape on the streets." His conclusion was that the ordinance was unconstitutional; for, he said, "this simply demonstrates the power of pornography as speech."[3]

Pornography, on this view, depicts subordination and causes it. A closer look at the words of the ordinance shows us that MacKinnon is saying something more. Before describing what pornography depicts, the ordinance begins: "We define pornography as the graphic sexually explicit subordination of women in pictures or words." Besides depicting and causing subordination, as Easterbrook allowed, pornography *is,* in and of itself, a form of subordination.[4]

This latter aspect of the legislation provoked the ire of judges and philosophers alike. In proposing that pornography actually is subordination, the drafters of the ordinance were tricksters, guilty of "a certain sleight of hand," said Judge Barker, in the District Court.[5] They were guilty of conceptual confusion, and their claim was "philosophically indefensible," said William Parent in the *Journal of Philosophy.*[6] It is all very well to talk about what pornography depicts; and it is all very well to talk about the effects it has on the lives of women. It is all very well to say, with Easterbrook, that pornography depicts subordination and causes it. Such claims may be unnerving, and they may be empirically false, but they are not, at least, incoherent. MacKinnon wants to say something more; she wants to attend not simply to the content of pornographic speech, nor simply to its effects, but to the actions constituted by it.

What she says may strike a chord of recognition among those who recall an older, more tranquil debate in the philosophy of language, and a philosopher who took as his starting point the slogan that "to say something is to *do* something." In *How to Do Things with Words,* J. L. Austin complained of a "constant tendency in philosophy" to overlook something of great importance: a tendency to consider the content of a linguistic utterance, and its effects on hearers, but to overlook the action constituted by it.[7] Austin encouraged philosophers to shift their gazes away from statements considered in isolation, sentences that describe, truly or falsely, some state of affairs, and look instead at "the issuing of an utterance in a speech situation."[8] Words, he said, were used to perform all kinds of actions—warning, promising, marrying, and the like—that philosophy had blithely ignored.

To say something is usually to do a number of different things. An example (from Austin):[9] Two men stand beside a woman. The first man turns to the second, and says "Shoot her." The second man looks shocked, then raises a gun and shoots the woman. You witness the scene and describe it later. The first man said to second, "Shoot her," meaning by "shoot" to shoot with a gun, and referring by "her" to the woman nearby. That description roughly captures the content of what was said: it captures what

Austin called the *locutionary* act. To perform a locutionary act is to utter a sentence that has a particular meaning, as traditionally conceived.[10] However, there is more to what you witnessed, so you describe the scene again. *By* saying "shoot her," the first man *shocked* the second; by saying "shoot her," the first man *persuaded* the second to shoot the woman. That description captures some of the effects of what was said: it captures what Austin called the *perlocutionary* act. But if you stop there you will still have left something out. You will have ignored what the first man did in saying what he said. So you go on. *In* saying "shoot her," the first man *urged* the second to shoot the woman. That description captures the actions constituted by the utterance itself: it captures what Austin called the *illocutionary* act. The actions listed earlier—warning, promising, marrying—are illocutionary acts. Austin's complaint was that this latter dimension to speech was often ignored, that there was "a tendency in philosophy to elide [illocutions] in favour of the other two."[11]

Pornography is not always done with words. Yet Easterbrook's description exemplifies the tendency of which Austin complained. Pornography depicts subordination and causes it. That—in Austin's terms—is to describe its locutionary and perlocutionary dimensions. What is missing is a description of the actions constituted by pornographic utterances: in Austin's terms, pornography's *illocutionary* force. MacKinnon supplies such a description when she says that pornography is an act of subordination.

Like Austin, MacKinnon wants to undermine the dichotomy between word and action. "Which is saying 'kill' to a trained guard dog, a word or an act?" she asks, in a passage that echoes Austin's example.[12] MacKinnon has accordingly been interpreted as saying that pornography is unprotected conduct rather than protected speech,[13] and one might imagine that Austin's approach gives this idea some support. If pornography is a kind of act, and action is conduct, then, one might think, pornography is unprotected by the First Amendment. But that interpretation of MacKinnon is wrong. "To state the obvious," she says, "I do not argue that pornography is 'conduct' in the First Amendment doctrinal sense."[14] In any case Austin's approach would give it no support, for it does not help us to distinguish conduct from speech. If there is a line that divides speech from conduct in the law, it does not divide speech from action in Austin's philosophy. On his view, *all* speech acts are actions. To say that pornography is a kind of act is not to say that pornography is conduct, and nothing that I say will turn on that claim. The important point is that actions, whether speech or conduct, can be protected or unprotected by law.[15] Whether they are protected should depend, in general, on the effects they have, and the actions they are.

Austin and MacKinnon are emerging as close, if unlikely, cousins. In this paper I exploit the work of the former to illuminate and defend the latter. . . .

The claim that pornography subordinates women, however interpreted, is a claim that pornography determines women's inferior civil status. Viewed thus, the ordinance poses an apparent conflict between liberty and equality:

the liberty of men to produce and consume pornography, and the rights of women to equal civil status. That is how the case was viewed by the courts. It posed a conflict between the right to free speech guaranteed by the First Amendment, and the right to equality guaranteed by the Fourteenth Amendment. . . .

. . . Once we consider pornographic images and texts as speech acts, we are in a position to apply to them Austin's distinctions between locutionary, illocutionary, and perlocutionary acts. We can make good sense of some central feminist claims when we focus on the illocutionary aspect of pornographic speech. . . .

I. "Pornography Subordinates"

Speech Acts

Before considering whether pornographic speech acts may subordinate, we will first look at speech acts in closer detail, and then ask whether in principle speech acts may subordinate.

Austin's chief concern was with illocutionary speech acts, and much labor in *How to Do Things with Words* is devoted to discovering what is distinctive about them. An illocutionary act is the action performed simply *in* saying something. A perlocutionary act is the action performed *by* saying something. A perlocutionary act is an utterance considered in terms of its consequences, such as the effects it has on its hearers. Austin took pains to distinguish illocutions from perlocutions, and he thought that the phrases "in saying" and "by saying" were typical—though by no means infallible— markers of the two. "In saying 'I do' I was marrying; by saying 'I do' I greatly distressed my mother." Saying "I do" in the right context counts as— constitutes—marrying: that is the illocutionary act performed. It does not count as distressing my mother, even if it has that effect: that is the perlocutionary act performed.

The illocutionary act bears certain relations to the other two. It can be thought of as a *use* of the locution to perform an action. In the earlier example, the first man used the locution "shoot her" to *urge* the second to shoot, whereas he might have used the very same locution to perform a different action: to *order* the second, or to *advise* perhaps. An illocutionary act may have a particular perlocutionary effect as its goal. When the first man urged the second to shoot, he may have aimed to *persuade* the second to shoot.

Austin's belief that there is something distinctive about illocutionary acts seems right. What we have here are utterances whose force is something more than the semantic content of the sentence uttered—the locution— and something other than the effects achieved by the utterance—the perlocution.

What is responsible for this important third dimension? Austin's answer was that an utterance has illocutionary force of a certain kind when it satisfies certain felicity conditions. These are typically set by conventions, written or unwritten, and typically require that the speaker is intending to do something with his words. Speech acts are a subset of actions in general, so there will always be some description under which a speech act is intentionally performed, and not mere noise and motion of lips.[16] The intention to perform an illocution of a particular kind often has an important role to play in determining what illocution is performed. Whether in saying "I do" the speaker is marrying depends on the felicity conditions of marriage, which require that the speaker intends to marry, and that the utterance takes place in the course of a particular conventional procedure, with appropriate participants (adult heterosexual couple, unmarried, plus priest or registrar). The speaker will also need to secure "uptake": that is to say, the hearer must recognize that an illocution of a certain kind is being performed. So, at any rate, the typical cases run. . . .

Subordinating Speech Acts

We turn now to the second preliminary task: the question of whether speech acts can, in principle, subordinate. Austin placed his theory of speech and action firmly in the arena of social activity, and there is a political dimension to this arena. People manage to do all kinds of things with words. Besides advising, warning, and marrying one another, people also manage to hurt and oppress one another. A child may chant that "sticks and stones may break my bones, but names will never hurt." Names do hurt, though. That is just why she chants. And that is why the law regards some speech as injury. Words can break bones. "Shoot her!" might break a few, as a perlocutionary act at any rate. ("By saying 'shoot her' he caused her skull to be fractured.") Speech can do more than break bones. It can determine civil status, as Easterbrook agreed, interpreting the idea in perlocutionary terms: by depicting subordination, pornographers perpetuate subordination.

When MacKinnon says that speech can subordinate, she means something more: that pornography can have the illocutionary force of subordination, and not simply have subordination as its locutionary content, or as its perlocutionary effect: *in* depicting subordination, pornographers subordinate. This is the alleged "sleight of hand."[17]

We need to evaluate this charge. Can a speech act be an illocutionary act of subordination? The answer, I think, is yes. Consider this utterance: "Blacks are not permitted to vote." Imagine that it is uttered by a legislator in Pretoria in the context of enacting legislation that underpins apartheid. It is a locutionary act: by "blacks" it refers to blacks. It is a perlocutionary act: it will have the effect, among others, that blacks stay away from polling booths. But it is, first and foremost, an illocutionary act: it makes it the case that blacks are not permitted to vote. It—plausibly— subordinates blacks. So does this utterance: "Whites only."[18] It too is a locutionary act: by "whites" it refers to whites. It has some important perlocutionary effects: it keeps blacks away from white areas, ensures that only whites go there, and perpetuates racism. It is—one might say—a perlocutionary act of subordination. But it is also an illocutionary act: it orders blacks away, welcomes whites, permits whites to act in a discriminatory way towards blacks. It subordinates blacks.[19] If this is correct, then there is no sleight of hand, no philosophical impropriety, about the claim that a certain kind of speech can be an illocutionary act of subordination.

In virtue of what do the speech acts of apartheid subordinate? In virtue of what are they illocutionary acts of subordination? In virtue of at least the following three features, I suggest. They *rank* blacks as having inferior worth. They *legitimate* discriminatory behavior on the part of whites. And finally, they *deprive* blacks of some important powers: for example, the power to go to certain areas and the power to vote. Here I am in broad agreement with MacKinnon, who says that to subordinate someone is to put them in a position of inferiority or loss of power, or to demean or denigrate them.[20]

There are two brief caveats before I go on. First, on the notion of legitimating: the illocutionary act of legitimating something is to be distinguished from the perlocutionary act of making people believe that something is legitimate. Certainly one effect of legitimating something is that people believe it is legitimate. But they believe it is legitimate because it has been legitimated, not vice versa. People believe discriminatory behavior to be legitimate because it has indeed been made legitimate in that particular arena of activity (though there may still be some perspective outside that arena from which one can say that discriminatory behavior is never truly legitimate).[21] Second, I do not suggest that all acts of ranking, legitimating, or depriving of powers are acts of subordination. Someone may rank an athlete as the fastest, legitimate beer drinking on campus, or deprive a driver of his license. These may be illocutionary acts that rank, legitimate, or deprive people of powers, yet they are not acts of subordination. But, unlike these, the speech acts of apartheid are acts of subordination: they *unfairly* rank blacks as having inferior worth; they legitimate *discriminatory* behavior on the part of whites; and they *unjustly* deprive them of some important powers.

Speech acts of this kind belong to an important class of illocutions discussed by Austin towards the end of his work. Some illocutions involve the authoritative delivery of a finding about some matters of fact or value. Actions of ranking, valuing, and placing are illocutions of this kind, labeled *verdictive* by Austin. For example: An umpire calls "Fault" at a tennis match. He expresses his opinion. He describes the world as he sees it. But he does much more than that: he gives his verdict. A bystander says "Fault." He expresses his opinion. He describes the world as he sees it. What he says has just the same content as what the umpire says: they perform the same locutionary act. But the bystander's utterance makes no difference to the score. The umpire's does. A government's action of ranking members of a certain race as inferior to others can be compared to the speech of the umpire, rather than the bystander. The authoritative role of the speaker imbues the utterance with a force that would be absent were it made by someone who did not occupy that role.

Close relatives of verdictives are illocutions that confer powers and rights on people, or deprive people of powers and rights. Actions of ordering, permitting, prohibiting, authorizing, enacting law, and dismissing an employee are illocutions of this kind, labeled *exercitive* by Austin.[22] The speech acts of apartheid that legitimate discriminatory behavior and unjustly deprive blacks of certain rights have an exercitive force that would be absent if they were made by speakers who did not have the appropriate authority.

It is in virtue of these particular verdictive and exercitive dimensions, then, that the speech acts of apartheid subordinate. This already tells us something important about any claim that a certain kind of speech subordinates. For the crucial feature of verdictive and exercitive illocutions is their sensitivity to the speaker's authority, and we can accordingly group them together under the label *authoritative* illocutions: actions whose felicity conditions require that the speaker occupy a position of authority in a relevant domain. Sometimes that authority is officially recognized. That is true of the utterances of the legislator enacting the laws of apartheid, and it is true of the umpire giving a verdict on a fault. But the principle that illocutionary force can vary with the authority of the speaker is more general. A slave may say to his master, "Is there anything to eat?" and the utterance may have the force of an entreaty. The master may say to the slave, "Is there anything to eat?" and the utterance may have the exercitive force of an order. And the domains of authority can vary in size and scope. The domain of the legislator's authority is vast—the entire population of a nation, present and future. There are [also] smaller domains. A parent who prohibits a child from venturing barefoot into the snow has authority in the local domain of the family. A patient who prohibits a doctor from administering life-saving medication has authority in the very local domain of his own life, his own body. In all these cases the action performed depends on the authority of the speaker in the relevant domain. Subordinating speech acts are authoritative speech acts, so if we are ever to count some class of speech acts as subordinating speech, the speakers in question must have authority. This is something to bear in mind in what follows.

Pornography

MacKinnon thinks that pornography in particular subordinates. The courts sometimes view this claim as a description of pornography's content. "Those words and pictures which *depict women in sexually subordinate roles* are banned by the Ordinance," said Judge Barker in the District Court, giving this as grounds for the Indianapolis Ordinance's unconstitutionality.[23] Barker is mistaken: the ordinance does not ban material simply in virtue of its content, for at this locutionary level there is nothing particularly distinctive about pornography. Not all sexually explicit depictions of subordination are pornography, as MacKinnon herself points out.[24] Utterances whose locutions depict subordination do not always subordinate. Locutions that depict subordination could in principle be used to perform speech acts that are a far cry from pornography: documentaries, for example, or police reports, or government studies, or books that protest against sexual violence, or perhaps even legal definitions of pornography. It all depends, as Austin might have said, on the *use* to which the locution is put. If we are to find what is distinctive about pornography, it seems that we must look elsewhere.

The perlocutionary aspect of pornographic utterances has rightly attracted much attention. This, as we saw, is how Easterbrook interpreted MacKinnon's claim when he said that pornography "perpetuates" subordination. At the perlocutionary level, pornographic speech can be variously described. Some hearers are entertained and sexually aroused by it. At this level a difference between pornography and documentaries that depict subordination does emerge. Although similar locutions may be used in both cases, different effects are achieved in the hearers: sexual arousal in the one case, indignation, perhaps, in the other. Pornography does more than arouse. Some of its hearers are distressed by it, as was made evident at the 1983 Minneapolis hearings. Some, it seems, have their attitudes and behavior altered by it in ways that ultimately hurt women: they can become more likely to view women as inferior, more disposed to accept rape myths (for example, that women enjoy rape), and more likely to view rape victims as deserving of their treatment, more likely to say that they themselves would rape if they could get away with it.[25] This in turn means that some women are hurt by it. In Easterbrook's words, pornography perpetuates the cycle of "insult and injury at home, battery and rape on the streets."

The claim that pornography harms women is not yet the perlocutionary claim conceded by the court that pornography perpetuates women's subordination. Plenty of people are harmed by cigarettes, but they are not thereby subordinated. A link between harm and subordination is made, though, when we shift our perspective on the asymmetric pattern of sexual violence and view it afresh, not simply as harm or as crime, but as an aspect of women's subordinate status.[26] To view it otherwise would be to obscure its systematically discriminatory nature, and to obscure the fact that the perpetrators are nearly always members of one class of citizens, the victims nearly always members of another. This shift in perspective is an important feature of feminist political analysis, and it affects how we are to characterize pornography in perlocutionary (and, we shall see shortly, illocutionary) terms. If pornography has sexual violence as its effect and sexual violence is an aspect of women's subordination, then pornography is a *perlocutionary* act of subordination. That is how we reach the claim conceded by Easterbrook: pornography perpetuates women's subordination.

However, the claim that pornography subordinates women is an illocutionary claim that goes beyond these locutionary and perlocutionary dimensions, and it is related to other illocutionary claims that feminists have made about pornography. Pornography is said to *rank* women as sex objects, "defined on the basis of [their] looks . . . [their] availability for sexual pleasure."[27] Pornography represents degrading and abusive sexual behavior "in such a way as to *endorse* the degradation."[28] MacKinnon has a striking list of illocutionary verbs: "Pornography sexualizes rape, battery, sexual harassment . . . and child sexual abuse; it . . . *celebrates, promotes, authorizes* and *legitimates* them."[29] These descriptions bear on the claim that pornography subordinates. Recall that we found three features in virtue of which the speech acts of apartheid were plausibly described as illocutionary acts of subordination. They rank certain people as inferior; they legitimate discriminatory behavior towards them; and they deprive them of powers and rights. The feminist claims we have just considered ascribe to pornography the first two of the three features. Pornography is, first, verdictive speech that ranks women as sex objects, and, second, exercitive speech that legitimates sexual violence. Since sexual violence is not simply harm, not simply crime, but discriminatory behavior, pornography subordinates because it legitimates this behavior. (Now we see how the feminist shift of perspective on violence affects our characterization of pornography at the illocutionary level as well.) For these two reasons, then, pornography is an *illocutionary* act of subordination. That, at any rate, is the claim.

However, there is disagreement—to put it mildly—about the correct ascription of pornography's illocutionary force. And this raises some questions. How, in general, do we discover what illocutionary force an utterance has? And what do we do in the face of disagreement? These are difficult questions, whose difficulty Austin acknowledged and sought—with limited success—to alleviate. Disagreements about the ascription of illocutionary force can be hard to settle, the utterances in question needing to have "a construction put upon them by judges."[30]

In situations of disagreement, the disputed illocution usually falls short of the paradigm case for the given illocution. In the paradigm case, one knows just what the felicity conditions for the given illocution are, and one knows that they are all satisfied. She said "I do" in the presence of priest and groom, the ceremony was uninterrupted, she intended to marry, etc., so in saying "I do," she must have been marrying. Moreover, in the paradigm case, one knows that appropriate uptake is secured: all present took the parties to have been marrying. And one knows about the perlocutionary effects: the later beliefs of others that the parties were married, the mother's distress, the grandmother's joy, and so forth. But when a speech act falls short of the paradigm, though not far short, there may be dispute as to what illocutionary act was performed. Suppose the marriage ceremony is interrupted at the very end by the priest's sudden heart attack. Not quite all the felicity conditions for marriage are satisfied, and doubtless the event is infelicitous in our usual sense of that term, but it may be near enough, perhaps, to count as a marriage nonetheless. Or suppose it is not known for certain that the priest's qualifications meet the required standard, for he is a refugee whose papers are missing. Not all the felicity conditions for marriage are known to be satisfied, but near enough, perhaps, to count as a marriage nonetheless. The first case presents a problem of vague boundaries: we know that not all conditions have been satisfied, but perhaps it is close enough. The second presents a problem of ignorance: we do not know that all conditions have been satisfied, but again, perhaps it is close enough. In both cases, what we have resembles but falls short of the paradigm, and we have to ask ourselves, how close is close enough? Here there is scope for argument.

One may argue in different ways. First, one may argue that, vagueness or ignorance notwithstanding, *some* felicity conditions—important ones—are satisfied, and that is good enough. "Shoot her" might count as an order, even if it failed exactly to match the paradigm—e.g., if it was intended merely as advice, but was spoken by someone in authority, in an appropriate context. Second, one may argue that *uptake* appropriate for the claimed illocution has been secured. "Coming from him, I took it as an order," as the hearer may have said. Its being taken as an order may be a reason for thinking it was an order. Third, one may argue that a speech act's effects are best *explained* by supposing that it has a certain illocutionary force. Part of the explanation for whites' discriminatory behavior is that such behavior has been legitimated by law. Part of the explanation for blacks keeping away from certain areas is that they have been ordered away. In such cases the illocutionary acts explain the perlocutionary effects.

All three ways of arguing are fallible, and they come in an ascending order of fallibility. The first, which says that at any rate *some* important felicity conditions have been satisfied, is tolerably secure. It is certainly a part of our practice of ascribing illocutions in everyday life, where the problems of vagueness and ignorance do not halt us in our tracks. "In ordinary life," as Austin says, "a certain laxness . . . is permitted."[31] The second is more fallible: securing appropriate uptake may not be sufficient for the illocution in question. The third is also fallible, since there may be other possible explanations for the known effects: I may have come to your party uninvited. However, each of the three, or some combination of them, may be useful, depending on the evidence we have.

We are now in a position to consider the disputed question: does pornography subordinate? Since there is a dispute, it may be that pornography fails to match exactly the illocutionary paradigm. I have not tried to say exactly what the paradigm for subordination is, but I have suggested that the speech acts of apartheid offer a clear example. They have verdictive and exercitive force: they rank a class of people, legitimate discrimination against them, and deprive them of rights and powers. Their felicity conditions include the condition that the speakers occupy a position of authority. They are speech acts that achieve a certain uptake: they are taken to be verdictive and exercitive acts (though not all hearers will take them to be subordinating acts). They are illocutions that have a pattern of perlocutionary effects on the beliefs and behavior of the population: whites believe blacks to be inferior, believe discrimination against them to be legitimate, and believe them to have fewer rights; whites discriminate against blacks, and blacks stay away from polling booths. Such speech acts are clearly acts of subordination.

Pornography falls short of this devastating paradigm in a number of important respects, but it may nonetheless be subordination. There is scope for argument in all three of the ways I discussed above. I begin with the third. We might find *explanations* for pornography's perlocutionary effects in terms of its illocutionary force. If the earlier claims are right, then pornography has a certain pattern of perlocutionary effects. It can affect attitudes and behavior, making its hearers more likely to view women as inferior, more disposed to accept rape myths, more likely to view rape victims as deserving of their treatment, and more likely to say that they themselves would rape if they could get away with it. Part of the explanation for this pattern might be that pornography has a particular illocutionary force: it ranks women as sex objects, and legitimates that kind of behavior. If pornography has the perlocutionary effects MacKinnon claims, then there is some reason for thinking it has the illocutionary force she and other feminist writers have ascribed to it.

This conclusion is reached by inference to the best explanation, and it is fallible. The hypothesis that you invited me to your party may best explain my arrival, but there are other possible explanations. Similarly, the hypothesis that pornography ranks women and legitimates certain attitudes and behavior may well explain the presence of these attitudes and behavior, but there are other possible explanations. The feminist claim would be strengthened if there were other ways to argue for the conclusion that pornography subordinates.

Let us consider the second way of arguing. What *uptake* does pornography secure in its hearers? What act do its hearers take it to be? The answer is mixed. Some hearers take it to be entertainment, escapist storytelling. Other hearers take it to be subordination. They take pornography to be something that ranks them, judges them, denigrates them, and legitimates ways of behaving that hurt women. Here we find vivid disagreement among the hearers as to just what the speech act is. Austin said that in such cases utterances are liable to have "a construction put upon them by judges," but who is in a position to judge? We might say that those women who take pornography to be subordination are in a better position to judge, that they can tell better than some other hearers what ranks them, what demeans and denigrates them, and what seems to legitimate ways of acting that are violent. But unless we privilege one group of hearers in this way, our result with this way of arguing will be inconclusive, though it may give some support to the claim that pornography subordinates.

We come now to the first way of arguing. The task of discovering whether some important *felicity conditions* are met looks more hopeful, for at least we know one felicity condition for subordination, and could in principle know whether pornography satisfies it. Since verdictives and exercitives are both *authoritative* illocutions, we know that the ability to perform them depends on the speaker's authority. The umpire, and not the bystander, can call a fault. The government, and not the private citizen, can enact law that ranks and legitimates. The authority in question need not be as formally recognized as in those cases, but it needs to be there. This means that in order to answer the question "Does pornography subordinate?" one must first answer another: "Do its speakers have authority?" If they do, then a crucial felicity condition is satisfied: pornographers' speech acts may be illocutions that authoritatively rank women, legitimate violence, and thus subordinate.

This question is, I think, at the heart of the controversy. If you believe that pornographic utterances are made by a powerless minority, a fringe group especially vulnerable to moralistic persecution, then you will answer negatively. Not so if you believe, with MacKinnon, that pornography's voice is the voice of the ruling power. Liberal debate about pornography has typically been premised on the former belief and part of MacKinnon's task is to persuade us that it is false. Just as the speech of the umpire is authoritative, within a certain domain—the game of tennis—so pornographic speech is authoritative, within a certain domain—the game of sex. The authors of pornographic speech are not mere bystanders to the game; they are speakers whose verdict counts. Pornography tells its hearers what women are worth: it ranks women as things, as objects, as prey. Pornography tells its hearers which moves are appropriate and permissible: if it tells them that certain moves are appropriate because women want to be raped, it legitimates violence. If pornography is authoritative speech it may subordinate.

Does pornographic speech have the authority required to substantiate MacKinnon's claim? Is this crucial felicity condition satisfied? These are not really questions to be settled from the philosopher's armchair. To answer them one needs to know about the role pornographers occupy as authoritative speakers about the facts, or supposed facts, of sex. What is important here is not whether the speech of pornographers is universally held in high esteem: it is not—hence the common assumption among liberals that in defending pornographers they are defending the underdog. What is important is whether it is authoritative in the domain that counts—the domain of speech about sex—and whether it is authoritative for the hearers that count: people, men, boys, who in addition to wanting "entertainment" want to discover the right way to do things, want to know which moves in the sexual game are legitimate. What is important is whether it is authoritative for those hearers who—one way or another—do seem to learn that violence is sexy and coercion legitimate: the fifty percent of boys who "think it is okay for a man to rape a woman if he is sexually aroused by her," the fifteen percent of male college undergraduates who say they have raped a woman on a date, the eighty-six percent who say that they enjoy the conquest part of sex, the thirty percent who rank faces of women displaying pain and fear to be more sexually attractive than faces showing pleasure.[32] In this domain, and for these hearers, it may be that pornography has all the authority of a monopoly.[33]

I have tried to show that pornography may subordinate, even if it falls short of the illocutionary paradigm. We earlier distinguished two ways in which actions may fall short. There may be vague boundaries in a situation where we know that not all conditions are satisfied and wonder whether what we have is close enough. There can be ignorance, where we do not know whether all conditions are satisfied. It may be that pornography falls short in both ways. We have the problem of ignorance: we are not certain that pornography is authoritative, and hence not certain whether it satisfies a crucial felicity condition for subordination. But supposing the problem of ignorance were remedied and pornography was known to satisfy this condition, the problem of vague boundaries might still remain. We might know that pornography satisfied many, but not all, the usual conditions for subordination. One typical feature of actions of ranking and legitimating, for example, is that the speakers *intend* to rank and legitimate. I have not argued that pornography satisfies that condition. But if pornography conforms closely enough to the paradigm in other respects, it may subordinate nonetheless.

The claim that pornography subordinates has good philosophical credentials: it is not trickery, or "sleight of hand"; it is by no means "philosophically indefensible." Moreover, considerations about explanation, uptake, and the felicity conditions for subordination give us reasons—though not conclusive ones— for thinking that the claim may be true. Pornography's effects may be best explained by supposing that it has the illocutionary force of subordination. An important group of pornography's hearers—even if not its intended hearers—take it to be subordination. And if the empirical premise about pornography's authority turns out to be true, then pornography satisfies a crucial felicity condition for subordination.

What we have not yet considered, however, is whether speech that subordinates should be restricted by law. As we noted at the outset, it does not immediately follow from the claim that pornography subordinates women that censorship is the best answer. What follows is that there is a conflict between liberty and equality, just as the courts declared. One possible response to this conflict might be to fight for equality in ways compatible with respecting the liberty of pornographers. What I have said leaves open that possibility. If pornography subordinates women, then it is not in virtue of its content but of its authority that it does so. It need not have that authority. There are imaginable circumstances where material just like pornography in other respects would have no authority, and in such circumstances such speech would not subordinate. MacKinnon's claim is that those circumstances are not ours, though one can hope that someday they will be.

This way of understanding the subordination claim thus has implications for policy. There may be ways of undermining pornography's authority that fall short of outright censorship, ways that would eventually relegate pornographers to the status of mere bystanders to the game, whose speech does not count. Perhaps pornographic speech could be fought with more speech: the speech of education to counter pornography's falsehoods, where women tell the world what women are really like,[34] or with the speech of competition to counter pornography's monopoly, where women themselves become authors of erotica that is arousing and explicit but does not subordinate.[35]

All this may be possible if women can indeed fight speech with more speech. But if pornography not only subordinates but *silences* women, it is not easy to see how there can be any such fight. At this point the second feminist claim demands our attention. Whether women can fight speech with more speech depends on whether, and to what extent, women can speak. . . .

NOTES

1. In, e.g., Catharine MacKinnon, "Linda's Life and Andrea's Work," *Feminism Unmodified* (Cambridge, Mass.: Harvard University Press, 1987), p. 130. Pornography, as defined by MacKinnon, and as discussed in this paper, is not the same as obscenity. See MacKinnon, "Not a Moral Issue," ibid.; and Frank Michelman, "Conceptions of Democracy in American Constitutional Argument: The Case of Pornography Regulation," *Tennessee Law Review* 56 (1989): 294 n. 8. MacKinnon drafted an ordinance that was passed in Indianapolis in 1984, but was then challenged and defeated. See *American Booksellers, Inc. v. Hudnut*, 598 F. Supp. 1327 (S. D. Ind. 1984). The ordinance made trafficking in pornography civilly actionable, rather than simply prohibiting it. I do not address this admittedly important feature of the legislation here.

2. MacKinnon, "Francis Biddle's Sister," p. 176, in *Feminism Unmodified*.

3. *Hudnut*, 771 F.2d 329 (7th Cir. 1985).

4. Easterbrook's omission has been commented upon by Melinda Vadas in "A First Look at the Pornography/Civil Rights Ordinance: Could Pornography Be the Subordination of Women?" *Journal of Philosophy* 84 (1987): 487–511. Vadas is interested, as I am, in saving the "subordinating" claim from charges of conceptual confusion, and she develops an interesting analysis which differs from that offered here. She says that some predicates can apply to a representational depiction because they apply to the scene depicted. "Subordinates" is such a predicate, in her view, so pornographic depictions of subordination can

themselves subordinate. My view is that the link is not as close as she sees it: an utterance's depicting subordination is neither necessary nor sufficient for its having the force of subordination. The reasons for this should emerge shortly.

5. *Hudnut,* 1316.

6. W. A. Parent, "A Second Look at Pornography and the Subordination of Women," *Journal of Philosophy* 87 (1990): 205–11. Parent's article is a response to Vadas's. He argues, by means of the following remarkable non sequitur, for the different conclusion that pornography is morally evil (p. 211). "Evil" means "depraved." "To deprave" means "to debase." "To debase" means "to bring into contempt." Pornography brings women into contempt, ergo pornography is evil. What actually follows from Parent's lexicographical premises is of course that *women* are evil. Women are brought into contempt (by pornography), therefore debased, therefore depraved, therefore evil.

7. J. L. Austin, *How to Do Things with Words* (London: Oxford University Press, 1962).

8. Ibid., p. 139.

9. Ibid., p. 101 (my version is a slight elaboration).

10. Ibid., p. 109.

11. Ibid., p. 103.

12. MacKinnon, "Not a Moral Issue," *Feminism Unmodified,* p. 156.

13. For example by Barker, 598 F. Supp. 1316, 1330 (1984).

14. "Francis Biddle's Sister," *Feminism Unmodified,* p. 300 n. 155.

15. Expressive conduct is protected; speech of various kinds—libel, for instance—is unprotected. See Laurence Tribe, *American Constitutional Law,* 2d ed. (Mineola, N.Y.: Foundation Press, 1988), chap. 12. Tribe also comments: "The trouble with the distinction between speech and conduct is that it has less determinate content than is sometimes supposed. . . . It is . . . not surprising that the Supreme Court has never articulated a basis for its distinction; it could not do so, with the result that any particular course of conduct may be hung almost randomly on the 'speech' peg or the 'conduct' peg as one see fit" (p. 827). Speech act theory gives some grounds for being dubious about the distinction, but that is not the point of what I have to say.

16. See Jennifer Hornsby, "Philosophers and Feminists on Language Use," *Cogito* (Autumn 1988): 13–15. For a similar approach to some of the questions addressed in this article, see Hornsby's excellent piece "Illocution and Its Significance," in *Foundations of Speech Act Theory: Philosophical and Linguistic Perspectives,* ed. S. L. Tsohatzidis (London and New York: Routledge, 1994). Hornsby develops a sophisticated and somewhat different account of illocutions, and uses it to explain how women can be silenced. She too considers the examples of refusal and giving testimony.

17. Judge Barker's accusation, see 598 F. Supp. 1316 (1984).

18. MacKinnon uses this example to make the point that words can be "an integral act in a system of segregation, which is a system of force" (MacKinnon, "On Collaboration," *Feminism Unmodified,* p. 202).

19. Here I depart from Vadas ("A First Look"), for it is not in virtue of depicting subordination that the "whites only" sign subordinates, if it does. That utterance does not depict subordination, any more than "I do" depicts a marriage. So something can subordinate without depicting subordination. The converse is also true. Something can depict subordination without subordinating (a documentary, for example). . . .

20. MacKinnon, "Francis Biddle's Sister," p. 176.

21. Compare an example borrowed from David Lewis. A master says to a slave: "It is now permissible to cross the white line." In saying that, the master makes a certain move, performs a certain illocutionary act: he makes it legitimate for the slave to cross the white line. The boundaries of what is legitimate and what is not change immediately. The beliefs of the slave as to what is legitimate will also change—that is to speak of the action's effects, its perlocutionary dimension. Here too there may also be some perspective from which we might say that it was never truly illegitimate for the slave to cross the line, but that would be to move outside the bounds of the language game in question. See Lewis, "Scorekeeping in a Language Game," *Philosophical Papers,* vol. 1 (Oxford: Oxford University Press, 1983), pp. 233–49.

22. Austin's discussion of verdictives and exercitives is in lecture 11, especially sections 1 and 2, pp. 152–56. The description I give of exercitives is used by him for what is strictly a proper subset of that class (p. 155).

23. 598 F. Supp. 1316 (1984), my italics.

24. MacKinnon, "Francis Biddle's Sister," p. 176.

25. So I interpret the available evidence. See Edward Donnerstein, Daniel Linz, and Steven Penrod, *The Question of Pornography: Research Findings and Policy Implications* (New York: Free Press; London: Collier Macmillan, 1987). Note that material that is sexually arousing and violent but *not* sexually explicit may also have these effects. See also *Public Hearings on Ordinances to Add Pornography as Discrimination Against Women,* Committee on Government Operations, City Council, Minneapolis, Minn. (Dec. 12–13, 1983); transcript of hearings published as *Pornography and Sexual Violence: Evidence of the Links* (London: Everywoman, 1988); and the *Report of the Attorney General's Commission on Pornography* (Washington, D.C.: United States Government Printing Office, 1986).

26. MacKinnon argues for this change of perspective in "Francis Biddle's Sister" and elsewhere.

27. "Francis Biddle's Sister," p. 173.

28. Helen E. Longino, "Pornography: Oppression and Freedom: A Closer Look," in *Take Back the Night: Women on Pornography,* ed. Laura Lederer (New York: William Morrow, 1980), p. 29. (Longino has the entire phrase in italics.)

29. MacKinnon, "Francis Biddle's Sister," p. 171, emphasis mine. I do not italicize "sexualizes" because I think it may be a perlocutionary rather than an illocutionary verb, meaning something like "makes viewers find the thought of rape, etc., sexually arousing." But perhaps it is an illocutionary verb meaning something like "legitimates rape, etc., in describing it as if it were normal sex."

30. Austin, *How to Do Things with Words,* p. 114.

31. Ibid., p. 37. Austin is speaking in particular here about failures to satisfy completely the procedural felicity conditions for an illocution.

32. The first statistic comes from a UCLA study, Jacqueline Goodchild et al. cited in Warshaw, *I Never Called It Rape* (New York: Harper and Row, 1988), p. 120; the second and third from studies by Alfred B. Heilbrun, Emory University, and Maura P. Loftus, Auburn University, cited in Naomi Wolf, *The Beauty Myth* (New York, Vintage, 1990), p. 166; the fourth from research done by Virginia Greenlinger, Williams College, and Donna Byrne, SUNY–Albany, cited in Warshaw, p. 93.

33. For a good discussion of the effect of this monopoly on the fantasy lives of these hearers and women as well, see Wolf, *The Beauty Myth,* esp. pp. 162–68.

34. Edward Donnerstein advocates education to counteract pornography's harmful effects in the final chapter of *The Question of Pornography.*

35. This is advocated by the Women Against Censorship group, who, as *amici curiae,* protested against the MacKinnon ordinance; see also *Pleasure and Danger: Exploring Female Sexuality,* ed. Carol Vance (London: Routledge and Kegan Paul, 1984); and the collection *Sex Exposed: Sexuality and the Pornography Debate,* ed. Lynne Segal and Mary McIntosh (New Brunswick, N.J.: Rutgers University Press, 1993).

JENNIFER HORNSBY

Speech Acts and Pornography

Jennifer Hornsby is professor of philosophy at Birkbeck College,
University of London. She is author of Actions (1980) *and of*
articles on the philosophy of mind.

In isolating some ground to make this discussion of manageable proportions, I have come to focus my remarks in the direction of a specific target.
The target is Ronald Dworkin. I argue that, in his work on free speech,
Dworkin misses the point of those women whom he addresses on the subject
of pornography.[1] He misses the point, I believe, because he helps himself to
some erroneous views about the workings of language. I shall try to show
this by challenging Dworkin's interpretation of Catharine MacKinnon's
claim that "pornography silences women."[2]

My remarks come in five parts: the first three prepare the ground for an
account of *silencing* which I offer in the fourth and by reference to which I
criticize Dworkin in the fifth.

1: Pornography

In 1984, Catharine MacKinnon and Andrea Dworkin brought an amendment
to Indianapolis's civil rights ordinance. If they had eventually been successful
in the courts, the legislation would have made it possible for individual citi-

---

Reprinted by permission.

zens of Indianapolis to sue in civil court both to put a future ban on the publication of specified sexually explicit material and to collect damages for the
harm that its publication had done. Their idea was that women have a right
not to be silenced, and should be empowered to defend that right.

One of the objections to the MacKinnon-Dworkin amendment that
Dworkin (Ronald Dworkin now) has elaborated on at some length is that it
is contrary to the First Amendment of the U.S. Constitution. This particular
objection is irrelevant to the argument I am concerned with here. Dworkin
gives an account of what justifies the protection of free speech, and he supposes that his account vindicates a liberal, anti-censorship attitude towards
pornography. Insofar as Dworkin was concerned to show this, the precise
constitutional situation is neither here nor there. I want to assess some of
Dworkin's thinking on its merits. The Indianapolis legislation enters the debate because it raises the good question, on which we can bring theory to
bear, of whether citizens might ever make the case that publication of certain
material is contrary to their civil rights. This question, not the possible practical implications of an answer to it, is my concern here.

The MacKinnon-Dworkin legislation comes in for another reason. It
contained a definition of pornography, which I shall take over, as follows:

> Pornography . . . is the graphic sexually explicit subordination of women
> through pictures or words. . . . [It] includes women dehumanized as
> sexual objects, things or commodities;
>> enjoying pain or humiliation or rape;
>> being tied up, cut up, mutilated, bruised, or physically hurt;
>> in postures of sexual submission or servility or display;
>> reduced to body parts, penetrated by objects or animals, or pre-
>>> sented in scenarios of degradation, injury, torture;
>> shown as filthy or inferior;
>> bleeding, bruised or hurt in a context which make these conditions
>>> sexual.

2: Free Speech

Speech is not the main ingredient in the definition of pornography, which
may be "pictures or words." And this aspect of the definition seems right:
most of the material that we think of as pornographic is photographic or cin-
ematic, even if text, written or spoken, attaches to it. On the face of it, then,
a defense of people's right to speak freely (or more generally their right to
produce verbal material, whether spoken or written) is not automatically a
defense of their right to publish pornographic material. Consider Mill's famous argument. Mill said that if someone's opinion is right, then preventing
him from expressing it "deprives [others] of the opportunity of exchanging
error for truth," if wrong, then "[another] loses the livelier impression of

truth produced by its collision with error"; so either way, it will be better if people can state their opinions than if they cannot.[3] This argument finds value in free speech which derives from the value of truth. It does not work to protect people's freedom to publish photographs, because photographs are not things we can readily assess for truth and falsehood. So it might seem as if arguments concerned with free *speech* will not be especially important in relation to pornography.

Part of the answer to this is simple: of course what liberals defend is the right to free speech *and expression*. Mill's is only one argument. Many traditional liberal arguments in the area are clearly intended to bring speech and other modes of expression under a single head. Dworkin says, in outlining what he calls the constitutive justification of the right to free speech, "It is a feature of a just political society that government treat all its adult members as responsible moral agents." Dworkin's idea is that a person would be treated as less than responsible if his expressive powers were curbed; it makes no difference now whether that person wants to express himself in speech, or wants to take photographs (say of women being cut up, tied up, mutilated, and shown as filthy or inferior) as a means of expressing himself.

Well, Dworkin's introduction of the idea of responsibility seems to me to provide only a feeble attempt at legitimizing the activities of pornography's purveyors. For his conception of the responsible citizen is of someone who has "a responsibility to express his convictions out of respect and concern for others, and out of a compelling desire that truth be known, justice served and the good secured"; and I doubt that those who profit materially from the pornography industry can be credited with such high-minded motives. But the present point is that it has to be acknowledged that there are aspects of the liberal justification of people's right to publish pornography which do not use the idea of freedom in the use of language as such. And with that acknowledged, it may be unclear why consideration of language use and of *speech acts* can play a part in evaluating Dworkin's arguments against feminists on the subject of pornography.

To understand the different sorts of arguments that liberals use, I think we need to distinguish, in the area of human expression, between what works cognitively and conveys some propositional message, and what does not work like that. Where language is used to make statements, it comes under the first head. But where language is used in writing fiction, it comes, with graphic material, under the second head. The distinction is between forms of expression which straightforwardly evince the beliefs of the expresser and forms of expression which do not do that. An extreme example of the first sort would be explicitly advocational speech—for instance where I try to persuade you of something by arguing for it. An extreme example of the second sort would be abstract art—for instance, were someone paints a picture but (as we might put it) there is nothing she is saying in painting it.

There could be debate about how sharp this distinction is. (I think myself that it is not a very sharp one, but that it is needed nonetheless to appreciate the different goals of arguments like Mill's and Dworkin's.) But what we need to notice here is that even if the distinction were a sharp one, so that there were two utterly different forms of human expression, that would not show that the distinction served to divide up two separate areas of human activity. For it is not as if the advocational use of language was one self-contained institution, and any other use of our expressive resources was something quite else. In the actual practice of life, cognitive expression and other forms of expression are in obvious ways interdependent. What people say affects the moral and aesthetic climate in which they say things; and the aesthetic and moral climate can affect what they see fit to say. So when it is maintained, for instance, that "pornography silences women," we have to recognize the influence of one group's non-cognitive expression on another group's cognitive, linguistic expression.

The pornographers' right which is in question is the right freely to go in for expression which typically is not speech; but the freedom of women we have to consider really does include their freedom of (literally) speech.

3: *Language Use*

Dworkin, in good liberal company, conceives protection of the right to free speech as the promotion of a negative liberty, where a negative liberty is something you have unless someone interferes with you. Free speech is easily achieved on this model: having the usual human cognitive resources, and a vocal apparatus, a person just is free to speak unless someone else presents actual obstacles. But I think that the model is founded in a misconception about the way language operates: it is as if uttering words which make up a sentence of a language were always enough to get a thought across. To put my criticism in the terms of J. L. Austin's "speech act theory," the model assumes that speech is a matter of *locution* simply; and it ignores *illocution*. I want then to present an account of *illocution* in order to expose the inadequacy of Dworkin's conception.[4]

A speech act account of language use is one which imposes a coherent pattern on all the very many things that may be done on any of the very many possible occasions when a bit of language may be used. When someone makes an utterance there is an *action* of hers (what Austin called a "fixed physical thing"). But in the case of any such action, there are many things that the speaker does—many *acts* she performs. Each speech act corresponds to a grouping of speech actions. And a principled way of organizing speech acts provides a framework into which the particularities of occasions on which one or another is done can potentially be fitted so as to provide for full and fully illuminating redescriptions of speech actions. The classification of speech acts into sorts which Austin got started can be thought of as a means of imposing system onto the actual data of linguistic communication.

Austin's own overall classification was a three-fold one: into locutionary, illocutionary and perlocutionary acts. There is little agreement about how exactly these classes should be marked out, and especially about the boundary between illocutionary and perlocutionary. My own suggestion is that the distinction between illocutionary and perlocutionary is a distinction between what is of proprietary concern to an account of language and what is not: some features of speech actions flow from something in the nature of linguistic communication itself, and those features constitute those actions as of certain illocutionary acts; but there are acts people do using language that no account of language as such can be expected to cover, and those are perlocutionary acts. Illocution may then be seen as at the heart of language use: a concern with locution is a concern with language-specific meaning, and a concern with perlocution is a concern with effects that uses of language may have. But whatever specific set of sounds people use—so that they do specific locutionary things—and whatever they may be trying to achieve by using language—so that they may do specific perlocutionary things—people have to do illocutionary things to communicate.

I think that Searle brought to notice the crucial element of illocution (though he did not see that as what he was doing). He illustrated it for the particular illocutionary speech act of *telling A that p:* "If I am trying to tell someone something . . . , as soon as he recognizes [that I am trying to tell it to him], I have succeeded. . . . Unless he recognizes that I am trying to tell him [it], I do not fully succeed in telling it to him."[5] What a person relies on, then, to tell someone something is the hearer's being open to the idea that she might be telling him what in fact she means to tell him: unless he can readily entertain the idea that she might be doing this, he could hardly take her to be doing it; when he does take her so, he is in a state of mind sufficient, with her utterance, for her having done it.

On this account of *telling*, it invokes (what I call) reciprocity. Reciprocity is the condition of linguistic communication. It obtains when people are such as to recognize one another's speech as it is meant to be taken, and thus to ensure the success of attempts to perform speech acts. When reciprocity obtains, there are things that speakers do simply by being heard as doing them. The hearer is now a complementary party to speech actions: the speaker's doing what she does with her words is the product of her attempt and the hearer's recognition of it.

When reciprocity is seen as the key to illocution, illocution can assume its proper place in an account of language use. Communication by words requires that speakers should produce recognizable sounds: a language, or system of locution, needs to be in place; and a hearer obviously relies upon knowing what thought a speaker's sounds are such as to express. But communication is a relation between people, and it requires understanding on an audience's part attuned not only to the significance of the sounds the speaker produces, but also to her intended performances. Whatever the particular language, it is a condition of its normal successful use—of speakers' intended communicative acts actually being performed—that people be sufficiently in harmony, as it were, to provide for recognition of speaker meaning. The speaker then exploits, in addition to a language (a way of interpreting patterns of sounds) the existence of reciprocity.

I think that the illocutionary is best circumscribed in a way that presupposes a background of reciprocity. We can say: X-ing is an illocutionary act if and only if the following gives a sufficient condition of its being done: the speaker's attempt at X-ing results in an audience's taking the speaker to X. If that is right, then illocutionary acts, like nearly all other acts, are characterized by reference to certain sorts of effects (or results, or consequences, or upshots) that actions may have. But the relevant effects where illocutionary acts are concerned are very special: they are effects on listeners of taking them some way, and the way an action is required to be taken to be (if it is to be some illocutionary one) is precisely the way that it is meant, by the speaker, to be. (Someone's doing what she wants with words, which may consist in her having further [perlocutionary] effects beyond the immediate illocutionary ones, is then dependent on her doing the illocutionary thing that she intends.)

The definition I have suggested does not require much of an illocutionary act: it says only that it is enough to do one to be correctly thought to do it. It gives no guarantee that any hearer will actually realize that a speaker did what she in fact meant to do; and it does not rule it out that a speaker might do some illocutionary thing even where no one thought she meant to. So the definition says that your recognizing that I meant to tell you something is enough for me to have told it [to] you, but it does not say that you have to have recognized that I meant to tell you something in order for me to have told it [to] you. Searle allowed for the possibility of an illocutionary act (like telling) being done without any help from a hearer by introducing "full success." His idea (I think) was that an illocutionary act not recognized by the hearer as done is not fully successful. What Searle said was, "Unless [my hearer] recognizes . . . I have not *fully succeeded* in telling him [something]." And there is surely something right about thinking of illocutionary acts performed without the use of reciprocity as in some sense defective (or less than fully successful): someone who performs an illocutionary act despite the fact that her action does not have the effect characteristic of that act, is not understood. Shared understanding is illocution's point. "Perfect" illocutionary acts are done invoking reciprocity, we might say.

4: Silencing

Relating illocutionary acts (like telling someone something) to reciprocity shows how such acts can be peculiarly easy to perform: provided that you can get the words out and have a suitably receptive audience, there is no possible obstacle to your full success. The relevant effect, which is simply its being understood by the person addressed, and which constitutes the action as e.g. *telling someone something,* is an effect that it will ordinarily have without any contrivance on the speaker's part. But there is a counterpart of the fact that illocutionary acts can be peculiarly easy to perform: they can be *impossible* successfully to perform. Just as it is more or less automatic that your attempt at an illocutionary act is successful when certain socially defined conditions obtain; so, when certain conditions do not obtain, you simply cannot perform any such act. Just as reciprocity may secure communication, so the absence of conditions that ensure reciprocity may prevent communication. To the extent that reciprocity fails you, you have been deprived of illocutionary potential.

I believe that we can understand silencing by thinking of the silenced person as someone deprived of illocutionary potential. The silenced person does not have it in her power to do with language what she might want to.

An example, which may fit such a description of a silenced person, is the woman dealing with a sexual advance from a man.

Judge David Wild once said:

Women who say no do not always mean no. It is not just a question of saying no.

This was in the process of recommending the acquittal of a man accused of rape.[6] The judge wanted the court to believe that the woman had meant "yes" by *No.* But there is another construction to put upon his idea that "it is not just a question of saying no." To perform the illocutionary act of refusal successfully, an utterance of the word "no" is not enough: to refuse successfully a woman must be understood as attempting to refuse. But a woman may mean to refuse, but be unable succesfully to refuse, because a condition of her having successfully refused—that she be recognized as attempting to refuse—is not satisfied.

(Notice how "successfully" works here. There can be an illocutionary act even when the speaker has not been fully successful in Searle's sense. And taking the woman's part against the judge, of course we shall say that she did refuse, and say this assuming that she was sincere and without thinking about how she was actually taken. The judge, however, wanted to put the woman's sincerity into question. He hoped to create a presumption of the woman's having been insincere; and if she had been insincere, then indeed there would not have been any act of refusal on the woman's part. Where such a presumption is in place, the demands on the audience lapse, and it becomes impossible for a speaker with however much sincerity she actually utters "No" to be *taken* to refuse. Thus can the Judge sow the seeds of doubt about sincerity: where she might have hoped to rely upon reciprocity, the Judge can exploit the possibility of a lack of reciprocity.)

It requires some explaining, of course, how there could be circumstances in which a word that is suited for refusal cannot be used to perform a perfectly good illocutionary act of refusing. But this is easily explained if we believe that embedded within the social practices in which our speech actions happen is an unwritten code of behavior. I mean a code according to which men have uncontrollable sexual urges; women who do not behave and dress with great circumspection are ready and willing to gratify those urges, but will feign unwillingness, whether through decency, or through deceitfulness, or through a desire to excite. If the idea were widespread that this is how men are and how women conduct themselves, and if the code informed men's expectations, then situations in which the reciprocity of intention and recognition required for a woman to refuse a man were lacking would be common. A woman confronted by a man with sex on his mind could not (successfully) refuse him by saying "No."

Silencing is the process of depriving of illocutionary potential. We now see how it might work: it may work by affecting people's mind-sets and expectations in such a way that reciprocity fails. Where reciprocity does fail, what someone might attempt to do, she will not be recognized as attempting to do, thus cannot be understood as having done, and therefore, given the nature of illocution, simply cannot (successfully) do.

Sexual refusal is the chosen example here for two reasons. It is a relatively straightforward example to describe. And it is plausible that pornography might have effected the silencing. (For this to seem plausible, it is not necessary to suppose that each individual man who cannot take attempted refusals for what they are is himself a big consumer of pornography, but only that pornography assumes its place in an endemic system of subordination.) Sexual refusal is only an example, however.

In order to see silencing as widespread—to see that there may be examples of very different sorts—one needs to appreciate that illocution embraces such apparently simple acts as *stating,* and to appreciate too that reciprocity can be a matter of degree. In the straightforward case, on which linguistic communication depends, speakers simply are taken to be doing the illocutionary things that they mean to do. In a certain climate, women, in certain situations (I have suggested) will not be taken to be doing the illocutionary things that they mean to. But there can be cases where, though it is not impossible for someone to do an illocutionary thing, the expectations she confronts ensure that her doing it is not the straightforward matter that communicating might ordinarily be: a person may be partially silenced, as it were.

And silencing is typically a *cumulative* process: we cannot readily point to particular instances which are pieces of silencing, though we may be able to think of things that some people regularly do which plausibly contribute to the process. At the level of the meanings of individual words, we are familiar with the idea of cumulative linguistic change: a word acquires a new meaning when it has been used enough by enough speakers as if it had that meaning; speakers' intentions then determine what other speakers are saying. Just as non-standard usages of individual words can cumulatively affect our locutionary acts (our language), so the distribution of pornographic material may affect our illocutionary acts (our use of our language). Pornography's dissemination may create, or may sustain, sets of expectations that bear on how people are taken when they speak. (So too of course may the distribution of superficially inoffensive material. It would take me far afield to consider the relative influences of different sorts of cultural products—the banally sexist and the notably misogynist.)

Catharine MacKinnon did not have anything so specific as my example in mind. She was concerned quite generally with the role of pornography in demeaning women. To put it in a style that Dworkin understands, she was concerned about a mechanism that works to reduce women's voice in democratic politics. My claim is that the promulgation of a demeaning view of women can have the effect of rendering women relatively powerless parties in communicative exchanges because it affects the reciprocity that is a precondition of illocution. For women as for men, the illocutionary acts that they are able to perform are only those they may be taken to be performing. But men more than women have determined when reciprocity obtains. I think that much of the rhetoric of silencing, as it is used in writings about the oppression of women and of other groups, not only in those of MacKinnon's writings where pornography is the agent of silencing, might be understood by reference to this sort of account.

5. R. Dworkin v. Feminists

Dworkin thinks that the claim that pornography silences women has an especially important place in the debate between liberals and some feminists about pornography and freedom. He is right about this. If the feminist is going to address the liberal in his own terms, then her most powerful challenge will come when she claims that pornography presents a conflict *within* the liberty of free speech-and-expression. And when we say that pornography silences women, we are not saying merely that the ills inherent in pornography's production and consequent upon its publication *compete* with those other goods which are constituted by citizens' possession of free speech and expression. The idea that women are silenced is, rather, the idea that pornographic publication can present an obstacle to free speech itself—to its possession by women. What this means is that however strong a justification of free speech and expression could be offered (however "absolute" a citizen's right to it), it could not remain unchallenged that pornography's producers and purveyors ought to have it, so long as it is allowed that women ought to too.

Dworkin considers the argument that

> some speech, including pornography, is silencing, so that its effect is
> to prevent other people from exercising their negative freedom to
> speak. . . . A woman's speech may be silenced not just by noise intended

to drown her out by also by argument and images that change her audience's perceptions of her character, needs, desires, and standing, and also, perhaps, change her own sense of what she wants.

But he thinks that the argument relies on a confusion. He accepts that private citizens who took away other citizens' liberty by preventing them from *saying* what they wish would need to be stopped. And he even accepts that the consequence of allowing some ideas to be heard is that "other ideas will be misunderstood, or given little consideration, or even not be spoken at all because those who might speak them are not in control of their own public identities and therefore cannot be understood as they wish to be." But these consequences, Dworkin claims, are not themselves curtailments of the liberty to speak. He says:

> Only by characterizing certain ideas as themselves "silencing" ideas—only by supposing that censoring pornography is like stopping people from drowning out other speakers—can they hope to justify censorship within the constitutional scheme that assigns a pre-eminent place to free speech. But the assimilation is nevertheless a confusion.

The account of silencing provides a ready answer to this. No confusion is involved in thinking that stopping pornographic publication is relevantly like stopping people from drowning out speakers. Silencing is an act whose effect is to render difficult or impossible certain illocutionary acts. In that respect it is exactly like drowning out. And that means that it is like drowning out in exactly the respects in which advocates of free speech object to drowning out. Silencing works more subtly than drowning out, it is true: silencing renders people not literally inaudible but unable to communicate. So it is not quite right to say of the silenced speaker, what can evidently be said of the drowned out speaker, that she might just as well have kept her mouth shut. But from the point of view of the silenced person herself, who will not be taken as she would mean to be taken, there is evidently something pointless about her making the noises she does—she cannot do what she intends to do by making them. If caring about free speech is a matter of caring about people's powers of communication, about an ability to do illocutionary things, then there is reason to stop the cumulative process of silencing if there is reason to stop people drowning one another out.

One further similarity between drowning out and silencing must be noticed. But this is now a similarity which might be thought to spoil the argument against Dworkin. Although drowning out and silencing both work on language, neither of them needs to use language. To drown someone out, you do not have to speak: you can use drums if you want to; you have only to make enough noise to render the speaker inaudible. Similarly you do not have to use language to silence; and when pornography is thought of as silencing, then (as I noted) it is usually not language, but the publication and scrutiny of graphic material, which is the silencing agent. This means that, if we were contemplating empowering people to put a halt to pornography which silences them, we could not simply compare pornographers' freedom of speech as against women's freedom of speech. We have rather to consider the pornographers' right to express themselves freely as set against women's right of free speech.

Well, Dworkin speaks of citizens as "having as much right to contribute to the formation of the moral or aesthetic climate as they do to participate in politics." And that makes it seem that he thinks that a right to free expression (to have one's productions contribute to the climate) is on a par with the right to free speech. I quoted some remarks of Dworkin defending all citizens' right to free expression; they struck me as feeble used in relation to pornography. And if all Dworkin's arguments here were as feeble as I found that one, then in a competition between pornographers' desire to express themselves and women's desire to communicate, the free speech of women would win out.

Yet Dworkin himself appears to think it goes the other way. It seems that he thinks that someone's right to free expression can actually trump someone else's right to have the freedom of speech which participatory politics requires. What he has said (and it is a thought he has expressed more than once) is this:

> It would plainly be unconstitutional to ban speech directly advocating
> that women occupy inferior roles . . . even if that speech fell on willing
> male ears and achieved its goals. So it cannot be a reason for banning
> pornography that it contributes to an unequal economic or social struc-
> ture, even it we think that it does.

Setting aside the appeal to the U.S. Constitution (whose irrelevance here I noted initially), and paraphrasing, we find Dworkin saying this: "You wouldn't want people who believed that women are inferior stopped from trying to persuade others of women's inferiority, would you? So if there are people who express themselves in such ways as to perpetuate arrangements in which women are treated as inferior, but who do not actually ever come out explicitly with the opinion that women are inferior, then you would want even less to stop them." This is a curious sort of inference. And when it is acknowledged that the "unequal economic or social structure" is one in which the losers are deprived of powers of communication, it results in the idea that pornography, working as it does in subtle ways to render women unfree to speak, requires more protection than advocational speech, whose processes and effects are more transparent.

I suggest that Dworkin argues as he does because he has not understood what is claimed about the mechanism of silencing. He fails to see that communication using speech is not a matter merely of getting out some audible sentences (it is not a matter merely of *locution*); so he cannot admit that there could be processes which played the same role in shaping *illocutionary* possibilities as advocational speech plays in shaping beliefs, but whose playing of that role might ordinarily be more or less hidden from most of us.

If I am right in my diagnosis of Dworkin, then we must not allow the liberal to help himself to the superficial account of speech which ignores illocution and which has made it possible to think of freedom to speak as a negative liberty. It is an important task for feminists to situate the debate about pornography in an account of language which takes it seriously as a social institution among others. What I have said about silencing is meant as a contribution to that task.

Postscript

Since writing "Liberty and Pornography" (which I have attended to above), Dworkin has reviewed Catharine MacKinnon's *Only Words* (Harvard University Press, 1993) in an article called "Women and Pornography" (*New York Review of Books,* Oct 21, 1993). This article attaches great importance to the feminist argument from equality which Dworkin had previously answered swiftly (see the quotation in my third to last paragraph). That argument is called a "new argument" now, and it is treated at greater length. It is no longer countered by saying that pornographers' claims to their negative liberty countervail against women's claims to be treated equally; it is countered now by saying that egalitarianism favors the pornographers. So whereas considerations of liberty were supposed to weigh most heavily on pornographers' side in "Liberty and Pornography" (and Dworkin said that was a confusion to count them on the women's side—see above), they are considerations of equality which are supposed to win the day for the pornographers in "Women and Pornography."

How can Dworkin . . . think that freedom of speech is the U.S. Constitution's "fundamental *egalitarian* command" ("Women and Pornography") having said that it was to be "conceived and protected as a fundamental *negative liberty*" in "Liberty and Pornography," where he carefully reminded us that "freedom is not equality"? Well, the answer could be that Dworkin takes the right to free speech to be part of a right to moral autonomy, and takes the foundation of that right to be a principle with "Equal" in its name. That being so, negative liberty itself can be defended as "egalitarian" in Dworkin's view. So his latest writing on pornography can be understood by seeing it as a defense of his old position—the one which Rae Langton criticized so effectively in "Whose Right?"

One novel theme does enter in 1993, however. Dworkin appears to show a new concern about whether pornographers' products are really speech. He elaborates now on his idea that the category of speech is wider than we might have thought—as if he had noticed the mismatch between the graphic sexually explicit material he defends and speech as he speaks of it. (One can be aware of the mismatch by asking: What are pornographers *"minded to say"*? When do they *"write or speak or broadcast"*? What *"convictions"* do they *"state"*? What *"opinions about the right way to lead one's life"* do they *"express"*? But it is actually not clear to me why, if a right to free speech really were a part of the right to moral autonomy, as Dworkin understands it, it would make any difference to someone's defense of his right whether he would "speak" by telling someone something or by putting out sadistic films that he makes of women in scenarios of degradation. So "Women and Pornography" seems to me to raise with a new urgency the question of what category of behavior is speech—where (we may assume) *speech* is that which a good justification of free speech justifies us in protecting. I believe that we shall need the account of illocution sketched above to answer this question: the philosophy of language may have more to offer the debate than an understanding of *silencing*. (MacKinnon uses the speech act idea in *Only Words* to oppose much recent U.S. First Amendment doctrine; and she is billed as an opponent of free speech. I like to think that attacks on the doctrine need not be attacks on free speech [when that is correctly understood].)[7]

NOTES

1. Dworkin's defense of the views I have contested is in "Liberty and Pornography," reprinted [in Part Two], and in "The Coming Battles Over Free Speech," *New York Review of Books,* June 11 '92.

2. For the claim of Catharine MacKinnon I have interpreted, see "Francis Biddle's Sister: Pornography, Civil Rights and Speech," in her *Feminism Unmodified* (Harvard, '87), parts of which are reprinted [in Part One]. Rae Langton's work has been a source of inspiration. In "Speech Acts and Unspeakable Acts" she treats the example of sexual refusal; I treat it (rather differently) below.

3. John Stuart Mill *On Liberty* (London, 1859).

4. It is an account I believe in independently of thinking about issues of pornography or freedom. I defend the notions of *illocution* and *reciprocity* as I use them below, in my "Illocution and Its Significance," *Foundations of Speech Act Theory: Philosophical and Linguistic Perspectives,* ed. S. L. Tsohatzidis (Routledge, 1994). The idea of *illocution* was in J. L. Austin, *How To Do Things With Words* (Oxford, 1962).

5. J. R. Searle, *Speech Acts: An Essay in Philosophy of Language* (Cambridge, 1969), p. 58.

6. As reported in *The Sunday Times,* 12 Dec. 1982. He was not the last to speak in this vein: Judge Dean, 1990, also summing up (quoted in *The Times,* 10 June 1993), said "As the gentlemen on the jury will understand, when a woman says 'No' she does not always mean it. Men can't turn their emotions on and off like a tap like some women can."

7. The . . . above, except the Postscript, is a slightly revised version of a paper printed in *Women's Philosophy Review* (issue no. 10) Nov. 1993, pp. 38–45.

Legal Appendix

One of the aims of this book is to encourage and facilitate an interdisciplinary exploration of the topic of pornography. Thus, this Appendix is designed to provide students and instructors with a simple reference guide to the treatment of pornography in a legal context. In it you will find brief descriptions of several important U.S. and Canadian Supreme Court decisions that bear on the current discussion of pornography. These are chronologically arranged and are interspersed with a number of salient "legal milestones"—for example, the definition of pornography employed in the model anti-pornography ordinance drafted by Catharine MacKinnon and Andrea Dworkin. Naturally, this is not an exhaustive coverage of the relevant jurisprudence; readers are encouraged to consult the Bibliography, I: Pornography and the State, for further references.

From Part Two, "Rights, Equality, and Free Speech," you will have seen that pornography raises very complex questions in legal theory—for example: What is the scope of our constitutional or Charter right to free speech? Such questions, and answers to them can appear rather abstract. But regardless of your position on the matter of whether pornography ought to be censored or restricted, the ways in which courts deal with these issues are of direct practical importance. Legal decisions have immediate concrete consequences and set precedents. Hence, in order to think seriously about pornography, it is imperative that we acquaint ourselves with the central decisions that our courts have rendered regarding pornography.

Furthermore, because a useful way of grasping both the strengths and weaknesses of an argument is to consider alternatives to it, our understanding of judicial reasoning about pornography will be enhanced if we adopt a transnational perspective. As it turns out, although there are similarities in the ways in which the United States Supreme Court and the Canadian Supreme Court have dealt with pornography, there are also some instructive differences. For example, the Canadian Supreme Court's 1992 decision, *R. v. Butler*, manifests that Court's very different understanding of the right to free speech compared with that of the U.S. Supreme Court (see below).

Neither the United States nor the Canadian law contains specific criminal provisions regarding pornography (with the exception of child pornography, which is prohibited in both countries). Thus in both the United States and Canada, pornography has been addressed under the rubric of obscenity. This explains, in part, why so much attention has been paid to questions about the precise definition of obscenity. In order to determine whether a criminal provision prohibiting obscenity applies to some material (for example, a film), a judge needs to be able to assess whether that material is obscene. Judges and law enforcement officials (including the police and customs agents) could, of course, simply rely on their intuitions here. Indeed, that may be all such people have to go on, as Justice Stewart appears to have suggested in *Jacobellis v. Ohio* when he said of obscenity, "I know it when I see it." But this would be unsatisfactory, for one thing, because people's intuitions about what is obscene vary greatly. Thus, both Courts have struggled with articulating more objective tests of obscenity that could be applied reliably to suspect material.

Until the late 1950s, all judicial discussion of obscenity in the United States concerned the statutory definition, or tests, of obscenity. Constitutional challenges to obscenity laws began in 1957, with *Roth v. United States*. It is hard to say precisely what caused this change. Perhaps, prior to the late 1950s, most people in the United States shared a conservative view about sexual morality, where part of that view held that sexually explicit representations are obscene by virtue of their sexual content alone. But community standards about sex and sexuality change. Thus the onset of constitutional challenges to obscenity laws, especially as they apply to pornography, might be explained (at least partly) in terms of the shift in prevailing sexual mores that occurred in the United States around 1960. Similarly, there is no jurisprudential discussion of the constitutionality of the obscenity provisions of the Criminal Code in Canada until after 1982. But we need not speculate about the reason for the extreme recency of constitutional challenges here: the Canadian Charter of Rights and Freedoms, with its explicit guarantee of freedom of speech, was not adopted until 1982.

Obscenity is not protected under the First Amendment of the U.S. Constitution. However, not all pornography is obscene (at least, on the statutory definition of obscenity). In any case, we must consider whether pornography, in all or any of its forms (including magazines, videos and films, and paraphernalia), is a form of speech or expression. If it is, then pornography is *prima facie* protected under the First Amendment and under section 2(b) of the Canadian Charter of Rights and Freedoms. To say that a form of expression is *prima facie* protected is simply to say that any legislation whose effect is to restrict or prohibit such expression must be subject to strict scrutiny by the courts. "Strict scrutiny" is the name for a standard or procedure of review that has been adopted over the years by federal courts in the United States (including the Supreme Court); it is employed when a court is deciding on the constitutionality of government legislation. A law or ordinance that is determined to pose a threat to freedom of expression must pass strict scrutiny in order to be deemed constitutional. In other words, the default assumption is that *all* expression[1] is protected against state interference unless the state can prove two things. First, it must show that the restriction is required in order to protect a compelling state interest—for example, public health or safety. Second, it must demonstrate that the restrictive measure to be employed is the least intrusive means of achieving the desired end. (A similar procedure is followed by the Supreme Court in Canada, although it is not called strict scrutiny.[2])

The respective guarantees of freedom of expression in the United States and Canada are:

Amendment I to the U.S. Constitution
Congress shall make no law respecting an establishment of religion, or prohibiting the free exercise of thereof; or abridging the freedom of speech, or of the press; or the right of the people peaceably to assemble, and to petition the Government for a redress of grievances.

---

[1]With the exception, of course, of that speech which the Court has already determined to be "unprotected"—for example, "fighting words." See the Introduction.
[2]See, for example, *R. v. Oakes* [1986] 1 S.C.R. 103.

Section 2 of the Canadian Charter of Rights and Freedoms
Everyone has the following rights and freedoms:
   (a) the freedom of conscience and religion;
   (b) freedom of thought, belief, opinion and expression, including
       freedom of the press and other media of communication;
   (c) freedom of peaceful assembly; and
   (d) freedom of association.

A central issue in U.S. constitutional theory is whether or not the First
Amendment provides an absolute guarantee of free speech, in other words,
whether its force is that speech may *never* be restricted. Justice Hugo Black
is often cited as the paradigm First Amendment absolutist, but the actual
practice of the Court has never been absolutism. The Court has sometimes
adopted a balancing approach, arguing that the right to free speech must
give way to other social values, such as freedom from harm. But rarely has
the Court determined that free speech interests must give way to other *political* values, such as equality. In Canada, the situation is different. The issue of
absolutism does not arise, for section 1 of the Charter of Rights and Freedoms reads:

> The Canadian Charter of Rights and Freedoms guarantees the rights
> and freedoms set out in it subject to reasonable limits prescribed by law
> as can be demonstrably justified in a free and democratic society.

Section 1 has scope over all the rights set out in the Charter. Its direct effect
is to render all those rights *non*absolute. Thus, the idea that free speech can
collide with (or even hinder the exercise of) other rights is built into the
Charter itself.
   This difference in approach to free speech is illuminated by comparing
two recent cases concerning pornography, one in the United States and one
in Canada. In 1984, Catharine MacKinnon and Andrea Dworkin presented
to the Indianapolis City Council a slightly modified version of the civil rights
anti-pornography ordinance they had previously drawn up for the city of
Minneapolis (see below for details). The ordinance was passed, signed by the
mayor, and immediately challenged as unconstitutional. In *American Booksellers, Inc. v. Hudnut*, the district court ruled that the ordinance was indeed
unconstitutional, and this decision was upheld by the Seventh Circuit Court
of Appeals. Supporters of the ordinance claimed that pornography has a

number of negative effects for women: it portrays women as inferior, it promotes and maintains false beliefs about women's capacities, and so on. In his opinion for the Seventh Circuit Court, Judge Frank Easterbrook argued that, if the supporters of the ordinance were right about the effects of pornography on women, then pornography must be understood as a form of speech. For only speech—something which expresses ideas—could have these kinds of effects. So understood, pornography is due the protection of the First Amendment. Thus Easterbrook concluded, because the ordinance would have the effect of curtailing free speech, it is unconstitutional.[3]

The contrast case in Canada is *R. v. Butler*. In this case, the Supreme Court was called on to examine the obscenity provision of the Canadian Criminal Code, section 163(8). It determined that the provision constitutes an infringement of the right to free speech guaranteed by section 2(b) of the Charter. However, it ruled that this infringement is justified under section 1. The reasoning in the case is complex, but simply put, section 1 gives the Canadian Supreme Court a way of explicitly taking into account pornography's alleged effects on other Charter rights—for example, equality rights. In its ruling in *Butler*, the Court did suggest that when it comes to some types of pornography (for example, pornography that is degrading or dehumanizing), there is good reason to think that the wide availability of this kind of material poses a threat to women's equality. Hence, it concluded that with respect to pornography of this kind, free speech interests must give way to other values.

On the basis of these cases, we might say that the essential difference between the Canadian Supreme Court and the U.S. Supreme Court with respect to the discussion of free speech and pornography is this: The U.S. Supreme Court's task is to assess whether or not pornography is speech protected by the First Amendment. If it is, then the burden of proof falls on those would seek to restrict or prohibit it. It must be conclusively demonstrated by the state (i) that it has a compelling interest in controlling pornography—for example, the protection of public health, and (ii) that the restrictive legislation is the least intrusive way of achieving that end. In Canada considerably less hangs on determining whether or not pornography is speech. Even if it is, and is thus protected, section 1 gives the Court the

---

[3]See the introduction to and essays in Part Four. Arguably, Judge Easterbrook misunderstood the meaning of the model ordinance.

power to assess directly whether the liberty to publish and circulate pornography is consistent with the values of "a free and democratic society"—for example, equality. Moreover, as the Canadian Court made clear in the *Butler* case, merely a *reasonable* apprehension of the harm(s) of pornography is sufficient to warrant the conclusion that its restriction is justified under section 1. In the United States, strict scrutiny requires the conclusive demonstration that pornography causes harm.

Pornography continues to pose pressing legal questions in both Canada and the United States. It is impossible to canvas them all here, and so the reader is invited to use the following annotated chronology as an initial guide into the legal literature.

Annotated Chronology

United States

1821   Vermont enacts the first state obscenity statute. Vermont Laws, ch. 23, no. 1, section 23 (1815).

1842   First federal obscenity statute. Act of 30 August 1842, ch. 270, section 28, 5 Stat. 548 (1842).

Britain

1868   *R. v. Hicklin*, L.R. 3 Q.B. 360
Obscenity is given its influential definition by Lord Cockburn:
"I think the test of obscenity is this, whether the tendency of the matter charged as obscenity is to deprave and corrupt those whose minds are open to such immoral influences, and into whose hands a publication of this sort may fall (371)."

United States

1879   *United States v. Bennett*, 24 F. Cas. 1093 (No. 14,571) (C.C.S.D.N.Y. 1879)
Federal courts adopt the *Hicklin* definition of obscenity.

1933   *United States v. One Book Called Ulysses*, 5 F. Supp. 182 (S.D.N.Y. 1933)
The *Hicklin* test of obscenity is rejected, and courts are advised to take into account an author's intentions, the literary merit of the

material, and the effect of the material on the average person, or "reasonable man."

1942   *Chaplinsky v. New Hampshire,* 315 U.S. 568
The Court outlines a rationale for distinguishing between protected and unprotected speech. It determines that obscenity, lewdness, fighting words, and libel do not have First Amendment protection, on the grounds that "such expressions are no essential part of any exposition of ideas, and are of such slight social value as a step to truth that any benefit that may be derived from them is clearly outweighed by the social interest in order and morality (572)."

1952   *Beauharnais v. Illinois,* 343 U.S. 250
The Court sustains the constitutionality of a state statute making it unlawful to disseminate or display publicly any "lithography, moving picture, play, drama or sketch" portraying "depravity, criminality, unchastity, or lack of virtue of a class of citizens, of any race, color, creed or religion" thereby either exposing these citizens to "contempt, derision or obloquy" or producing a "breach of the peace or riots."

1957   *Roth v. United States,* 354 U.S. 476
This case represents one of the earliest constitutional challenges to obscenity law. Prior to *Roth,* obscenity laws and their enforcement had not been taken to implicate the First Amendment, because it was thought that obscenity was not *prima facie* protected by that amendment. In this case, the Court reaffirmed that view, and ruled that both state and federal provisions concerning obscenity were constitutional. Justice Brennan, writing for the majority, argues that obscenity is not protected by the First Amendment, because obscenity is "utterly without redeeming social importance (484)." Wary to protect other forms of speech, Brennan attempts to articulate a definition of obscenity such that its constitutionally legitimate restriction does not entail the permissibility of restricting other types of speech. Brennan defines obscenity in the following way: "material which deals with sex in a manner appealing to prurient interest" where the prurient interest refers to "having a tendency to excite lustful thoughts . . . [or] as [a] shameful and morbid interest in sex (487)." In addition, Brennan argues that the appropriate test for obscenity is "whether to the average person, applying contemporary

community standards, the dominant theme of the material taken as a whole appeals to the prurient interest (489)." *Roth* remains an important and controversial case for at least two reasons. First, the Court likens obscenity to conduct rather than speech. The effect of this is to weaken the stringency of the requirements of what needs to be shown about the effects of obscenity in order that it can be constitutionally restricted. Second, this decision set the stage for the doctrinal exclusion of obscenity from First Amendment protection, with the subsequent effect that the Court has paid little attention to obscenity, and thus to pornography—particularly its effects.

Canada

1959   The current obscenity provision comes into force as section 150, subsection (8), which sets out the statutory definition of obscenity as follows: "For the purposes of this Act, any publication a dominant characteristic of which is the undue exploitation of sex, or of sex and any one or more of the following subjects, namely, crime, horror, cruelty and violence, shall be deemed to be obscene."

1962   *Brodie v. The Queen* [1962] S.C. R. 681
In this decision the Court sets out the principal tests for the determination of whether some material is obscene. In particular, the Court emphasizes that obscenity is to be measured against prevailing community standards and that it needs to be determined whether the emphasis on sex in the material under consideration is required for the serious treatment of a theme. This has come to be known as the internal necessities test.

United States

1964   *Jacobellis v. Ohio*, 378 U.S. 184
Justice Brennan emphasizes that, in order to count as obscene, material must be *utterly* without redeeming social value. Hence, if it can be demonstrated that a work has some literary merit, then it is not obscene.

Canada

1964   *Dominion News and Gifts (1962) Ltd. v. R.* [1964] S.C.R. 251
On the grounds that the community standards test of obscenity be

responsive to changing social mores, the Court declares that the community standards against which something is to be tested as obscene must be *contemporary*.

United States

1966   *A Book Named John Cleland's "Memoirs of a Woman of Pleasure" v. Attorney General of Massachusetts*, 383 U.S. 413
In this decision, Justice Brennan introduces a stricter test of obscenity than that found in *Roth*. Material is obscene if (1) its dominant theme is prurient; (2) it is "patently offensive because it affronts contemporary community standards"; (3) it is "utterly without redeeming social value (419–420)." With this decision the emphasis in the determination of obscenity shifted from mere prurience to offensiveness.

Canada

1969   *R. v. Rioux* [1969] S.C.R. 599
The Court determines that the obscenity provision (section 150) does not extend to the obscene films shown in the privacy of an individual's home, and that showing such films in this context does not constitute the intention to put the film into circulation.

United States

1969   *Stanley v. Georgia*, 394 U.S. 557
The Court determines that the constitutional right to privacy ensures the right to use pornography in one's own home, even if that material is legally obscene. "If the First Amendment means anything, it means that a State has no business telling a man sitting in his own house, what books he may read or what films he may watch. Our whole constitutional heritage rebels at the thought of giving government the power to control men's minds." However, the right to purchase this material or to make it available for commercial purposes is not so protected.

1970   The United States Commission on Obscenity and Pornography releases its report. It concludes that the findings of empirical research on the effects of pornography are insufficient to establish that pornography is a central causal factor in acts of sexual violence. On this basis, it recommends the repeal of many laws that restrict adult access to sexually explicit material. A small minority of the commission disagrees and argues that some studies do establish the role of pornography in deviant sexual behavior.

1973   *Paris Adult Theater I v. Slaton,* 413 U.S. 49

The Court again reaffirms its finding in *Roth*—namely, that obscenity falls outside the ambit of First Amendment protection. Chief Justice Burger, writing for the majority, argues that state interference in matters of the sexual conduct of adults is not necessarily constitutionally suspect. And Brennan reiterates the difficulty associated with articulating a workable test for obscenity, arguing that the vagueness of the notion of obscenity makes judgments concerning the constitutionality of certain state actions difficult to determine. This decision is also important for the fact that it was here that the Court set out its position regarding the necessity of establishing a causal link between obscenity and harm to society.

Miller v. California, 413 U.S. 15

Burger's majority opinion sets out the following test for obscenity: Material is obscene only if "(a) the average person, applying contemporary community standards, would find that the work, taken as whole, appeals to the prurient interest; [and] (b) the work depicts or describes, in a patently offensive way, sexual conduct specifically defined by the applicable state law; and (c) the work, taken as a whole, lacks serious literary, artistic, political, or scientific value [LAPS test] (25)." An important part of the *Miller* decision is that the Court declared that the relevant community standards concerning prurience and offensiveness should be local, not nationwide. This test of obscenity is still central in the Court's treatment of obscenity cases.

Canada

1974   *R. v. Dechow* [1978] 1 S.C.R. 951

The Court declares that subsection 159 (8) of the Criminal Code (see above; now subsection 163 (8)) provided an exhaustive test for obscenity. The term *publication* is given a broad interpretation to include sexual paraphernalia, as well as books, magazines, and films.

1978   The Report on Pornography by the Standing Committee on Justice and Legal Affairs (the MacGuigan report) is released. It declares,

"The clear and unquestionable danger of this type of material is that it reinforces some unhealthy tendencies in Canadian society. The effect of this type of material is to reinforce male-female stereotypes to the detriment of both sexes. It attempts to make degradation, humiliation, victimization, and violence in human relationships appear normal and acceptable. A society which holds that egalitarianism, non-violence, consensualism, mutuality are basic to any human interaction, whether sexual or other, is clearly justified in controlling and prohibiting any medium of depiction, description or advocacy which violates these principles (18:4)."

United States

1982 *New York v. Ferber,* 458 U.S. 747
The Court rules that a New York statute that prohibits the knowing distribution of pornography made with minors as actors or models is constitutional.

1983 Catharine MacKinnon and Andrea Dworkin draft an amendment to the Minneapolis Civil Rights Ordinance. They define pornography thus: "Pornography is the sexually explicit subordination of women, graphically depicted, whether in pictures or in words, that also includes one or more of the following: (i) women are presented dehumanized as sexual objects, things or commodities; or (ii) women are presented as sexual objects who enjoy pain or humiliation; or (iii) women are presented as sexual objects who experience sexual pleasure in being raped; or (iv) women are presented as sexual objects tied up or cut up or mutilated or bruised or physically hurt; or (v) women are presented in postures of sexual submission; or (vi) women's body parts—including but not limited to vaginas, breasts, and buttocks—are exhibited, such that women are reduced to those parts; or (vii) women are presented as whores by nature; or (viii) women are presented as being penetrated by objects or animals; or (ix) women are presented in scenarios of degradation, injury, abasement, torture, shown as filthy or inferior, bleeding, bruised, or hurt in a context that makes those conditions sexual." Moreover, the ordinance says, "The use of men, children, or transsexuals in the place of women in . . . (i)–(ix) above is pornography. . . ." The MacKinnon–Dworkin anti-pornography ordinance, as it has come to be known, has it that pornography "is a form of discrimination on the basis of sex." It makes four discriminatory practices actionable: (i) discrimination by trafficking in pornography; (ii) coercion into pornographic performances; (iii) forcing pornography on a person; and (iv) assault or attack due to pornography. The ordinance was passed by the Minneapolis City Council but subsequently vetoed (twice) by the mayor. (See Bibliography, I: Pornography and the State. F. The Model Anti-Pornography Ordinance.)

1984 A slightly modified version of the model ordinance is passed by the Indianapolis City and County Council. The modifications include the elimination of subsections (i), (v), (vi), and (vii) of the definition above, and the substitution of (vi) "women are presented as sexual objects for domination, conquest, violation, exploitation, posses-sion, or use, or through postures or positions of servility or submis-sion or display." Most significantly, the Indianapolis version allowed that only violent material was actionable; material satisfying just the new subsection (vi) would not be. The ordinance is immediately challenged: the district court rules it unconstitutional, and the In-dianapolis City Council appeals. (See immediately below.)

American Booksellers Association, Inc. v. Hudnut, 598 F. Supp. 1316 The Seventh U.S. Circuit Court of Appeals upholds the district court's ruling that the Indianapolis ordinance is unconstitutional. The decision is again appealed to the Supreme Court, which sum-marily dismisses the appeal without hearing oral argument (*Ameri-can Booksellers Association, Inc. v. Hudnut*, 771 F2d. 323, *aff'd* S. Ct. 1172 [1986]).

Canada

1985 *Towne Cinema Theatres Ltd. v. R.* [1985] 1 S.C.R. 494
Chief Justice Dickson, for the majority, argues that the community standards test is a test of tolerance and not taste: "It is a standard of *tolerance*, not taste, that is relevant. What matters is not what Cana-dians think is right for themselves to see. What matters is what Ca-nadians would not tolerate other Canadians seeing because it would be beyond the contemporary Canadian standard of tolerance to al-low them to see it (508)." Unlike the U.S. decision in *Miller*, the majority in this case refused to consider that obscenity could vary

from place to place. Thus the relevant standards were taken to be national, not local.

The Special Committee on Pornography and Prostitution releases its report—the Fraser Report. It concludes that there is insufficient evidence to posit "that pornography is a significant causal factor in the commission of some forms of violent crime, in the sexual abuse of children, or the disintegration of communities and society (99)." Nonetheless, it recommends the criminalization of pornography: "Because of the seriousness of the impact of this sort of pornography on the fundamental values of Canadians, we are prepared to recommend that the Criminal Code has an important role to play in defining what material may be available within our society (103)."

United States

1986   The Attorney General's Commission on Pornography (the Meese Commission) releases its report. Its conclusions are directly at odds with those of the United States Commission on Obscenity and Pornography (1970). It concludes: "The available evidence strongly supports the hypothesis that substantial exposure to sexually violent materials as described here bears a causal relationship to antisocial acts of violence and, for some subgroups, possibly to unlawful acts of sexual violence (vol. 1, 326)." The proceedings of this Commission and its report remain highly controversial, especially among psychologists whose research was cited in support of the above conclusion. (See the Bibliography, III: Empirical Research. C. Discussion about Empirical Work.)

1987   *Pope v. Illinois,* 481 U.S. 497
        The Court narrows the definition of obscenity, doing away with the idea that the value of a work could "vary from community to community based on the degree of acceptance it has won." The so-called LAPS test, outlined in *Miller,* now refers to a "reasonable" person and not to the "average" person.

Canada

1989   *Irwin Toy Ltd. v. Quebec (Attorney General)* [1989] 1 S.C.R. 927
        The Court holds that some human activity is purely physical, and is thus devoid of meaning. Therefore, such material is not protected by

section 2(b) of the Charter. Crucially, the Court argues that, in the absence of conclusive proof of a causative link between obscenity and harm, the legislature can determine on the basis of whatever evidence is available whether the relevant material is likely to produce adverse effects.

United States

1990   *Osborne v. Ohio,* 495 U.S. 103

The Court upholds a statute making it illegal to possess child pornography. This case stands in contrast with *Stanley v. Georgia* (above), in which the Court argued that the possession of legally obscene material is protected by the right to privacy. In *Osborne* the Court argues that the legislation seeks not to "control men's minds" but rather to protect children from exploitation and harms involved in the production of child pornography.

Canada

1990   *R. v. Keegstra* [1990] 3 S.C.R. 697

This case was the first constitutional challenge to the Hate Propaganda provisions of the Criminal Code (section 319). Here it is unanimously agreed that the mere content of a person's expression, no matter how offensive it is, does not constitute sufficient grounds for removing that expression from section 2(b) protection. So hate speech is *prima facie* protected speech. The Court, however, following its ruling in *Irwin Toy* concerning the necessity of demonstrating harm from certain types of expression, argues that it is reasonable to proceed on the assumption that there is a connection between hate speech and hatred towards members of the target group.

1992   *R. v. Butler* [1992] 1 S.C.R. 452

The Court holds that section 163(8) of the Criminal Code (see above) seeks restriction on the basis of content and thus represents a violation of section 2(b) of the Charter. But it argues that this infringement is justified under section 1 of the Charter. That is, it represents a constraint on free speech that is demonstrably justified in a free and democratic society. This decision is of interest for several other reasons. First, the Court explicitly considers the relationship between the three existing tests of obscenity in Canada: (i) the community standards test; (ii) the degradation and dehumanization test; and (iii) the internal necessities test. Second, it defines *harm* in terms of predisposing people to act in an antisocial manner—that is, in a manner that is inconsistent with the proper functioning of society. Third, the Court holds that the community should be the final arbiter of what is likely to be harmful. Finally, the Court introduces a tripartite distinction between types of pornography: (i) explicit sex with violence, horror, or cruelty; (ii) explicit sex in which one or more of the participants is degraded or dehumanized; and (iii) explicit sex without violence that is neither degrading nor dehumanizing. And it argues that only the first two types are vulnerable to restriction, because those kinds of pornography will "necessarily fail" the community standards test of tolerance.

Bibliography

This is by no means a complete bibliography of work on pornography. Instead it represents material that is accessible and useful to students and instructors across a range of disciplines in both the United States and Canada. One of the aims of this book is to make clear just how many issues the topic of pornography raises. Among other things, pornography requires that we think about the meaning and place of sex in our society; when we ask what if anything, ought to be done about pornography, we are forced to consider the proper relationship between the state and the individual, between morality and the law. Pornography has become a central issue for feminists, though not all feminists agree about the effects of pornography or about whether it ought to be restricted or censored. Many feminists insist that pornography cannot be considered in abstraction from the realities of women lives. In particular, they argue that it must be assessed against the backdrop of the systemic violence against women. However, recent years have seen the emergence of feminist critiques of feminist critiques of pornography. Finally, there is the matter of empirical research: What have psychologists and social scientists discovered about the effects of pornography? How credible are their results?

This bibliography, then, is arranged to facilitate tracking down material that bears directly on each of the major topics above. Thus, a student interested in pursuing the various arguments that feminists have made about pornography should consult section II: Feminism and Pornography, which is further subdivided into A. Feminist Critiques of Pornography, B. Feminist Critiques of Feminist Critiques, and so on. A student who wishes to find out more about freedom of expression as it bears on pornography should consult subsection C. Freedom of Expression in section I: Pornography and the State.

Crucially, the bibliography is aimed at encouraging an interdisciplinary and transnational approach to thinking about pornography. Philosophy students are often unaware of the information available to them in law journals. Law students may be ignorant of the vast feminist literature on pornography and violence against women. Students from more empirical disciplines, such as psychology and social work have much to learn from theory, while others more theoretically inclined should consider some of the empirical research on the effects of pornography. Researchers on both sides of the border can benefit from reading about how differently pornography and free speech are considered in both Canada and the United States.

I. PORNOGRAPHY AND THE STATE
    A. Law—United States
    B. Law—Canada
    C. Freedom of Expression
    D. Pornography and Political Theory
    E. Morality and the Law
    F. The Model Anti-Pornography Ordinance
    G. Government Reports—United States
    H. Government Reports—Canada
    I. Government Report—Britain

II. FEMINISM AND PORNOGRAPHY
    A. Feminist Critiques of Pornography
    B. Feminist Critiques of Feminist Critiques
    C. Other Critiques of Feminist Critiques
    D. General Discussion of Feminism and Pornography
    E. Feminism and Sexuality

III. EMPIRICAL RESEARCH
    A. Studies
    B. Content Analyses
    C. Discussion about Empirical Work

IV. LESBIAN AND GAY PORNOGRAPHY

V. MEN ON PORNOGRAPHY

I. PORNOGRAPHY AND THE STATE

A. Law—United States

Arthur, John. *The Unfinished Constitution: Philosophy and Constitutional Practice.* Belmont, Calif.: Wadsworth, 1989, chap. 4.

Dunlap, Mary. "Sexual Speech and the State: Putting Pornography in Its Place." *Golden Gate University Law Review* 17 (1987): 359–378.

Michelman, Frank. "Conceptions of Democracy in American Constitutional Argument: The Case of Pornography Regulation." *Tennessee Law Review* 56 (1989): 291–319.

Schauer, Frederick. "Speech and 'Speech'—Obscenity and 'Obscenity': An Exercise in the Interpretation of Constitutional Language." *Georgetown Law Journal* 67 (1979): 899–933.

Spaulding, Christina. "Anti-Pornography Laws as a Claim to Equal Respect: Feminism, Liberalism, and Community." *Berkeley Women's Law Journal* 4 (1988-89): 128–165.

Sunstein, Cass R. "Pornography and the First Amendment." *Duke University Law Journal* (1986): 589–627.

B. Law—Canada

Arbour, Louise. "The Politics of Pornography: Towards an Expansive Theory of Constitutionally Protected Speech." In *Litigating the Values of a Nation: The Canadian Charter of Rights and Freedoms,* ed. Joseph M. Weiler and Robin M. Elliot. Toronto: Carswell, 1986.

Beckton, Clare. "Obscenity and Censorship Re-examined under the Charter of Rights." *Manitoba Law Journal* 13 (1983): 351–369.

Dyzenhaus, David. "Obscenity and the Charter: Autonomy and Equality." (1991) 1 C.R. (4th) 367.

Lahey, Kathleen. "The Charter and Pornography: Toward a Restricted Theory of Constitutionally Protected Speech." In *Litigating the Values of a Nation: The Ca-*

nadian Charter of Rights and Freedoms, ed. Joseph M. Weiler and Robin M. Elliot. Toronto: Carswell, 1986.

McCormack, Thelma. "Must We Censor Pornography? Civil Liberties and Feminist Jurisprudence." In *Freedom of Expression and the Charter*, ed. David Schneiderman. Canada: Thomson Professional Publishing, 1991.

Mahoney, Kathleen. "Canaries in a Coal Mine: Canadian Judges and the Reconstruction of Obscenity Law." In *Freedom of Expression and the Charter*, ed. David Schneiderman. Canada: Thomson Professional Publishing, 1991.

———. "Obscenity, Morals and the Law: A Feminist Critique." *Ottawa Law Review* 17 (1985): 33–71.

C. Freedom of Expression

Berger, Fred. *Freedom of Expression*. Belmont, Calif.: Wadsworth, 1980.

Bork, Robert. "Neutral Principles and Some First Amendment Problems." *Indiana Law Journal* 47 (1971): 1–35.

Dworkin, Ronald. "The Coming Battles over Free Speech." *New York Review of Books*, 11 June 1992, 55–58, 61–64.

Elliot, Robin M. "Freedom of Expression and Pornography: The Need for a Structured Approach to Charter Analysis." In *Litigating the Values of a Nation: The Canadian Charter of Rights and Freedoms*, ed. Joseph M. Weiler and Robin M. Elliot. Toronto: Carswell, 1986.

Meiklejohn, Alexander. *Free Speech and Its Relation to Self-Government*. New York: Harper, 1948.

Redish, Martin H. "The Value of Free Speech." *University of Pennsylvania Law Review* 130 (1982): 591–645.

Scanlon, Thomas. "Freedom of Expression and Categories of Expression." *University of Pittsburgh Law Review* 40 (1979): 519–550.

———. "A Theory of Free Speech." *Philosophy and Public Affairs* 2 (1972): 204–226.

Trau, Jane Mary. "Limitation of Artistic Expression and Public Funding of the Arts." *International Journal of Applied Philosophy* 6 (1991): 57–83.

Tribe, Lawrence H. "Speech as Power: Of Swastikas, Spending and the Mask of Neutral Principles." In *Constitutional Choices*. Cambridge, Mass.: Harvard University Press, 1985.

Vadas, Melinda. "The Pornography/Civil Rights Ordinance versus the BOG: And the Winner Is . . . ?" *Hypatia* 7 (1992): 94–109.

Wendell, Susan. "Pornography and Freedom of Expression." In *Pornography and Censorship*, ed. David Copp and Susan Wendell. Buffalo, N.Y.: Prometheus Books, 1983.

D. Pornography and Political Theory

Clark, Lorenne. "Liberalism and Pornography." In *Pornography and Censorship*, ed. David Copp and Susan Wendell. Buffalo, N.Y.: Prometheus Books, 1983.

Dyzenhaus, David. "Liberalism, Pornography, and the Rule of Law." In *Canadian Perspectives on Legal Theory*, ed. Richard F. Devlin. Toronto: Emond Montgomery, 1991.

Kahane, David. "The Limits of Shared Understandings: Sandel on Community and Pornography." Department of Philosophy, Cambridge University, Cambridge. Photocopy.

Sandel, Michael. "Morality and the Liberal Ideal." *The New Republic,* 7 May 1984, 15–17.

E. Morality and the Law

Devlin, Patrick. "Morals and the Criminal Law." In *The Enforcement of Morals.* Oxford: Oxford University Press, 1965.

Gardbaum, Stephen. "Why the Liberal State Can Promote Moral Ideals after All." *Harvard Law Review* 104 (1991): 1350–1371.

Hart, H. L. A. *Law, Liberty, and Morality.* London: Oxford University Press, 1963.

Leiser, Burton M. *Liberty, Justice and Morals.* 3rd ed. New York: Macmillan, 1986.

Richards, David A. J., ed. *The Moral Criticism of Law.* Encino, Calif: Dickenson Publishing Co., 1977.

F. The Model Anti-Pornography Ordinance

Baldwin, Margaret. "The Sexuality of Inequality: The Minneapolis Pornography Ordinance." *Law and Inequality: A Journal of Theory and Practice* 2 (1984): 629–653.

Brest, Paul, and Ann Vandenberg. "Politics, Feminism, and the Constitution: The Anti-Pornography Movement in Minneapolis." *Stanford Law Review* 39 (1987): 607–661.

Cole, Susan G. "The Minneapolis Ordinance: Feminist Law Making." *Resources for Feminist Research* 14 (1986): 30–32.

Duggan, Lisa, Nan Hunter, and Carole S. Vance. "False Promises: Feminist Antipornography Legislation in the U.S." In *Women against Censorship,* ed. Varda Burstyn. Vancouver: Douglas and MacIntyre, 1985.

Dworkin, Andrea. "Against the Male Flood: Censorship, Pornography, and Equality." *Harvard Women's Law Journal* 8 (1985): 1–19.

Gershel, Michael A. "Evaluating a Proposed Civil Rights Approach to Pornography: Legal Analysis as If Women Mattered." *William Mitchell Law Review* 11 (1985): 41–80.

Hoffman, Eric. "Feminism, Pornography, and Law." *University of Pennsylvania Law Review* 133 (1985): 497–534.

MacKinnon, Catharine A. "On Collaboration." In *Feminism Unmodified: Discourses on Life and Law.* Cambridge, Mass.: Harvard University Press, 1987.

Manning, Rita C. "Redefining Obscenity." *Journal of Value Inquiry* 22 (1988): 193–205.

Parent, W. A. "A Second Look at Pornography and the Subordination of Women." *Journal of Philosophy* 87 (1990): 202–211.

Pornography and Sexual Violence: Evidence of the Links. London: Everywoman, 1988; being "The complete transcript of the Public Hearings on Ordinances to Add Pornography as Discrimination Against Women: Minneapolis City Council, Government Operations Committee, December 12 and 13, 1983."

Vadas, Melinda. "A First Look at the Pornography/Civil Rights Ordinance: Could Pornography Be the Subordination of Women?" *Journal of Philosophy* 84 (1987): 487–511.

G. Government Reports—United States

Attorney General's Commission on Pornography. *Final Report*, 2 vols. Washington, D.C.: U.S. Government Printing Office, July 1986. [The Meese Commission.]
Public Hearings on Ordinances to Add Pornography as Discrimination against Women, Committee on Government Operations, City Council, Minneapolis, Minn., 12–13 Dec. 1983.
United States Commission on Obscenity and Pornography. *Report of the Commission on Obscenity and Pornography.* Washington, D.C.: U.S. Government Printing Office, 1970.

H. Government Reports—Canada

Canada. House of Commons. Standing Committee on Justice and Legal Affairs. *Report on Pornography*, no. 18, 22 March 1978. [The MacGuigan Report.]
Canada. Special Committee on Pornography and Prostitution. *Pornography and Prostitution in Canada: Report of the Special Committee on Pornography and Prostitution*, vol. 1. Ottawa: Supply and Services, 1985. [The Fraser Report.]
MacDonald, D. "Pornography—Reviewed." Ottawa: Library of Parliament, Research Branch, 1987.
"Pornography: An Analysis of Proposed Legislation (Bill C-54)." Ottawa: Canadian Advisory Council on the Status of Women, 1988.
"Pornography in the Northwest Territories." Whitehorse: Northwest Territories Advisory Council on the Status of Women, 1986.
Robertson, James R. "Obscenity: The Decision of the Supreme Court of Canada in R. v. Butler." Ottawa: Library of Parliament, Research Branch, 1992.
———. "Pornography—Rev." Ottawa: Library of Parliament, Research Branch, 1991.

I. Government Report—Britain

Williams, Bernard, ed. *Obscenity and Film Censorship.* An abridgement of the Williams Report. Cambridge: Cambridge University Press, [1979] 1981.

II. FEMINISM AND PORNOGRAPHY

A. Feminist Critiques of Pornography

Brown, Beverley. "A Feminist Interest in Pornography: Some Modest Proposals." In *The Woman in Question: M/f*, ed. Parveen Adams and Elizabeth Cowie. Cambridge, Mass.: MIT Press, 1990.
Brownmiller, Susan. *Against Our Will: Men, Women and Rape.* New York: Simon & Schuster, 1975.

Cole, Susan. *Pornography and the Sex Crisis*. Toronto: Amanita, 1989.

———. "A View from Another Country." In *The Sexual Liberals and the Attack on Feminism*, ed. Dorchen Leidholdt and Janice Raymond. New York: Pergamon Press, 1990.

Dworkin, Andrea. *Pornography: Men Possessing Women*. New York: Plume, 1989.

Garry, Ann. "Pornography and Respect for Women." *Social Theory and Practice* 4 (1978): 395–421.

Griffin, Susan. *Pornography and Silence: Culture's Revenge against Nature*. New York: Harper & Row, 1981.

Hill, Judith M. "Pornography and Degradation." *Hypatia* 2 (1987): 39–54.

Jeffreys, Sheila. *Anticlimax: A Feminist Perspective on the Sexual Revolution*. New York: New York University Press, 1990, chap. 5.

Kerr, Alison. "Pornography: What's Out There Now." *Canadian Women's Studies* 11 (1991): 51–53.

———. "Pornography: What's to Be Done." *Canadian Women's Studies* 11 (1991): 100–102.

Lederer, Laura, ed. *Take Back the Night: Women on Pornography*. New York: William Morrow & Co., 1980.

MacKinnon, Catharine. *Feminism Unmodified. Discourses on Life and Law*. Cambridge, Mass.: Harvard University Press, 1987.

———. "Liberalism and the Death of Feminism." In *The Sexual Liberals and the Attack on Feminism*, ed. Dorchen Leidholdt and Janice Raymond. New York: Pergamon Press, 1990.

———. *Only Words*. Cambridge, Mass.: Harvard University Press, 1993.

———. "Pornography as Defamation and Discrimination." *Boston University Law Review* 71 (1991): 793–815.

———. "Pornography: Not a Moral Issue." *Women's Studies International Forum* 9 (1986): 63–78.

———. "Sexuality, Pornography and Method: Pleasure under Patriarchy." *Ethics* 99 (1989): 314–346.

Manion, Eileen. "We Objects Object: Pornography and the Women's Movement." *Canadian Journal of Political and Social Theory* 15 (1991): 285–300.

B. Feminist Critiques of Feminist Critiques

Assister, Alison, and Avedon Carol, eds. *Bad Girls and Naughty Pictures*. London: Pluto Press, 1993.

Burstyn, Varda, ed. *Women against Censorship*. Vancouver: Douglas and McIntyre, 1985.

Califia, Pat. "Among Us, Against Us—The New Puritans." *The Advocate*, 17 April 1980, 14–18.

Ellis, Kate, Beth Jaker, Nan D. Hunter, Barbara O'Dair, and Abby Tallmer, eds. *Caught Looking: Feminism, Pornography and Censorship*. 3rd ed. East Haven, Conn.: Long River Books, 1992.

Elshtain, Jean Bethke. "The Victim Syndrome: A Troubling Turn in Feminism." *The Progressive*, June 1982, 42–47.

English, Deirdre. "The Politics of Porn: Can Feminists Walk the Line?" *Mother Jones*, Apr. 1980, 20–23, 43–50.

Tisdale, Sallie. "Talk Dirty to Me." *Harper's Magazine,* Feb. 1992, 37–39.

Willis, Ellen. "Feminism, Moralism, and Pornography." In *Beginning to See the Light.* Hanover, N.H.: University Press of New England, 1992.

C. Other Critiques of Feminist Critiques

Beis, R. H. "Pornography: The Harm It Does." *International Journal of Moral and Social Studies* 2 (1987): 81–92.

Christensen, F. M. *Pornography: The Other Side.* New York: Praeger, 1990.

Dority, Barbara. "Feminist Moralism, 'Pornography,' and Censorship." *Humanist* 49 (1989): 8–9.

Dworkin, Ronald. "Liberty and Pornography." *The New York Review of Books,* 15 Aug. 1991, 12–15.

———. "Women and Pornography." Review of *Only Words,* by Catharine A. MacKinnon. *The New York Review of Books,* 21 Oct. 1993, 36, 37, 40–42.

Gould, James. "Why Pornography Is Valuable." *International Journal of Applied Philosophy* 6 (1991): 53–55.

Gracyk, Theodore A. "Pornography as Representation: Aesthetic Considerations." *Journal of Aesthetic Education* 21 (1987): 103–121.

Irving, John. "Pornography and the New Puritans." *The New York Times Book Review,* 29 Mar. 1992, 1, 24–25, 27.

Rhodes, Jane. "Silencing Ourselves? Pornography, Censorship and Feminism in Canada." *Resources for Feminist Research* 17 (1988): 133–135.

Russo, Ann. "Conflicts and Contradictions among Feminists over the Issue of Pornography and Sexual Freedom." *Women's Studies International Forum* 10 (1987): 103–112.

Soble, Alan. "Pornography: Defamation and the Endorsement of Degradation." *Social Theory and Practice* 11 (1985): 61–87.

———. *Pornography: Marxism, Feminism and the Future of Sexuality.* New Haven: Yale University Press, 1986.

D. General Discussion of Feminism and Pornography

Assister, Alison. "Autonomy and Pornography." In *Feminist Perspectives in Philosophy,* ed. Morwenna Griffiths and Margaret Whitford. Bloomington: Indiana University Press, 1988.

———. *Pornography, Feminism and the Individual.* London: Pluto Press, 1989.

Berger, Ronald J. *Feminism and Pornography.* New York: Praeger, 1992.

Berger, Ronald J., Patricia Searles, and Charles E. Cottle. "Ideological Contours of the Contemporary Pornography Debate—Divisions and Alliances." *Frontiers* 11 (1990): 30–38.

Chester, Gail, and Julienne Dickey, eds. *Feminism and Censorship.* London: Prism, 1988.

Collins, Barbara G. "Pornography and Social Policy: Three Feminist Approaches." *Affilia* 5 (1990): 8–26.

DeCew, Judith Wagner. "Violent Pornography: Censorship, Morality and Social Alternatives." *Journal of Applied Philosophy* 1 (1984): 79–94.

Eckersley, Robin. "Whither the Feminist Campaign? An Evaluation of Feminist Critiques of Pornography." *International Journal of the Sociology of Law* 15 (1987): 149–178.

Ellis, Kate, Barbara O'Dair, and Abby Tallmer. "Feminism and Pornography." *Feminist Review* 36 (1990): 15–18.

Fox-Genovese, Elizabeth. "Pornography and Individual Rights." In *Feminism without Illusions*. Chapel Hill, N.C.: University of North Carolina Press, 1991.

Hornsby, Jennifer. "Speech Acts and Pornography." *Women's Philosophy Review*, no. 10 (Nov. 1993): 38–45.

Langton, Rae. "Speech Acts and Unspeakable Acts." *Philosophy and Public Affairs* 22 (1993): 293–330.

———. "Whose Right? Ronald Dworkin, Women, and Pornographers." *Philosophy and Public Affairs* 19 (1990): 311–359.

Ramos, Norma, Andrea Dworkin, Gloria Jacobs, Marcia Ann Gillespie, Barbara Findlen, Marilyn French, and Ntozake Shange. "Where Do We Stand on Pornography?" *Ms.*, Jan./Feb. 1994, 32–41.

Read, Daphne. "(De)constructing Pornography: Feminisms in Conflict." In *Passion and Power: Sexuality in History*, ed. Kathy Peiss and Christina Simmons. Philadelphia: Temple University Press, 1989.

Russell, Diana E., ed. *Making Violence Sexy: Feminist Views on Pornography*. New York: Teachers College Press, 1993.

Smith, Anna Marie. "'What Is Pornography?': An Analysis of the Policy Statement of the Campaign Against Pornography and Censorship." *Feminist Review* 43 (1993): 71–87.

West, Robin. "The Feminist-Conservative Anti-Pornography Alliance and the 1986 Attorney General's Commission on Pornography Report." *American Bar Foundation Research Journal* 4 (1987): 681–711.

Yanni, Denice A. "The Pornography Debate in the Women's Community: A Clash of Cultures." *Women and Language* 11 (1987): 22–25.

E. Feminism and Sexuality

Bar On, Bat-Ami. "The Feminist 'Sexuality Debates' and the Transformation of the Political." *Hypatia* 7 (1992): 45–58.

Bartky, Sandra. *Femininity and Domination: Studies in the Phenomenology of Oppression*. New York: Routledge, 1990.

Bell, Laura, ed. *Good Girls, Bad Girls: Sex Trade Workers and Feminists Face to Face*. Toronto: The Women's Press, 1987.

Cohen, Cheryl H. "The Feminist Sexuality Debate: Ethics and Politics." *Hypatia* 3 (1986): 71–86.

Delacoste, Frederique, and Priscilla Alexander, eds. *Sex Work: Writings by Women in the Sex Industry*. Pittsburgh, Pa.: Cleis Press, 1987.

Dworkin, Andrea. *Intercourse*. New York: The Free Press, 1987.

English, Deirdre, Amber Hollibaugh, and Gayle Rubin. "Talking Sex: A Conversation on Sexuality and Feminism." *Socialist Review* 58 (1981): 43–62.

Ferguson, Ann, Ilene Philipson, Irene Diamond, Lee Quinby, Carole Vance, and Ann Barr Snitow. "Forum: The Feminist Sexuality Debates." *Signs* 10 (1984): 106–135.

Freccero, Carla. "Notes of a Post-Sex Wars Theorizer." In *Conflicts in Feminism*, ed. Marianne Hirsch and Evelyn Fox Keller. New York: Routledge, 1990.

Jeffreys, Sheila. *Anticlimax. A Feminist Perspective on the Sexual Revolution*. New York: New York University Press, 1990.

Leidholdt, Dorchen, and Janice Raymond, eds. *The Sexual Liberals and the Attack on Feminism*. New York: Pergamon Press, 1990.

Linden, Robin Ruth, Darlene R. Pagano, Diana E. H. Russell, and Susan Leigh Star, eds. *Against Sadomasochism: A Radical Feminist Analysis*. San Francisco: Frog in the Well, 1982.

Lorde, Audre. "Uses of the Erotic: The Erotic as Power." In *Sister Outsider*. Freedom, Calif.: The Crossing Press, 1984.

Rich, Adrienne. "Compulsory Heterosexuality and Lesbian Existence." In *Women: Sex and Sexuality,* ed. Ethel Spector Person and Catherine R. Simpson. Chicago: University of Chicago Press, 1980.

Rich, B. Ruby. "Review Essay: Feminism and Sexuality in the 1980's." *Feminist Studies* 12 (1986): 525–561.

Valverde, Mariana. "Beyond Gender Dangers and Private Pleasures: Theory and Ethics in the Sex Debates." *Feminist Studies* 15 (1989): 237–254.

———. *Sex, Power, and Pleasure*. Toronto: The Women's Press, 1985.

Vance, Carole, ed. *Pleasure and Danger: Exploring Female Sexuality*. London: Pandora Press, 1992.

III. EMPIRICAL RESEARCH

A. Studies

Burgess, A., ed. *Handbook of Research on Pornography and Sexual Assault*. New York: Garland Publishing Inc., 1984.

Cowan, Gloria. "Feminist Attitudes toward Pornography Control." *Psychology of Women Quarterly* 16 (1992): 165–177.

Cowan, Gloria, Cheryle J. Chase, and Geraldine B. Stahly. "Feminist and Fundamentalist Attitudes toward Pornography Control." *Psychology of Women Quarterly* 13 (1989): 97–112.

Donnerstein, Edward. "Pornography: Its Effects on Violence against Women." In *Pornography and Sexual Aggression,* ed. Neil M. Malamuth and Edward Donnerstein. Orlando, Fla.: Academic Press, 1984.

Donnerstein, Edward, and Leonard Berkowitz. "Victim Reactions in Aggressive Erotic Films as a Factor in Violence against Women." *Journal of Personality and Social Psychology* 41 (1981): 710–724.

Kutchinsky, B. "Pornography and Rape: Theory and Practice: Evidence from Crime Data in Four Countries Where Pornography Is Easily Available." *International Journal of Law and Psychiatry* 14 (1991): 47–64.

Linz, Daniel G., Edward Donnerstein, and Steven Penrod. "The Effects of Long-Term Exposure to Violent and Sexually Degrading Depictions of Women." *Journal of Personality and Social Psychology* 55 (1988): 758–768.

Malamuth, Neil M., and John H. Check. "The Effects of Mass Media Exposure on Acceptance of Violence against Women: A Field Experiment." *Journal of Research on Personality* 15 (1981): 436–446.

Malamuth, Neil M., and Edward Donnerstein. "The Effects of Aggressive-Porno-
graphic Mass Media Stimuli." *Advances in Experimental Social Psychology* 15
(1982): 103–136.

Malamuth, Neil M., and Edward Donnerstein, eds. *Pornography and Sexual Aggression*. Orlando, Fla.: Academic Press, 1984.

Mayerson, Suzin E., and Dalmas A. Taylor. "The Effects of Rape Myth Pornography
on Women's Attitudes and the Mediating Role of Sex Role Stereotyping." *Sex
Roles* 17 (1987): 321–338.

Russell, Diana. "Pornography and Rape: A Causal Model." *Political Psychology* 9
(1988): 41–73.

Yaffe, Maurice, and Edward Nelson, eds. *The Influence of Pornography on Behavior*.
New York: Academic Press, 1982.

Zillman, Dolph. *Connections between Sex and Aggression*. Hillsdale N.J.: Lawrence
Erlbaum Associates, 1984.

Zillman, Dolph, and Jennings Bryant. "Pornography, Sexual Callousness, and the
Trivialization of Rape." *Journal of Communication* 32 (1982): 10–21.

B. Content Analyses

Cowan, Gloria, Carole Lee, Daniella Levy, and Debra Snyder. "Dominance and Inequality in X-rated Video Cassettes." *Psychology of Women Quarterly* 12 (1988):
299–311.

Dietz, Park Elliot, and Barbara Evans. "Pornographic Imagery and Prevalence of
Paraphilia." *American Journal of Psychiatry* 139 (1982):1493–1495.

Malamuth, Neil M., and Barry Spinner. "A Longitudinal Content Analysis of Sexual
Violence in the Best Selling Erotic Magazines." *Journal of Sex Research* 16
(1980): 226–237.

Matacin, Mala L. "A Content Analysis of Sexual Themes in *Playboy* Cartoons." *Sex
Roles* 17 (1987): 179–186.

Palys, T. S. "Testing the Common Wisdom: The Social Content of Video Pornography." *Canadian Psychology* 27 (1986): 22–35.

Slade, Joseph W. "Violence in the Hard-Core Pornographic Film: A Historical Sur-
vey." *Journal of Communication* 34 (1984): 148–163.

Smith, Don D. "The Social Content of Pornography." *Journal of Communication* 26
(1976): 16–33.

Smith, M., J. V. P. Check, and M. J. Henry. *Sexual Violence in the Mass Media: A Content Analysis of Feature Length Films*. Paper presented at the annual meeting of
the Canadian Psychological Association, Ottawa. 1984.

Stein, Michael Carl. *The Ethnography of an Adult Bookstore*. Mellen Studies in Sociology, vol. 7. Lewiston, N.Y.: Edwin Mellen Press, 1990.

C. Discussion about Empirical Work

Christensen, Ferrel M. "Cultural and Ideological Bias in Pornography Research."
Philosophy of the Social Sciences 20 (1990): 351–375.

Cottle, Charles E., Patricia Searles, Ronald J. Berger, and Beth Ann Pierce. "Conflicting Ideologies and the Politics of Pornography." *Gender and Society* 3 (1989):
303–333.

Donnerstein, Edward, et. al. *The Question of Pornography: Research Findings and Policy Implications.* New York: Free Press, 1987.

Linz, Daniel G., and Edward Donnerstein. "The Role of Social Scientists in Policy Decision Making about Pornography." *Canadian Psychology* 31 (1990): 368–370.

Linz, Daniel G., Edward Donnerstein, and Steven Penrod. "The Findings and Recommendations of the Attorney General's Commission on Pornography: Do the Psychological 'Facts' Fit the Political Fury?" *American Psychologist* 42 (1987): 946–953.

Page, Stewart. "On Linz and Donnerstein's Pornography Research." *Canadian Psychology* 31 (1990): 371–373.

———. "The Turnaround on Pornography Research: Some Implications for Psychology and Women." *Canadian Psychology* 31 (1990): 359–367.

Russell, Diana. "Pornography and Violence: What Does the New Research Say?" In *Take Back the Night: Women on Pornography*, ed. Laura Lederer. New York: William Morrow & Co., Inc., 1980.

Segal, Lynne. "Pornography and Violence: What the 'Experts' Really Say." *Feminist Review* 36 (1990): 29–41.

Soble, Alan. "Pornography and the Social Sciences." *Social Epistemology* 2 (1988): 135–44.

IV. LESBIAN AND GAY PORNOGRAPHY

Barrington, Judith, ed. *An Intimate Wilderness: Lesbian Writers on Sexuality.* Portland, Ore.: The Eighth Mountain Press, 1991.

Dunn, Sara. "Voyage of the Valkyries: Recent Lesbian Pornographic Writing." *Feminist Review* 34 (1990): 161–170.

Henderson, Lisa. "Lesbian Pornography: Cultural Transgression and Sexual Demystification." *Women and Language* 14 (1991): 3–12.

Samois, ed. *Coming to Power.* Boston: Alyson Publications, 1982.

Smith, Cherry. "The Pleasure Threshhold: Looking at Lesbian Pornography on Film." *Feminist Review* 34 (1990): 152–159.

Stoltenberg, John. "Gays and the Pro-Pornography Movement: Having the Hots for Sex Discrimination." In *Men Confront Pornography*, ed. Michael S. Kimmel. New York: Penguin USA/Meridian, 1991.

Tucker, Scott. "Gender, Fucking, and Utopia: An Essay in Response to John Stoltenberg's *Refusing to Be a Man.*" *Social Text* 27 (1990): 3–34.

Watney, Simon. *Policing Desire: Pornography, AIDS and the Media.* Minneapolis: University of Minnesota Press, 1987, chap. 4.

V. MEN ON PORNOGRAPHY

Brod, Harry. "Pornography and the Alienation of Male Sexuality." *Social Theory and Practice* 14 (1988): 265–284.

Kimmel, Michael S., ed. *Men Confront Pornography.* New York: Penguin USA/Meridian, 1991.

Soble, Alan. "Why Do Men Enjoy Pornography?" In *Rethinking Masculinity*, ed. Larry May. Lanham, N.J.: Rowman & Littlefield, 1992.

Stoltenberg, John. *The End of Manhood: A Book for Men of Conscience.* New York: Dutton, 1993.

———. *Refusing to Be a Man: Essays on Sex and Justice.* Portland, Ore.: Breitenbush Books Inc., 1989.

VI. CHILD PORNOGRAPHY

Burgess, Ann Wolbert, and Marieanne Lindeqvist Clark, eds. *Child Pornography and Sex Rings.* Lexington, Mass.: Lexington Books, 1984.

Campagna, Daniel S. *The Sexual Trafficking in Children: An Investigation of the Child Sex Trade.* Dover, Mass.: Auburn House Publishing Co., 1988.

Kelly, Liz. "Pornography and Child Sexual Abuse." In *Pornography: Women, Violence and Civil Liberties, A Radical View,* ed. Catherine Itzin. Oxford: Oxford University Press, 1992.

Regan, Tom. *The Thee Generation.* Philadelphia: Temple University Press, 1991, chap. 4.

Tate, Tim. *Child Pornography: An Investigation.* London: Methuen, 1990.

VII. CULTURAL CRITIQUES AND AESTHETICS

Brigman, William E. "Pornography as Political Expression." *Journal of Popular Culture* 17(1983): 129–134.

Elmer, Jonathon. "The Exciting Conflict: The Rhetoric of Pornography and Anti-Pornography." *Cultural Critique* (Winter 1987–88): 45–77.

Finn, Geraldine. "Nobodies Speaking: Subjectivity, Sex and the Pornography Effect." *Philosophy Today* 33 (1989): 174–182.

Gubar, Susan. "Representing Pornography: Feminism, Criticism and Depictions of Female Violation." *Critical Inquiry* 13 (1987): 712–741.

Gubar, Susan, and Joan Hoff. *For Adult Users Only: The Dilemma of Violent Pornography.* Bloomington: Indiana University Press, 1989.

Jaffe, Harold, Larry McCaffery, and Mel Freilicher, eds. "Pornography and Censorship." *Fiction International* 22 (1992).

Jarvie, Ian Charles. "The Sociology of the Pornography Debate." *Philosophy of the Social Sciences* 17 (1987): 257–275.

Kappeler, Susanne. *The Pornography of Representation.* Minneapolis: University of Minnesota Press, 1986.

Kurti, Laszlo. "Dirty Movies—Dirty Minds: The Social Construction of X-Rated Films." *Journal of Popular Culture* 17 (1983): 187–192.

Modleski, Tania. *Feminism without Women: Culture and Criticism in a "Postfeminist" Age.* New York: Routledge, 1991.

Nead, Lynda. "The Female Nude: Pornography, Art and Sexuality. Notes." *Signs* 15 (1990): 323–335.

Roberts, Nicki. "Sex, Class and Morality." In *Ethics: A Feminist Reader,* ed. Elizabeth Frazer, Jennifer Hornsby, and Sabina Lovibond. Cambridge, Mass.: Blackwell, 1992.

Sontag, Susan. "The Pornographic Imagination." In *A Susan Sontag Reader,* introduction by Elizabeth Hardwick. New York: Farrar, Strauss and Giroux, 1982.

Williams, Linda. *Hardcore: Power, Pleasure and the Frenzy of the Visible*. Berkeley, Calif.: University of California Press, 1989.

Zizek, Slavoj. *Looking Awry: An Introduction to Jacques Lacan through Popular Culture*. Cambridge, Mass.: MIT Press, 1991, chap. 6.

VIII. VIOLENCE AGAINST WOMEN

A. Rape

Brownmiller, Susan. *Against Our Will: Men, Women, and Rape*. New York: Simon & Schuster, 1975.

Burt, Martha R. "Cultural Myths and Supports for Rape." *Journal of Personality and Social Psychology* 38 (1980): 217–230.

Clark, Lorenne M. G., and Debra J. Lewis. *Rape: The Price of Coercive Sexuality*. Toronto: Canadian Women's Educational Press, 1977.

Frieze, Irene. "Investigating the Causes and Consequences of Marital Rape." *Signs: Journal of Women in Culture and Society* 8 (1983): 532–553.

Gager, Nancy, and Cathleen Schurr. *Sexual Assault: Confronting Rape in America*. New York: Grosset and Dunlap, 1976.

LaFree, Gary. "Male Power and Female Victimization: Towards a Theory of Interracial Rape." *American Journal of Sociology* 88 (1982): 311–328.

Medea, Andrea, and Kathleen Thompson. *Against Rape*. New York: Farrar, Straus and Giroux, 1974.

Pineau, Lois. "Date Rape: A Feminist Analysis." *Law and Philosophy* 8 (1989): 217–243.

Russell, Diana. *Rape in Marriage*. New York: Macmillan, 1982.

Russell, Diana, and Nancy Howell. "The Prevalence of Rape in the United States Revisited." *Signs: Journal of Women in Culture and Society* 8 (1983): 688–695.

B. Battery

Dobash, R. Emerson, and Russell Dobash. *Violence against Wives: A Case against the Patriarchy*. New York: Free Press, 1979.

Langley, Roger, and R. Levy. *Wife Beating: The Silent Crisis*. New York: Dutton, 1977.

Martin, Del. *Battered Wives*. Rev. ed. San Francisco: Volcano Press, 1981.

Walker, Leonore E. *The Battered Woman*. New York: Harper & Row, 1979.

C. Sexual Harassment

Benson, Donna J., and Gregg E. Thompson. "Sexual Harassment on a University Campus: The Confluence of Authority Relations, Sexual Interest and Gender Stratification." *Social Problems* 29 (1982): 236–251.

Crocker, Phyllis L., and Anne E. Simon. "Sexual Harassment in Education." *Capital University Law Review* 10 (1981): 541–584.

MacKinnon, Catharine A. *Sexual Harassment of Working Women: A Case of Sex Discrimination*. New Haven: Yale University Press, 1979.

U.S. Merit Systems Protection Board. *Sexual Harassment in the Federal Workplace: Is It a Problem?* Washington, D.C.: U.S.Government Printing Office, 1981. A report of the U.S. Merit Systems Protection Board, Office of the Merit Systems Review and Studies.

D. Incest and Child Abuse

Armstrong, Louise. *Kiss Daddy Goodnight: Ten Years Later.* New York: Pocket Books, 1987.
Brady, Katherine. *Father's Days: A True Story of Incest.* New York: Seaview Books, 1979.
Burgess, Ann Wolbert, et al. *Sexual Assault of Children and Adolescents.* Lexington, Mass.: Lexington Books, 1978.
Butler, Sandra. *Conspiracy of Silence: The Trauma of Incest.* San Francisco: New Glide Publications, 1978.
Finkelhor, David. *Child Sexual Abuse: New Theory and Research.* New York: Free Press, 1984.
———. *Sexually Victimized Children.* New York: Free Press, 1979.
Herman, Judith Lewis. *Father-Daughter Incest.* Cambridge, Mass.: Harvard University Press, 1981.
Rush, Florence. *The Best-Kept Secret: Sexual Abuse of Children.* Englewood Cliffs, N.J.: Prentice Hall, 1980.
Russell, Diana. *The Secret Trauma: Incest in the Lives of Girls and Women.* New York: Basic Books, 1986.

E. Prostitution

Barry, Kathleen. *Female Sexual Slavery.* New York and London: New York University Press, 1979.
James, Jennifer. *The Politics of Prostitution.* 2nd ed. Seattle: Social Research Associates, 1975.

F. General

Canadian Panel on Violence against Women. *Final Report of the Canadian Panel on Violence against Women.* Ottawa, Ont.: The Panel, 1993.
Edwards, Susan S. M. *Policing Domestic Violence: Women, the Law and the State.* London: Sage, 1989.
Long Laws, Judith, and Pepper Schwartz. *Sexual Scripts: The Social Construction of Female Sexuality.* Hinsdale, Ill.: Dryden Press, 1976.
Russell, Diana E. H.. *Sexual Exploitation: Rape, Child Sexual Abuse and Workplace Harassment.* Beverly Hills, Calif.: Sage Publications, 1984.
Russell, Diana, and Nicole Van de Ven. *Crimes against Women: Proceedings of the International Tribunal.* Millbrae, Calif.: Les Femmes, 1976.
Schur, Edwin M. *Labeling Women Deviant: Gender, Stigma, and Social Control.* Philadelphia: Temple University Press, 1984.
Tong, Rosemarie. *Women, Sex and the Law.* Totowa, N.J.: Rowman and Allanheld, 1984.

United States Congress. Senate. Committee on the Judiciary. *Violence against Women: Victims of the System:* Hearing before the Committee on the Judiciary, United States Senate, One hundred second Congress, First Session, on S 15, a bill to combat violence and crimes against women on the streets and in homes, 9 Apr 1991. Washington, D.C.: U.S. Government Printing Office, 1992.

Wilson, Elizabeth. *What Is to Be Done about Violence against Women?* Middlesex: Penguin Books, 1983.

IX. GENERAL WORKS AND ANTHOLOGIES

Baird, Robert M., and Stuart E. Rosenbaum, eds. *Pornography: Private Right or Public Menace?* Buffalo, New York: Prometheus Books, 1991.

Copp, David, and Susan Wendell, eds. *Pornography and Censorship.* Buffalo, NY: Prometheus Books, 1983.

Downs, Donald A. *The New Politics of Pornography.* Chicago: University of Chicago Press, 1989.

Hawkins, Gordon, and Franklin E. Zimring. *Pornography in a Free Society.* Cambridge: Cambridge University Press, 1991.

Hebditch, David, and Nick Anning. *Porn Gold: Inside the Pornography Business.* London: Faber and Faber, 1988.

Holbrook, David, ed. *The Case against Pornography.* New York: Library Press, 1973.

Hughes, Douglas A., ed. *Perspectives on Pornography.* New York: St. Martin's Press, 1970.

Hunt, Lynn, ed. *The Invention of Pornography. Obscenity and the Origins of Modernity, 1500–1800.* New York: Zone Books, 1993.

Hyde, H. Montgomery. *A History of Pornography.* London: Heineman, 1964.

Itzin, Catherine, ed. *Pornography: Women, Violence and Civil Liberties, a Radical View.* Oxford: Oxford University Press, 1992.

Kendrick, Walter M. *The Secret Museum: Pornography in Modern Culture.* New York: Viking, 1987.

Lacombe, Dany. *Ideology and Public Policy.* Toronto: Garamond Press, 1988.

Lapham, Lewis H., Al Goldstein, Midge Decter, Erica Jong, Susan Brownmiller, Jean Bethke Elshtain, and Aryeh Neier. "The Place of Pornography." *Harper's,* Nov. 1984, 31–45.

Lederer, Laura, ed. *Take Back the Night: Women on Pornography.* New York: William Morrow & Co., Inc., 1980.

Randall, Richard. *Freedom and Taboo: Pornography and the Politics of a Self Divided.* Berkeley, Calif.: University of California Press, 1989.

Rist, Ray C., ed. *The Pornography Controversy.* New Brunswick, N.J.: Transaction Publishers, 1975.

Segal, Lynne, and Mary McIntosh, eds. *Sex Exposed: Sexuality and the Pornography Debate.* New Brunswick, N.J.: Rutgers University Press, 1993.

Simons, G. L. *Pornography without Prejudice.* London: Abelard-Schuman Ltd., 1972.

X. BIBLIOGRAPHIES

Byerly, Greg, and Rick Rubin. *Pornography: The Conflict over Sexually Explicit Material in the United States. An Annotated Bibliography.* New York: Garland Publishing, Inc., 1980.

Nordquist, Joan. *Pornography and Censorship.* Contemporary Social Issues: A Bibliographic Series, No. 7. Santa Cruz, Calif.: Reference and Research Series, 1987.

————. *Violence against Women: A Bibliography.* Contemporary Social Issues: A Bibliographic Series, No. 26. Santa Cruz, Calif.: Reference and Research Series, 1992.

Sellen, Betty-Carol, and Patricia A. Young. *Feminists, Pornography and the Law: An Annotated Bibliography of Conflict, 1970–1986.* Hamden, Conn.: Library Professional Publications, 1987.

Slade, Joseph W. "Pornography." In *Handbook of American Popular Culture,* 2nd. ed., rev. and enlarged, ed. M. Thomas Inge. New York: Greenwood Press, 1989.